Latin Primer 2

Teacher's Edition

LATIN PRIMER SERIES

Latin Primer: Book 1, Martha Wilson
Latin Primer 1: Student Edition
Latin Primer 1: Teacher's Edition
Latin Primer 1: Flashcard Set
Latin Primer 1: Audio Guide CD

Latin Primer: Book 2, Martha Wilson
Latin Primer 2: Student Edition
Latin Primer 2: Teacher's Edition
Latin Primer 2: Flashcard Set
Latin Primer 2: Audio Guide CD

Latin Primer: Book 3, Martha Wilson *(coming 2011)*
Latin Primer 3: Student Edition
Latin Primer 3: Teacher's Edition
Latin Primer 3: Flashcard Set
Latin Primer 3: Audio Guide CD

Published by Canon Press
P.O. Box 8729, Moscow, ID 83843
800.488.2034 | www.canonpress.com

Martha Wilson, *Latin Primer Book 2 Teacher's Edition*
Copyright © 1993 by Martha Wilson.
Copyright © 2010 by Canon Press.
First Edition 1993, Second Edition 2003, Third Edition 2003,
Fourth Edition 2010

Cover design by Rachel Hoffmann.
Interior layout and design by Phaedrus Media.
Textual additions and edits by Laura Storm.
Printed in the United States of America.

For printable PDFs of the student Weekly Quizzes and Unit Tests found in the book, go to:
www.canonpress.com/latinprimer2

Library of Congress Cataloging-in-Publication Data

Wilson, Martha.
  Latin primer. 2 : teacher's edition / by Martha Wilson ; edited by Laura Storm. -- 4th ed.
    p. cm.
  Includes bibliographical references.
  ISBN-13: 978-1-59128-073-6 (pbk.)
  ISBN-10: 1-59128-073-7 (pbk.)
  1. Latin language--Study and teaching. 2. Latin language--Grammar. I. Storm, Laura, 1981- II. Title.
  PA2063.W55 2010
  478.2'421--dc22
                                            2010009983

10 11 12 13 14 15 16   10 9 8 7 6 5 4 3 2 1

BOOK 2

Latin
PRIMER

TEACHER'S EDITION

MARTHA WILSON / Edited by LAURA STORM

canonpress
Moscow, Idaho

CONTENTS

Unit 1: Weeks 1–8   1

Unit 2: Weeks 9–16   97

Unit 3: Weeks 17–24 196

Unit 4: Weeks 25–32 291

Appendices 390

INTRODUCTION

Welcome to the *Latin Primer 2!* You now have one year of Latin behind you—congratulations! Your main work last year was to memorize chants and learn vocabulary. All together you learned about four hundred words! This year, you'll notice that your Word Lists include not only new words, but old favorites as well. (And sometimes exercises will include old words you might not have seen since last year . . . just to keep you on your toes!)

Your main job this year is to begin to read and write more advanced Latin sentences. A large part of being able to read and write Latin is having lots of things (especially vocabulary!) tucked away in your memory, ready to use. By the end of this year you'll be able to translate sentences like, *Latrō quondam erat eques mīrus* ("The robber was once a wonderful knight") and *Lupī cervum nōn possunt oppugnāre* ("The wolves are not able to attack the deer").

As you learn more advanced Latin, you'll notice that you'll understand even better how our English language works. Since you're so used to using English, there are many things about it that you won't even notice until you see how Latin is different.

You may have realized last year that Latin appears in many places. I hope over the last year you've been able to recognize English names and other words that come from Latin. Maybe you've seen Latin on buildings, coins, or memorials. I've discovered that many colleges have Latin on their seals. You had a list of some of those in *Latin Primer 1,* and you'll be learning a couple more this year!

Once, at the end of a dinner I was having with my grandmother, she said with satisfaction, "*Fīnis.*" Learning Latin may not be quite as easy as eating dinner, but I hope you'll be able to say "*fīnis*" with satisfaction at the end of this year. Instead of being full of meat and potatoes, you'll be full of new knowledge!

Valēte,
Martha Wilson

PRONUNCIATION GUIDE

When approaching Latin for the first time, many teachers are concerned that they pronounce the words correctly. Due to a great variety of schools of thought on Latin pronunciation (classical, ecclesiastic, Italian, English, and any hybrid thereof), we would advise teachers not to worry, but to simply choose a pronunciation and stick with it. Spoken Latin has been dead so long that no one can be sure what a "proper" pronunciation would sound like, and there is no point in straining at gnats (or macrons). In this book, classical pronunciation is used.

Vowels:

Vowels in Latin have only two pronunciations, long and short. When speaking, long vowels are held twice as long as short vowels. Long vowels are marked with a "macron" or line over the vowel (e.g., ā). Vowels without a macron are short vowels.

When spelling a word, including the macron is important, as it can determine the meaning of the word (e.g., liber is a noun meaning *book*, and līber is an adjective meaning *free*).

Long Vowels:		*Short Vowels:*	
ā	like *a* in *father*: frāter, suprā	a	like *a* in *idea*: canis, mare
ē	like *e* in *obey*: trēs, rēgīna	e	like *e* in *bet*: et, terra
ī	like *i* in *machine*: mīles, vīta	i	like *i* in *this*: hic, silva
ō	like *o* in *holy*: sōl, glōria	o	like *o* in *domain*: bonus, nomen
ū	like *oo* in *rude*: flūmen, lūdus	u	like *u* in *put*: sum, sub
ȳ	like i in *chip:* grȳps, cȳgnus		

Diphthongs:

A combination of two vowel sounds collapsed together into one syllable is a dipthong:

ae	like *ai* in *aisle*	caelum, saepe
au	like *ou* in *house*	laudo, nauta
ei	like *ei* in *reign*	deinde
eu	like *eu* in *eulogy*	Deus
oe	like *oi* in *oil*	moenia, poena
ui	like *ew* in *chewy*	huius, hui

Consonants:

Latin consonants are pronounced with the same sounds with the following exceptions:

c	like *c* in *come*	never soft like *city*, *cinema*, or *peace*
g	like *g* in *go*	never soft like *gem*, *geology*, or *gentle*
v	like *w* in *wow*	never like *Vikings*, *victor*, or *vacation*
s	like *s* in *sissy*	never like *easel*, *weasel*, or *peas*
ch	like *ch* in *chorus*	never like *church*, *chapel*, or *children*
r	is trilled	like a dog snarling, or a machine gun
i	like *y* in *yes*	when used before a vowel at the beginning of a word, between two vowels within a word, otherwise it's usually used as a vowel

HOW TO USE THIS BOOK

Welcome to *Latin Primer 2.*

Congratulations on your continuing Latin journey!

The *Latin Primer* series covers the very essentials of classical Latin, based on the Trivium model of education. The Trivium sees students developing through varying stages of learning—namely, poll-parrot, pert, and rhetorical stages. These stages correspond roughly to elementary (ages five through ten), junior high, and high school. *Latin Primer 2* is designed for the poll-parrot/elementary stage in which children love to chant and memorize.

According to the Trivium, as explained by Dorothy Sayers in her essay "The Lost Tools of Learning," the poll-parrot stage is the time to store away large amounts of information which the students may not yet fully understand (like the meaning of the ablative case!). In the *Latin Primer* series, students start first by memorizing vocabulary, verb endings, noun endings, and so on; a strong emphasis is placed on learning these "building blocks" of the language. Bit by bit, they are introduced to the grammar behind the language, and each grammar concept is reinforced with basic translational exercises. The ease of a Trivium approach to Latin is this focus on absorbing the frame now and understanding it later. This may seem odd initially, but it has a long historical pedigree.

The *Latin Primer 2* Teacher's Edition follows the layout of the Student Edition, including the answers to the questions in the student text. Each lesson should take approximately one week to learn, review, and complete. Each week, you as the teacher will be given a weekly outline, typically following this pattern: Word List (vocabulary), Derivatives, Chant, Quotation, Worksheet, and Quiz. While helpful teaching notes will be included in each weekly outline, the next few pages will provide you with the overall framework for using the book. These will give both the classroom and homeschool teacher the proficiency to introduce beginning Latin with confidence.

Thank you for investing in the *Latin Primer* series, and may God bless you as you learn this incredible language!

Word Lists

Each week, students will be given a new list of Latin vocabulary to learn. The words are broken out into parts of speech (nouns, adjectives, verbs, adverbs, and so on). Then within those groupings, the words are listed alphabetically.

Derivatives

A derivative is not an "original" word, but a word that can be traced as coming directly from another word. (The word "derivative" itself has roots meaning "to flow downstream from" a source.) In the following example, the Latin word *māter* means "mother" in English. One of the English derivatives of *māter* is "maternal," meaning "motherly."

LATIN	ENGLISH	DERIVATIVE
māter	mother	maternal

The basic guidelines for determining if an English word is a derivative of a certain Latin word are:

1. In part or in whole, they have **similar spellings.**
2. They have **some of the same meaning.**

These are not foolproof tests—some words appear to be unlikely descendants, but in fact are, while others present themselves as heirs and are not. Discerning likely derivatives requires practice throughout the year. Some students take to it quickly; others need practice in applying the two little tests above. Working with derivatives is a good path to the growth of English vocabulary. It is also helpful for memorizing Latin vocabulary when the meaning of an English derivative is already known, and it is preferable to memorization based on fiction such as "I praise loudly" to help one remember the meaning of *laudō*. You may also find more derivatives in the Latin entries of a Latin dictionary, or refer to an English dictionary (such as *The Oxford English Dictionary*) that gives the history of the English word.

Working with derivatives should be part of the weekly routine. After introducing the weekly Word List, you may want to lead students in brainstorming possible derivatives. Included in the Teaching Notes for each weekly lesson are lists of derivatives for the current Word List. The lists are not exhaustive, but include words which will be most useful. There will be more derivatives given than you will want to use; these are for your reference rather than the students' use. Some words will not have any listed derivatives.

In the student text, on the page following each weekly Word List, is a section where students can list the derivatives you discuss together each week.

Chants

Chants are one of the basic building blocks for the foundation of Latin learning. This year, students will review and learn seventeen chants. If you used the *Latin Primer 1* last year, you'll probably want to continue chanting where you left off, adding the new chants from this year to your recitation. If you're just starting or switching to the *Primer 2* from another series, simply recite the chants in the order you learn them each week.

Students should practice their chants together verbally each day. They need to have the chants memorized thoroughly and accurately by the end of this year; however, they don't need to fully understand how all the chants are used. Only those parts that need to be understood will be pointed out.

All of the chants in this book are meant to be recited starting at the top left, proceeding by going first through the left column and then the right.

Complete listings of the chant charts can be found in two different places in this book. First, you'll find the charts listed with the weekly Word Lists and quotations. Second, the chant charts can be found in the back of this book (beginning on p. 391).

Quotations

Nearly every week, students will be given a new Latin quotation to learn. These are generally common phrases in everyday English speech (i.e., *verbatim*) or well-known phrases from literature and/or history (i.e., *Ecce homō!*). These quotations are intended to be fun and help students understand that Latin is still part of contemporary speech.

In the student text, on the page following each weekly Word List, is a section where students can copy each week's quotation.

Worksheets

Each week, students will be expected to complete a worksheet made up of different exercises intended to reinforce and review weekly concepts.

Quizzes

Weekly quizzes are included at the end of each lesson to test students' understanding and comprehension of each week's materials, as well as aid in reviewing older material. Teachers are permitted to copy and distribute these quizzes for use in the classroom. For printable PDFs of the student weekly quizzes, go to: www.canonpress.com/latinprimer2.

Unit Tests

This text contains four units (see the Table of Contents), comprised of eight weeks each. At the beginning of each unit, a list of goals is provided. At the end of each Unit is a comprehensive test, which allows the teacher to measure whether those goals have been reached. Teachers are permitted to copy and distribute these tests for use in the classroom. For printable PDFs of the student unit tests, go to: www.canonpress.com/latinprimer2.

Optional Games

At least once a week, you may want to play games to review and practice the vocabulary that has been covered. Four basic games are described below.

Circum Mundum (Around the World): Starting at some point in the room, two neighbors are given a Latin word. Whoever gives the English meaning first gets to go on to compete against the next student. If someone is in top form, he or she might make it *circum mundum*.

Puerī contra Puellās or Puellae contra Puerōs: The boys and girls line up in separate lines. The first girl in line competes against the first boy in line. They are given a Latin word; whoever is first with the English meaning goes to the back of the line and the loser sits down. The winning team is the one that still has at least one member standing, with the other team entirely seated.

Note: If there is a disparity in numbers, the smaller group is given "insurance" to make up for it (e.g., if there are two more boys than girls, the first two girls to lose don't have to sit down).

Graecī et Rōmānī: The class is divided into two groups and the first player from each team comes to the board. They face away from the board while a conjugated verb or simple sentence is written there. At a signal, they turn around and race to write a translation. The first one to do it correctly earns a point for their team.

Vincō: This is played the same as Bingo. To begin, the students are given a table as shown here, enlarged to fit a standard 8.5 x 11" sheet of paper.

V	I	N	C	O

From a list of words on the board such as conjugated verbs, nouns in singular or plural, or just words from the weekly lists, the students pick twenty-five to write in their squares, arranging them as they like. When the English translations are read, they find the corresponding Latin on their sheet, if it is there, and cross it out. The first one to have a row or diagonal of five crossed-out squares shouts *Vincō!* ("I conquer").

LATIN GRAMMAR BASICS

VERBS: Characteristics

Every verb has five different identifying characteristics: person, number, tense, mood, and voice. Below are some helpful explanations and questions to get your students thinking about the characteristics of verbs:

1. ***Person:*** Who is the subject? Who is doing the action?
    First Person: The speaker(s)—*I* or *we*
    Second Person: The person(s) spoken to—*you* or *you all*
    Third Person: The person(s) spoken about—*he/she/it* or *they*
2. ***Number:*** Is the subject singular or plural? How many?
3. ***Tense:*** When does the action take place?
4. ***Voice:*** A way to determine if the subject performs the action or receives it.
5. ***Mood:*** The method of expressing a verbal action or state of being.

Latin has six **tenses**:
    Present System—all tenses in this system are formed using the present stem
        Present: Action right now
            The elephant <u>is charging</u>.
        Future: Action that will happen in the future
            The elephant <u>will charge</u>.
        Imperfect: Continuous or sustained action in the past
            The elephant <u>was charging</u>.
    Perfect System—all tenses in this system are formed using the perfect (active or passive) stem
        Perfect (present perfect): Completed action in the past (short-term)
            The birds <u>have flown</u> south.
        Pluperfect (past perfect): Completed action prior to some time in the past
            The birds <u>had flown</u> south.
        Future Perfect: Completed action prior to some point in the future
            The birds <u>will have flown</u> south.

Latin has two **voices**:
        Active Voice: The subject is performing the action
            The ball <u>is bouncing</u>.
        Passive Voice: The subject is the receiver of the action
            The ball <u>is being bounced</u>.
Finally, Latin has **moods**:
        Indicative: Shows "real" action that has occurred, will occur, or is occurring
            I <u>have</u> a carrot.
        Imperative: Commands someone to take action that has not yet occurred
            <u>Give</u> me a carrot.
        Subjunctive: Describes potential, hypothetical action to take place or indirect action
            I wish carrots <u>were</u> blue.

In this book, you'll be dealing primarily with person, number, and tense, and voice will only be active. Mood is mentioned here purely for reference and will not be discussed in detail this year, although students will be translating in the indicative and imperative.

VERBS: Principal Parts

Nearly every Latin verb has four "principal parts." In this book, you will only be using the first and second principal parts. However, being aware of all four forms is good background to the language. The standard four principal parts are as follows:

1. Present Active Indicative: *amō,* I love (this is also the first person singular, present active form)
2. Present Active Infinitive: *amāre,* to love
3. Perfect Active Indicative: *amāvī,* I have loved/I loved
4. Perfect Passive Participle: *amātum,* loved/having been loved

VERBS: Stems

A *stem* is the underlying base of a word—an unchanging part, a root—to which endings may be added. The stem is the heart of verb—where you find out what action is being done. Is someone loving? Running? Exploring? Eating? The stem will tell you.

How do you find the stem? It's very simple. Go to the verb's second principal part, take off the *-re,* and there's your stem. Let's look at an example. The Latin word for "I love" is *amō* (first principal part). The second principal part is *amāre.* To find the stem, we take off *-re,* leaving us with the stem: *amā-.*

Let's look a little closer. In the box below, *amō* is conjugated in the present tense. First (of course), is the first principal part itself—*amō.* After that, the verb endings change, but the stem (*amā-*) remains.[1]

PRESENT ACTIVE

	SINGULAR	PLURAL
1ST	amō	**amā**mus
2ND	**amā**s	**amā**tis
3RD	**ama**t	**ama**nt

This same stem (bolded) is also used in the future and imperfect tenses.

---

1. *Notice that the macron disappears in the third person forms of the present active. This is true for both first and second conjugation verbs. When in doubt about macron placement, check the full conjugations on pages 396–398 and follow the examples given there.*

FUTURE ACTIVE

	SINGULAR	PLURAL
1ST	**amā**bō	**amā**bimus
2ND	**amā**bis	**amā**bitis
3RD	**amā**bit	**amā**bunt

IMPERFECT ACTIVE

	SINGULAR	PLURAL
1ST	**amā**bam	**amā**bāmus
2ND	**amā**bās	**amā**bātis
3RD	**amā**bat	**amā**bant

VERBS: Conjugations (Also Called Families, Paradigms, or Patterns)

A verb *conjugation* (also referred to as a *family)* is a group of verbs that share the same stem vowel. For example, in the chants above, you'll notice that the vowel "ā" exists in the middle of every form. This occurs because *amō* is in the first conjugation, or "ā" family. There are many verbs in the "ā" family—and they all have an "ā" at the end of their stem. Similarly, verbs in the "ē" family all have a long "e" at the end of their stem. To "conjugate" a verb means to list together, verbally or written, all of its forms. (In the above chants, *amō* has been "conjugated" in the future and imperfect tenses.)

In Latin, there are four different verb conjugations. Also, there are several irregular verbs which do not belong to a conjugation or family. The fourth conjugation will be introduced next year. In this book, the following will be covered:

1. *First Conjugation or "ā" Family*—represented by *amō*. Verbs in this family share an "ā" in the stem. They follow the same conjugating pattern as *amō*. Other examples are *laudō, dō,* and *portō*.

2. *Second Conjugation or "ē" Family*—represented by *videō*. Verbs in this family share an "ē" in the stem. They follow the same conjugating pattern as *videō*. Other examples are *doceō, habeō,* and *audeō*.

3. *Third Conjugation or "e" Family*—represented by *dūcō*. Verbs in this family share an "e" in the stem. They follow the same conjugating pattern as *dūcō*. Other examples are *scribō, agō,* and *currō*.

4. *Irregular Verbs*—*sum* and *possum*. These are the only irregularly conjugating verbs you'll learn this year.

VERBS: Endings

As you've seen in the *amō* chants, verb endings are added to verb stems to form complete verbs. These endings change to indicate person, number, tense, voice, and mood.

Students will only be translating using three tenses during this year, however, you can see three completely conjugated verbs in the appendices at the back of this book, on pages 396–398. *Amō* (first conjugation/"ā" family), *videō* (second conjugation/"ē" family), and *dūcō* (third conjugation/"e" family) are shown in each tense and translated, with the endings in bold.

The following three chants all use the present stem. In Unit 2, you'll learn about the third conjugation, which does its own riff on these endings; however, the third conjugation is an exception to the rule, so only the standard endings are listed below.

- *Present Active Verb Endings (-ō, -s, -t)*: Equally correct translations of the present tense include "I am loving," "I love" or "I do love"; "you are loving," "you love," or "you do love," etc.

- *Future Active Verb Endings (-bō, -bis, -bit)*: The entire stem appears in every form in both conjugations, whether ending in "ā" (first conjugation) or in "ē" (second conjugation). This typically translates, "I will love," "you will love," and so on.

- *Imperfect Active Verb Endings (-bam, -bas, -bat)*: Typically translated in this book as, "I was loving," "you were loving," etc. However, this is only one translation of the imperfect tense. The sense of it is an action that was ongoing in the past, so "I used to love" or " I kept loving" would also be correct.

The "perfect" stem is used when forming the following three chants.

- *Perfect Active Verb Endings (-ī, -isti, -it)*: Often translated, "I loved," there are also two other translations of this tense: "I have loved" and "I did love." In the first conjugation, the perfect stem for most verbs is the present stem + "v"; in the second conjugation there is less consistency.

- *Future Perfect Active Verb Endings (-erō, -eris, -erit)*: This tense is generally translated, "I will have loved." It illustrates action that will have been completed at a future time.

- *Pluperfect Active Verb Endings (-eram, -eras, -erat)*: This tense derives its name from the Latin for "more than perfect" and designates action completed prior to a time in the past. This is most clear when translated, "I had loved."

The following three chants are the Present, Future, and Imperfect tenses, in the passive voice. In the passive, the subject noun is acted upon, rather than acting itself. Again, you will not be conjugating using these tenses this year, so the following is simply grammatical background.

- *Present Passive Verb Ending (-r, -ris, -tur)*: With one exception, this tense is formed by adding the endings to the present stem. The exception is in the first person singular form (*laudor* and *movēor*) where the ending is added to the full present tense active form. A translation of the present passive is "I am being loved."

- *Future Passive Verb Ending (-bor, -beris, -bitur)*: To form this tense, the endings are simply added to the present stem. The translation is "I will be loved."

- *Imperfect Passive Verb Ending (-bar, -baris, -batur)*: Again, this tense is formed by adding the endings to the present stem. The translation is "I was being loved."

NOUNS: Endings, Bases, & Cases

Noun ending chants appear in Weeks 1, 2, 3, 13, 15 23, and 25; they also are listed in the back of this book, beginning on page 391 (p. 206 of the student text).

A noun's ending indicates which *case* the noun is in and, therefore, its function in the sentence. These noun endings attach to a noun's *base,* which is found by simply taking the genitive singular form and removing the genitive ending. For example, what is the base of *equus?* The genitive singular is *equī.* Remove the genitive singular ending *ī,* and you're left with the base—*equ-*.

Five cases are listed to the left of the noun chant: *nominative, genitive, dative, accusative,* and *ablative*. The endings in the example below are first declension endings (discussed further in the following section).

	LATIN			ENGLISH	
	SINGULAR	PLURAL		SINGULAR	PLURAL
NOMINATIVE	-a	-ae		a, the *noun*	the *nouns*
GENITIVE	-ae	-ārum		of the *noun*, the *noun's*	of the *nouns*, the *nouns'*
DATIVE	-ae	-īs		to, for the *noun*	to, for the *nouns*
ACCUSATIVE	-am	-ās		the *noun*	the *nouns*
ABLATIVE	-ā	-īs		by, with, from the *noun*	by, with, from the *nouns*

The **nominative** case is the basic noun form. Nouns appear in this form in your weekly Word Lists (as well as in Latin dictionaries). In a Latin sentence, the subject noun will *always* be in the nominative case.

The second case, the **genitive**, is typically used to show possession or ownership—i.e., "the *star's* brilliance" or "the father *of the boy*." The genitive is also the case that indicates a noun's declension. For this reason, the genitive singular is always listed after the nominative in Latin dictionary entries, as well as in this book.

The third case is the **dative**. It is mainly used for indirect objects. In the sentence, "Jane gave the donut to her mother," *mother* would be in the dative case, since she is the one *to whom* the donut is being given.

The fourth case is the **accusative**. The accusative is primarily used for direct objects and objects of some prepositions. In the sentence, "Her mother ate the donut," *donut* would be in the accusative case, since it is receiving the direct action of the verb (what is being eaten).

The final case is the **ablative.** Ablative case is often referred to as Latin's "junk drawer." Ablative is a bit of a grammatical daredevil, performing all sorts of functions, often in connection with prepositional phrases.

Not included in the chants are two less frequently used cases, the locative and vocative. You don't need to be concerned with them at this point in your Latin studies.

Although the students will only be working with the nominative and accusative cases in translation this year, it is important to have them learn the names of the cases. A mnemonic device used (and invented, I suspect) by my first Latin teacher is: **N**o **g**ood **d**ad **a**ttacks **a**pples. I confess to having used it myself. The kids enjoyed it.

NOUNS: Declensions & Gender

In Latin, every noun is in a specific declension, a noun family, where every member of that family functions in the same way. There are five declensions in Latin, four of which you'll be working with this year.

Every Latin noun also has a gender—it is either masculine, feminine, or neuter.

Let's start with how to recognize a noun's declension. To determine a noun's declension, check its *genitive singular ending*. This ending functions like a noun's DNA.

Nouns of the **first declension** (see Week 1) have the genitive singular ending -*ae*. Typically, these nouns are *feminine*. Of course, there are a few exceptions, representing people who had jobs that were traditionally male (e.g., *poeta*, poet; *nauta*, sailor; *agricola,* farmer). These nouns decline exactly like the feminine nouns, but their gender is masculine.

Second declension nouns have the genitive singular ending -*ī*. Nouns in this declension are usually *masculine* in gender (see Week 2).

However, there is also another category of second declension nouns: the **second declension** *neuter.* Neuter nouns are just that—neither masculine or feminine. These second declension nouns still have the identifying genitive singular ending -*ī*, but *you'll recognize them as neuter because they end in* -um *in the nominative singular* (see Week 3).

Nouns of the **third declension** (see Weeks 13 and 15) have the genitive singular ending -*is*. The genders of these nouns vary widely, so the only way to be sure you know their gender is to memorize it.

Fourth declension nouns (see Week 23) have the genitive singular ending *-ūs*. Like the second declension, there is also a specific group of **fourth declension *neuter*** nouns (see Week 25), which have the genitive singular *-ūs*, but can be identified as particularly neuter by the ending *-ū* in the nominative singular.

Last year, as a general rule, students went by the noun's endings to discern its gender. When you're only working with first and second declension nouns, this typically works. However, as they work with more declensions this year, they'll realize a noun's endings will no longer indicate its gender. It is important that they develop the habit of memorizing the entire noun entry—nominative, genitive, gender, and meaning.

ADJECTIVES: Endings

Adjectives are noun modifiers. They answer questions like *which?, what kind?,* and *how many?* Because they modify nouns, adjectives work very much like nouns. The adjectives you'll be using share the same endings as nouns—first, second, and second declension neuter.

Adjectives are copy cats. For an adjective to correctly modify a noun (e.g., "The *wild* girl laughed"), the adjective has to match the noun in three ways: gender, number, and case.

Gender: In Latin, the word *ferus* means "wild" and the word *puella* means "girl." But *ferus* has a masculine ending (*-us*) and *puella* is a feminine noun. How do you say "the wild girl" without having mismatched noun/adjective genders?

To match the noun they modify, most adjectives have a special trait: they come with three different endings! This gives them the ability to match the gender of any noun. So in our example, *ferus* is wearing the wrong ending to match *puella*. To match, the adjective takes off its *-us* ending, and puts on the *-a* ending: *fera*.

Number: *Puella* (girl) is singular, so the ending for *fera* (wild) is singular too.

Case: The subject of our example sentence is *puella,* so *puella* is in the nominative case (p. xviii); this means that the adjective, *fera,* also is in the nominative case. Voilà! *Puella fera* means "the wild girl" and it matches in gender, number, and case.

Here are a few more examples:

equus ferus	*the wild horse*
discipulus parvus	*a little student*
stella parva	*a little star*
caelum magnum	*the big sky*
lūdus magnus	*the big school*

ADVERBS

Adverbs are perhaps the easiest of Latin words. They answer the questions like *how?, where?, when?* and *to what extent?* They do not decline or conjugate and generally will appear before the adjective, adverb, or (most commonly) verb they modify. To translate, simply place the adverb where it sounds most natural. For example:

Aquila **bene** videt.	*The eagle sees well.*
Populus **nōn** probat.	*The people do not approve.*
Puerī **nōn satis** exercent.	*The boys do not exercise enough.*

This concludes our (brief!) overview of the basics of Latin grammar. You'll want to refer back to this section throughout the year as the students are introduced to new concepts; but for now, *valē!*

1 UNIT ONE

UNIT 1: GOALS

By the end of Week 8, students should be able to . . .

- Chant from memory the first declension, second declension, and second declension neuter noun endings
- Recognize and distinguish first declension, second declension, and second declension neuter nouns
- Decline any first declension, second declension, or second declension neuter noun
- Chant from memory the present, future, and imperfect verb ending chants
- Recognize and distinguish first and second conjugation verbs by their stems
- Translate simple present, future, and imperfect tense sentences (e.g., *Delphīnī properābant* means "The dolphins were rushing")

Unit 1 Overview (Weeks 1–8)

Welcome to Unit 1! During the next eight weeks, students will be reviewing the noun and verb endings they learned last year. This unit begins by reviewing first, second, and second declension neuter noun endings. In the weeks to follow, students will review the verb endings for present, future, and imperfect tenses. Weeks 7 and 8 are general review.

Teaching Notes: Week 1

1. Word List: Introduce the Word List for Week 1, asking students to carefully imitate the pronunciation. *Astō* is a combination of *ad* and *stō*, both words from last year's studies.

As in *Latin Primer 1,* each noun appears in its nominative singular form, followed by its genitive singular ending. (In the case of *puer,* the entire genitive form is given.) Beginning this year, the gender of each noun will also be provided. Students should memorize the entire entry, reading it off as, "amīcus, -ī, masculine, friend." Note that both *nauta* and *poeta,* though in the first declension, are masculine in gender.

Also like last year, each verb is followed by its second principal part. Now that students are familiar with the concept of the second principal part, the parentheses have been dropped. It will be helpful to remind students that the second principal part is the verb form you use to find a verb's stem (see p. xii).

Review the new Word List throughout the week on a regular basis.

2. Derivatives: Discuss the derivatives for this week's vocabulary (listed below). An explanation of derivatives appears on pages viii–ix in the "How to Use This Book" section of their student book.

1. amīcus, *friend:* amiable, amicable, amity
2. aqua, *water:* aquatic, aquarium, aqueduct
3. caelum, *sky, heaven:* celestial
4. cibus, *food*
5. colōnus, *settler:* colony, colonial
6. equus, *horse:* equestrian, equine
7. latebra, *hiding place*
8. mūrus, *wall:* mural, intramural
9. nauta, *sailor:* nautical
10. nimbus, *thundercloud, storm:* cumulonimbus, nimbus
11. poēta, *poet:* poetic, poet, poetry
12. pontus, *sea, seawater*
13. puella, *girl*
14. puer, *boy:* puerile
15. stella, *star:* stellar, constellation
16. taurus, *bull:* taurine
17. terra, *earth, land:* terrestrial, terra firma, subterranean, terrarium, inter, terra cotta
18. virga, *branch, twig:* virgate
19. astō, *I stand near, stand by*
20. peccō, *I sin:* peccadillo, peccant

Have the students write this week's derivatives in the Week 1 "Derivatives" section, which appears on the page after their Word List.

3. History: Under the Roman Empire, all countries were united by a common language: Latin. But when the Roman Empire fell, the Latin in different countries began to change, and modern languages started to develop. Romance languages—Italian, French, Spanish, Portuguese, and Romanian—all came from the language of the Romans and therefore have vocabularies that are often very similar.

3. Chants: This week you'll be reviewing first declension noun endings. The following chant information should all be familiar from last year!

At the top of the chant chart, you'll see the Singular and Plural columns. To the left are the case names—Nominative, Genitive, and so on. Each of these case endings, when applied to a noun, creates a different grammatical form of the noun. Students will be responsible to know all of the case names, though they will only be working with the nominative and genitive forms in this unit. (To review the basics of Latin nouns, see page xiv–xvi.)

To say the chant, begin in the top left corner and work down the column, then chant down the right column: *a, ae, ae, am, ā / ae, ārum, īs, ās, īs.* Run through the chant several times with the students to refresh their memories.

First Declension Noun Endings

Every Latin noun is in a specific declension, or family. Do your students remember how can to tell which nouns are in which declension? A noun may look like it's in one family when it's really in another!

Students should recall that the key is the ending that follows after a noun—the noun's genitive singular ending. **With a noun's genitive ending, you can discover what family that noun is in.** First declension nouns will *always* have -ae as their genitive singular ending. When you see the -ae genitive ending following a noun, you can be sure you have a *first declension* noun on your hands.

For example, what family is the word *nauta* in? If we look in this week's Word List, we can see that its genitive singular ending is -ae. Since only first declension nouns have an -ae genitive ending, we know *nauta* is in the first declension.

In the following chart, *nauta* has been declined. The endings are shown in bold. The part before the endings is called the *base*. The base of *nauta* is *naut-*. To decline *nauta*, each ending is applied to its base. A noun's base is very easy to determine: simply remove the genitive ending from the word, and you are left with the base!

(Note the variety of translations given for *nauta* in the nominative: a sailor, the sailor, sailor. This same flexibility also applies to the other cases because classical Latin does not have a word for the articles *a, an,* and *the.*)

	LATIN			ENGLISH	
	SINGULAR	PLURAL		SINGULAR	PLURAL
NOMINATIVE	naut**a**	naut**ae**		a sailor, the sailor, sailor	the sailors, sailors
GENITIVE	naut**ae**	naut**ārum**		of the sailor, the sailor's	of the sailors, the sailors'
DATIVE	naut**ae**	naut**īs**		to, for the sailor	to, for the sailors
ACCUSATIVE	naut**am**	naut**ās**		the sailor	the sailors
ABLATIVE	naut**ā**	naut**īs**		by, with, from the sailor	by, with, from the sailors

Students should remember that every noun has a gender. Last year, they used a very generalized rule of thumb, determining a noun's gender based on its declension. This year, as they learn more declensions, this will be too basic; they should memorize each noun's gender as they memorize the rest of the word and its definition.

Once students have gotten back into the rhythm of chanting the first declension endings, move on to declining whole nouns out loud.

4. Quotation: Juvenal was a Roman satrist, born in the first century A.D. He is credited with coining the phrase *rara avis*, "a rare bird." He used the phrase to refer to the perfect wife, but it has come to describe anything special and difficult to find—in this case, a true friend.

　　Have the students write this week's quotation in the Week 1 "Quotation" section, which appears on the page after their Word List.

5. Worksheet: Follow the directions given and complete the worksheet.

6. Quiz: Administer Quiz 1 at the end of the week.

WEEK 1

Word List

NOUNS

1. amīcus, -ī (m) . . . . friend
2. aqua, -ae (f) . . . . water
3. caelum, -ī (n) . . . . sky, heaven
4. cibus, -ī (m) . . . . food
5. colōnus, -ī (m) . . . . . . settler
6. equus, -ī (m) . . . . horse
7. latebra, -ae (f) . . . . . . hiding place
8. mūrus, -ī (m) . . . . wall
9. nauta, -ae (m) . . . . . . sailor
10. nimbus, -ī (m) . . . . . thundercloud, storm
11. poēta, -ae (m) . . . . . . poet

12. pontus, -ī (m) . . . . . . sea, seawater
13. puella, -ae (f) . . . . . . girl
14. puer, puerī (m) . . . . . boy
15. stella, -ae (f) . . . . star
16. taurus, -ī (m) . . . . . . bull
17. terra, -ae (f) . . . . earth, land
18. virga, -ae (f) . . . . . . branch, twig

VERBS

19. astō, astāre . . . . I stand near, stand by
20. peccō, peccāre . . . . . I sin

Chant:

First Declension Noun Endings

	LATIN			ENGLISH	
	SINGULAR	PLURAL		SINGULAR	PLURAL
NOMINATIVE	-a	-ae		a, the *noun*	the *nouns*
GENITIVE	-ae	-ārum		of the *noun*, the *noun's*	of the *nouns*, the *nouns'*
DATIVE	-ae	-īs		to, for the *noun*	to, for the *nouns*
ACCUSATIVE	-am	-ās		the *noun*	the *nouns*
ABLATIVE	-ā	-īs		by, with, from the *noun*	by, with, from the *nouns*

 Quotation:

Amīcus verus est rara avis—"A true friend is a rare bird"

Weekly Worksheet 1: Answer Key

A. Cross out the two wrong words in the definition below and write the correct words above them. Then, using the lines below, list all the Latin nouns from this week's Word List, their genitive ending, and gender. The first one is done for you.

names   **thing**

A noun ~~describes~~ a person, place, or ~~action~~.

1. _____ amīcus, -ī (m) _____
2. _____ **aqua, -ae (f)** _____
3. _____ **caelum, -ī (n)** _____
4. _____ **cibus, -ī (m)** _____
5. _____ **colōnus, -ī (m)** _____
6. _____ **equus, -ī (m)** _____
7. _____ **latebra, -ae (f)** _____
8. _____ **mūrus, -ī (m)** _____
9. _____ **nauta, -ae (m)** _____

10. _____ **nimbus, -ī (m)** _____
11. _____ **poēta, -ae (m)** _____
12. _____ **pontus, -ī (m)** _____
13. _____ **puella, -ae (f)** _____
14. _____ **puer, puerī (m)** _____
15. _____ **stella, -ae (f)** _____
16. _____ **taurus, -ī (m)** _____
17. _____ **terra, -ae (f)** _____
18. _____ **virga, -ae (f)** _____

B. Complete the review chant for this week and answer the questions about it.

	SINGULAR	PLURAL
NOMINATIVE	**-a**	**-ae**
GENITIVE	**-ae**	**-ārum**
DATIVE	**-ae**	**-īs**
ACCUSATIVE	**-am**	**-ās**
ABLATIVE	**-ā**	**-īs**

1. Are these endings for nouns or verbs? **nouns**

2. Which declension are these endings for? **first declension**

3. What is the gender of most nouns in this declension? **feminine**

4. Which ending tells you a noun's declension? **genitive singular**

C. Decline *virga, -ae* in the chart below, then answer the questions.

	SINGULAR	PLURAL
NOM.	virga	**virgae**
GEN.	**virgae**	**virgārum**
DAT.	**virgae**	**virgīs**
ACC.	**virgam**	**virgās**
ABL.	**virgā**	**virgīs**

1. The word *virga* means **branch or twig.**

2. Last year, you learned the word *virgō,* which means **maiden.**

D. Use your knowledge of Latin to answer the following questions about derivatives. Remember, a derivative is an English word with a Latin root.

1. The English word *noun* comes from the Latin word *nomen,* which means **name.**

2. An *aquarium* is like a zoo for sea animals. *Aquarium* is a derivative of the Latin word **aqua.**

3. A *peccadillo* is small mistake. *Peccadillo* is a derivative of the Latin word **peccō.**

Give an English derivative for each of these words. **Note: Answers may vary.**

4. mūrus _____ **mural, intramural** _____ 6. terra _____ **terrestrial, terrarium** _____

5. poēta _____ **poet, poetic, poetry** _____ 7. equus _____ **equine, equestrian** _____

The word for "friend" in Latin is *amīcus*. Look at the word for "friend" in these languages.

ITALIAN	amico
SPANISH	amigo
FRENCH	ami

8. Why do they look so much like *amīcus*? **Italian, Spanish, and French are Romance languages—languages that descended from Latin—so it makes sense that many of their words look similar to Roman words. *Amīcus* is an example of this.**

E. Complete the chart!

	ENGLISH: SINGULAR	LATIN: SINGULAR	LATIN: PLURAL
1.	**sailor**	nauta	**nautae**
2.	**girl**	puella	**puellae**
3.	wall	**mūrus**	**mūrī**
4.	**hiding place**	latebra	**latebrae**
5.	**sea**	**pontus**	pontī
6.	poet	**poēta**	**poētae**
7.	horse	**equus**	**equī**
8.	**settler**	**colōnus**	colōnī
9.	**food**	cibus	**cibī**
10.	bull	**taurus**	**taurī**

F. For each noun, give its declension and gender. Then decline each noun by adding the endings to the base that is given. Each noun's nominative and genitive singular forms are provided.

DECLENSION __1__   GENDER __F__

	SINGULAR	PLURAL
NOM.	aqua	aqu**ae**
GEN.	aquae	aqu**ārum**
DAT.	aqu**ae**	aqu**īs**
ACC.	aqu**am**	aqu**ās**
ABL.	aqu**ā**	aqu**īs**

DECLENSION __1__   GENDER __F__

	SINGULAR	PLURAL
NOM.	latebra	latebr**ae**
GEN.	latebrae	latebr**ārum**
DAT.	latebr**ae**	latebr**īs**
ACC.	latebr**am**	latebr**ās**
ABL.	latebr**ā**	latebr**īs**

1. How do you find the base of a noun? **To find the base of a noun, you remove the genitive singular ending from the noun. What remains is the base.**

G. Answer the questions about this week's quotation.

1. What does *Amīcus verus est rara avis* mean in English? **A true friend is a rare bird**

2. Which Latin word is the subject of this quotation? **amīcus**

3. What case does the subject noun always take? **nominative**

4. Which Latin word is the verb? (Hint: you should recognize it from last year!) **est**

H. On the lines below, give the Latin word for each object.

1. **nimbus**

2. **equus**

3. **taurus**

Week 1 Quiz

name:

A. Chant

Complete the chant chart, then answer the questions.

	SINGULAR	PLURAL
NOM.		
GEN.		
DAT.		-īs
ACC.		
ABL.	-ā	

1. The *subject* of a Latin sentence always takes the _____ case.

        a) accusative   b) singular   c) nominative

2. You can tell what declension a noun is in by looking at its _____.

        a) nominative plural ending   b) meaning   c) genitive singular ending

3. What declension is *terra, -ae* in?

        a) first   b) second   c) third

4. What is the gender of *terra, -ae?*

        a) masculine   b) feminine   c) neuter

5. What declension is *poēta, -ae* in?

        a) first   b) second   c) third

6. What is the gender of *poēta, -ae?*

 a) masculine b) feminine c) neuter

Decline *stella, -ae* and *puella, -ae* in the chart below. Give each noun's declension and gender.

DECLENSION _____ GENDER _____ DECLENSION _____ GENDER _____

	SINGULAR	PLURAL		SINGULAR	PLURAL
NOM.					
GEN.					puellārum
DAT.	stellae				
ACC.					
ABL.					

B. Vocabulary

Translate the Latin words into English, and the English words into Latin!

1. equus _____

2. sailor _____

3. peccō _____

4. cibus _____

5. caelum _____

6. seawater _____

7. storm _____

8. I stand by _____

Give the gender of each Latin noun: masculine (M), feminine (F), or neuter (N).

9. amīcus _____

10. puella _____

11. colōnus _____

12. nimbus _____

13. aqua _____

14. mūrus _____

15. virga _____

16. taurus _____

17. caelum _____

18. nauta _____

Week 1 Quiz: Answer Key

A. Chant

Complete the chant chart, then answer the questions.

	SINGULAR	PLURAL
NOM.	-a	-ae
GEN.	-ae	-ārum
DAT.	-ae	-īs
ACC.	-am	-ās
ABL.	-ā	-īs

1. The *subject* of a Latin sentence always takes the _____ case.

     a) accusative   b) singular   (c) nominative)

2. You can tell what declension a noun is in by looking at its _____.

     a) nominative plural ending   b) meaning   (c) genitive singular ending)

3. What declension is *terra, -ae* in?

     (a) first)   b) second   c) third

4. What is the gender of *terra, -ae?*

     a) masculine   (b) feminine)   c) neuter

5. What declension is *poēta, -ae* in?

     (a) first)   b) second   c) third

6. What is the gender of *poēta, -ae?*

(a) masculine)   b) feminine   c) neuter

Decline *stella, -ae* and *puella, -ae* in the chart below. Give each noun's declension and gender.

DECLENSION ___1___ GENDER ___F___

	SINGULAR	PLURAL
NOM.	stella	stellae
GEN.	stellae	stellārum
DAT.	stellae	stellīs
ACC.	stellam	stellās
ABL.	stellā	stellīs

DECLENSION ___1___ GENDER ___F___

	SINGULAR	PLURAL
NOM.	puella	puellae
GEN.	puellae	puellārum
DAT.	puellae	puellīs
ACC.	puellam	puellās
ABL.	puellā	puellīs

B. Vocabulary

Translate the Latin words into English, and the English words into Latin!

1. equus   **horse**   5. caelum   **sky, heaven**

2. sailor   **nauta**   6. seawater   **pontus**

3. peccō   **I sin**   7. storm   **nimbus**

4. cibus   **food**   8. I stand by   **astō**

Give the gender of each Latin noun: masculine (M), feminine (F), or neuter (N).

9. amīcus ___M___   13. aqua ___F___   17. caelum ___N___

10. puella ___F___   14. mūrus ___M___   18. nauta ___M___

11. colōnus ___M___   15. virga ___F___

12. nimbus ___M___   16. taurus ___M___

Teaching Notes: Week 2

1. Word List: Introduce the Word List for Week 2, asking students to carefully imitate your pronunciation. Word #6, *mālum,* means apple, but it looks very similar to the adjective *malus,* meaning evil. Students will be able to tell the two apart because *mālum* (apple) has a long "a."

Review the new Word List throughout the week on a regular basis.

2. Derivatives: Discuss the derivatives for this week's vocabulary:

1. ariēna, *banana*

2. cunīculus, *rabbit:* coney

3. folium, *leaf:* foliage, defoliate, exfoliation, foil, folio, portfolio

4. frāgum, *strawberry*

5. hortus, *garden:* horticulture

6. mālum, *apple*

7. pirum, *pear:* pear

8. ūva, *grape*

9. apricus, *sunny:* apricate

10. dēliciōsus, *delicious:* delicious

11. magnus, *large, big:* magnify, magnanimous, magnificent, magnitude, magnum

12. malus, *bad, evil:* malign, malignant, malevolence, malaria, malady, malpractice, malicious, malice, malodorous

13. parvus, *little, small*

14. gustō, *I taste:* gusto

Have the students write this week's derivatives in the Week 2 "Derivatives" section, which appears on the page after their Word List.

3. Chant: This week you'll be refreshing students on second declension noun endings. The chant works in exactly the same way as last week's. Run through the chant several times with the students to refamiliarize them with it.

Second Declension Noun Endings

Remember, with a noun's genitive ending, you can discover what family that noun is in. Second declension nouns will *always* have -*ī* as their genitive singular ending. Once you see the -*ī* genitive ending following a noun, you can be sure you are working with a noun in the second declension.

Let's look at an example. What family is the word *hortus* in? If we look in this week's Word List, we can see that its genitive singular ending is -*ī*. Only second declension nouns have an -*ī* genitive ending, therefore we know *hortus* is in the second declension.

In the chart below, *hortus* has been declined. To decline *hortus,* each ending is applied to the base, *hort-*. Remember, to find the base of any noun, simply remove the genitive singular ending—what remains is the noun's base. In the following chant chart, the endings are shown in bold.

	LATIN			ENGLISH	
	SINGULAR	PLURAL		SINGULAR	PLURAL
NOM.	hort**us**	hort**ī**		a, the *garden*	the *gardens*
GEN.	hort**ī**	hort**ōrum**		of the *garden*, the *garden's*	of the *gardens*, the *gardens'*
DAT.	hort**ō**	hort**īs**		to, for the *garden*	to, for the *gardens*
ACC.	hort**um**	hort**ōs**		the *garden*	the *gardens*
ABL.	hort**ō**	hort**īs**		by, with, from the *garden*	by, with, from the *gardens*

Once students have gotten back into the rhythm of chanting the second declension endings, lead them in declining second declension nouns out loud. Feel free to use the above chant chart as a guide if necessary.

4. Quotation: This week's Latin quotation may be one students have already encountered without realizing it was Latin. The Magna Carta is an English legal charter, issued in the year 1215. It was written by English barons in order to limit the power of the king, who at the time was King John of England. The Magna Carta is credited with being one of the most influential legal documents in all of history.

Have the students write this week's quotation in the Week 2 "Quotation" section, which appears on the page after their Word List.

5. Worksheet: Follow the directions given and complete the worksheet.

6. Quiz: Administer Quiz 2 at the end of the week.

WEEK 2

Word List

NOUNS

1. ariēna, -ae (f) . . . . banana
2. cunīculus, -ī (m). . . . . . rabbit
3. folium, -ī (n) . . . . leaf
4. frāgum, -ī (n) . . . . . . strawberry
5. hortus, -ī (m) . . . . . . garden
6. mālum, -ī (n). . . . . . . apple
7. pirum, -ī (n) . . . . pear
8. ūva, -ae (f) . . . . grape

ADJECTIVES

9. apricus, -a, -um . . . . . . sunny
10. dēliciōsus, -a, -um . . . delicious
11. magnus, -a, -um. . . . . large, big
12. malus, -a, -um . . . . . . bad, evil
13. parvus, -a, -um . . . . . little, small

VERBS

14. gustō, gustāre. . . . . . I taste

Chant:

Second Declension Noun Endings

	LATIN			ENGLISH	
	SINGULAR	PLURAL		SINGULAR	PLURAL
NOM.	-us	-ī		a, the *noun*	the *nouns*
GEN.	-ī	-ōrum		of the *noun,* the *noun's*	of the *nouns,* the *nouns'*
DAT.	-ō	-īs		to, for the *noun*	to, for the *nouns*
ACC.	-um	-ōs		the *noun*	the *nouns*
ABL.	-ō	-īs		by, with, from the *noun*	by, with, from the *nouns*

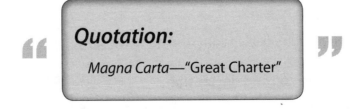

Quotation:

Magna Carta—"Great Charter"

Weekly Worksheet 2: Answer Key

A. Complete the chant chart and answer the questions about it.

	SINGULAR	PLURAL
NOMINATIVE	-us	**-ī**
GENITIVE	**-ī**	**-ōrum**
DATIVE	**-ō**	**-īs**
ACCUSATIVE	**-um**	**-ōs**
ABLATIVE	**-ō**	**-īs**

1. Is this a noun ending or a verb ending chant? **noun ending**

2. Which declension is it? **second declension**

3. Which gender are most of the nouns that take these endings? **masculine**

B. Decline *hortus, -ī* in the chart below, then answer the questions about it.

	SINGULAR	PLURAL
NOM.	**hortus**	**hortī**
GEN.	**hortī**	**hortōrum**
DAT.	**hortō**	**hortīs**
ACC.	**hortum**	**hortōs**
ABL.	**hortō**	**hortīs**

1. Which ending tells you a noun's declension? **the genitive singular**

2. Which declension is *hortus*? **second declension**

3. What does *hortus* mean? **garden**

Decline *ariēna, -ae* in the chart below, then answer the questions about it.

	SINGULAR	PLURAL
NOM.	ariēna	**ariēnae**
GEN.	**ariēnae**	**ariēnārum**
DAT.	**ariēnae**	**ariēnīs**
ACC.	**ariēnam**	**ariēnās**
ABL.	ariēnā	**ariēnīs**

2. Which declension is *ariēna?* **first declension**

3. What does *ariēna* mean? **banana**

C. For each noun, write in the blank whether it is in the first declension (1) or second declension (2).

1. cibus, -ī ____**2**____

5. pontus, -ī ____**2**____

2. stella, -ae ____**1**____

6. virga, -ae ____**1**____

3. cunīculus, -ī ____**2**____

7. poēta, -ae ____**1**____

4. aqua, -ae ____**1**____

8. puer, puerī ____**2**____

D. Translate these words into English. Can you do it from memory?

1. pirum   **pear**

6. apricus   **sunny**

2. latebra   **hiding place**

7. gustō   **I taste**

3. dēliciōsus   **delicious**

8. ūva   **grape**

4. nimbus   **storm, thundercloud**

9. astō   **I stand near, stand by**

5. peccō   **I sin**

10. folium   **leaf**

E. Answer the questions about this week's quotation.

    1. What does *Magna Carta* mean? **Great Charter**

    2. Who was king of England at the time the Magna Carta was written? **King John of England**

F. Write three sentences in English. In each sentence, replace two of the words with Latin words from this week. One sentence is given as an example. **Note: Student answers will vary and will need to be checked individually.**

    1. The *apple* is juicy and *delicious.*   The *mālum* is juicy and *deliciosus.*

    2. _____

    3. _____

    4. _____

G. Each sentence below uses a derivative (in italics). Use your knowledge of Latin vocabulary to finish each sentence by circling the correct answer!

    1. If someone writes a *malicious* letter, she is being _____.

        a) funny   (b) mean)   c) thoughtful

    2. "I'm going to go *apricate*" is just a fancy way to say "I'm going to go _____.

        (a) lay in the sun)   b) pick fruit   c) write a thank-you note

    3. *Coney* Island got its name because hundreds of _____ used to live there.

        a) circus animals   b) poets   (c) rabbits)

    4. *Horticulture* is the study of _____.

        a) how to raise toucans   (b) how to grow plants)   c) how to heal sicknesses

    5. When a person is *magnanimous*, it means that he is _____.

        (a) generous)   b) afraid   c) short

Week 2 Quiz

name:

A. Chant

Complete the chant chart, then answer the questions.

	SINGULAR	PLURAL
NOM.		
GEN.		
DAT.		
ACC.		-ōs
ABL.		

1. You can tell what declension a noun is in by looking at its _____ .

2. Which declension is *latebra, -ae* in? _____

3. Which declension is *cunīculus, -ī* in? _____

4. Which declension is *puer, puerī* in? _____

Decline *cunīculus, -ī* and *aqua, -ae* in the chart below.

	SINGULAR	PLURAL
NOM.	cunīculus	
GEN.		
DAT.		
ACC.		
ABL.		

	SINGULAR	PLURAL
NOM.	aqua	
GEN.		
DAT.		
ACC.		
ABL.		

B. Vocabulary

For each noun, write in the blank whether it is in the first declension (1) or second declension (2).

1. amīcus, -ī _____   5. puer, puerī _____

2. ariēna, -ae _____   6. hortus, -ī _____

3. cibus, -ī _____   7. virga, -ae _____

4. poēta, -ae _____   8. uva, -ae _____

Give the gender of each Latin noun: masculine (M), feminine (F), or neuter (N).

9. pirum, -ī _____   13. stella, -ae _____

10. ariēna, -ae _____   14. hortus, -ī _____

11. poēta, -ae _____   15. mūrus, -ī _____

12. mālum, -ī _____   16. caelum, -ī _____

Complete each sentence using one of the following words. One will be left over!

magnus   frāgum   cunīculus   apricus

virga   malus   gustō

1. I love to go to the beach in the summer when it's _____ and warm outside.

2. On his birthday, he asked for _____ shortcake for dessert.

3. Cinderella's slipper didn't fit her ugly stepsisters' _____ feet.

4. His brother found a robin's nest last autumn, up high on a tree _____ .

5. _____ some of everything at Thanksgiving, except the green beans!

6. Peter _____ ate lettuces, beans, and radishes from Mr. McGregor's garden.

Week 2 Quiz: Answer Key

A. Chant

Complete the chant chart, then answer the questions.

	SINGULAR	PLURAL
NOM.	**-us**	**-ī**
GEN.	**-ī**	**-ōrum**
DAT.	**-ō**	**-īs**
ACC.	**-um**	-ōs
ABL.	**-ō**	**-īs**

1. You can tell what declension a noun is in by looking at its **genitive singular ending.**

2. Which declension is *latebra, -ae* in? **first declension**

3. Which declension is *cunīculus, -ī* in? **second declension**

4. Which declension is *puer, puerī* in? **second declension**

Decline *cunīculus, -ī* and *aqua, -ae* in the chart below.

	SINGULAR	PLURAL		SINGULAR	PLURAL
NOM.	cunīculus	**cunīculī**	NOM.	aqua	**aquae**
GEN.	**cunīculī**	**cunīculōrum**	GEN.	**aquae**	**aquārum**
DAT.	**cunīculō**	**cunīculīs**	DAT.	**aquae**	**aquīs**
ACC.	**cunīculum**	**cunīculōs**	ACC.	**aquam**	**aquās**
ABL.	**cunīculō**	**cunīculīs**	ABL.	**aquā**	**aquīs**

B. Vocabulary

For each noun, write in the blank whether it is in the first declension (1) or second declension (2).

1. amīcus, -ī **2**

5. puer, puerī **2**

2. ariēna, -ae **1**

6. hortus, -ī **2**

3. cibus, -ī **2**

7. virga, -ae **1**

4. poēta, -ae **1**

8. uva, -ae **1**

Give the gender of each Latin noun: masculine (M), feminine (F), or neuter (N).

9. pirum, -ī **N**

13. stella, -ae **F**

10. ariēna, -ae **F**

14. hortus, -ī **M**

11. poēta, -ae **M**

15. mūrus, -ī **M**

12. mālum, -ī **N**

16. caelum, -ī **N**

Complete each sentence using one of the following words. One will be left over!

magnus	frāgum	cunīculus	apricus

| virga | malus | gustō | |

1. I love to go to the beach in the summer when it's **apricus** and warm outside.

2. On his birthday, he asked for **frāgum** shortcake for dessert.

3. Cinderella's slipper didn't fit her ugly stepsisters' **magnus** feet.

4. His brother found a robin's nest last autumn, up high on a tree **virga**.

5. **Gustō** some of everything at Thanksgiving, except the green beans!

6. Peter **cunīculus** ate lettuces, beans, and radishes from Mr. McGregor's garden.

Teaching Notes: Week 3

1. Word List: Introduce the Word List for Week 3, asking students to carefully imitate your pronunciation. Review the new Word List throughout the week on a regular basis.

2. Derivatives: Discuss the derivatives for this week's vocabulary:

1. aedificium, *building:* edifice
2. cēna, *dinner, meal:* cenacle
3. dominus, *lord, master:* dominate, domain, dominion
4. epistula, *letter:* epistle
5. fābula, *story, legend:* fable, fabulous
6. fēmina, *woman:* feminine, female
7. fīlia, *daughter*
8. fīlius, *son:* filial, affiliate
9. forum, *public square, marketplace:* forum
10. lingua, *tongue, language:* language, lingo, lingua, linguist, linguistics, bilingual
11. mensa, *table:* mesa
12. porta, *door, gate:* porter, portal, portcullis
13. sella, *seat, chair*
14. turba, *crowd, mob:* turbid
15. ambulō, *I walk:* amble, perambulator
16. amō, *I love:* amateur, amorous
17. exsultō, *I leap up, dance, rejoice:* exult, exultation
18. laudō, *I praise:* laud, laudatory
19. occultō, *I hide, conceal:* occult
20. probō, *I approve:* probation, probe, probable, probate, approbation, reprobate, reproof

Have the students write this week's derivatives in the Week 3 "Derivatives" section, which appears on the page after their Word List.

3. Chant: This week, you'll be reviewing the noun ending chant for the second declension *neuter*. Students should remember that the second declension neuter is a variation on the masculine second declension endings, reviewed last week. The endings function in exactly the same way; the difference is this week's chant is only for nouns of the second declension that are *neuter*.

Second Declension Neuter Noun Endings

Remember, with a noun's genitive ending, you can discover what declension that noun is in. Second declension nouns will *always* have -ī as their genitive singular ending. But the second declension neuter has a little twist. How can you tell whether you should use the usual second declension endings or the second declension neuter endings? **The key is to look at the nominative and genitive singular endings together**—in the second declension, only neuter nouns follow the -*um,* -*ī* progression. Once you see the -ī genitive ending following a noun, you know you are working with a noun in the second declension. *If the nominative singular ending of that word is -um, y*ou know you are working with a noun in the second declension *neuter.*

For example, what family is the word *aedificium* in? If we look in this Week's Word list, we see that *aedificium's* genitive singular ending is -*ī,* so we know *aedificium* is in the second declension. But *aedificium* also ends in -*um* in the nominative singular. Only second declension neuter nouns have an -*ī* in the genitive singular, plus -*um* in the nominative singular. Therefore, we know *aedificium* has to be a second declension neuter noun.

The second declension neuter endings are almost exactly the same as the standard second declension endings. Note the three endings where there is a difference—nominative singular, nominative plural, and accusative plural. A helpful trick to remember when declining these neuter nouns is the nominative and accusative endings (both singular and plural) will always match each other.

In the following chart, you can compare the similarities between the two. *Aedificium* has been declined alongside *taurus*. The endings are shown in bold. To decline *aedificium*, each ending is applied to the base, *aedifici-*. (To find the base of any noun, remove the genitive singular ending—what remains is the noun's base.)

SECOND DECLENSION

	SINGULAR	PLURAL
NOM.	taur**us**	taur**ī**
GEN.	taur**ī**	taur**ōrum**
DAT.	taur**ō**	taur**īs**
ACC.	taur**um**	taur**ōs**
ABL.	taur**ō**	taur**īs**

SECOND DECLENSION NEUTER

	SINGULAR	PLURAL
aedifici**um**	aedifici**a**
aedifici**ī**	aedifici**ōrum**
aedifici**ō**	aedifici**īs**
aedifici**um**	aedifici**a**
aedifici**ō**	aedifici**īs**

Once students have gotten into the rhythm of chanting the noun endings, begin applying the endings to whole nouns, as above with *aedificium*. Second declension neuter nouns from the last two weeks are: *caelum, folium, frāgum, mālum,* and *pirum*.

4. Quotation: This week's quotation is taken from Ruth 2:4 in the Latin Vulgate. The English translation is a common greeting in many Christian churches, to which the reply is "And with your spirit" (*Et cum spiritū tuō*) or "And also with you."

Have the students write this week's quotation in the Week 3 "Quotation" section, which appears on the page after their Word List.

5. Worksheet: Follow the directions given and complete the worksheet.

6. Quiz: Administer Quiz 3 at the end of the week.

WEEK 3

Word List

NOUNS

1. aedificium, -ī (n) . . . . . building
2. cēna, -ae (f) . . . . dinner, meal
3. dominus, -ī (m) . . . . . lord, master
4. epistula, -ae (f) . . . . . letter
5. fābula, -ae (f) . . . . . . story, legend
6. fēmina, -ae (f) . . . . . . woman
7. fīlia, -ae (f) . . . . daughter
8. fīlius, -ī (m) . . . . son
9. forum, -ī (n) . . . . public square, marketplace
10. lingua, -ae (f) . . . . . tongue, language
11. mensa, -ae (f) . . . . . table

12. porta, -ae (f) . . . . . . door, gate
13. sella, -ae (f) . . . . seat, chair
14. turba, -ae (f) . . . . . . crowd, mob

VERBS

15. ambulō, ambulāre . . . I walk
16. amō, amāre . . . . I love
17. exsultō, exsultāre . . . I leap up, dance, rejoice
18. laudō, laudāre . . . . . . I praise
19. occultō, occultāre . . . . I hide, conceal
20. probō, probāre . . . . . I approve

Chant:

Second Declension Neuter Noun Endings

	LATIN			ENGLISH	
	SINGULAR	PLURAL		SINGULAR	PLURAL
NOM.	-um	-a		a, the *noun*	the *nouns*
GEN.	-ī	-ōrum		of the *noun*, the *noun's*	of the *nouns*, the *nouns'*
DAT.	-ō	-īs		to, for the *noun*	to, for the *nouns*
ACC.	-um	-a		the *noun*	the *nouns*
ABL.	-ō	-īs		by, with, from the *noun*	by, with, from the *nouns*

(Continued on the next page)

Quotation:

Dominus vōbīscum—"The Lord be with you"

Weekly Worksheet 3: Answer Key

A. On the lines below, give the Latin word for each fruit.

1. **frāgum**

2. **mālum**

3. **ūva**

B. Write the declensions in the blanks, then complete the chants.

1st DECLENSION

	SINGULAR	PLURAL
NOM.	**-a**	**-ae**
GEN.	-ae	**-ārum**
DAT.	-ae	**-īs**
ACC.	**-am**	**-ās**
ABL.	**-ā**	**-īs**

2nd DECLENSION

	SINGULAR	PLURAL
NOM.	**-us**	-ī
GEN.	-ī	**-ōrum**
DAT.	**-ō**	**-īs**
ACC.	**-um**	**-ōs**
ABL.	**-ō**	**-īs**

2nd DECLENSION NEUTER

	SINGULAR	PLURAL
NOM.	-um	**-a**
GEN.	**-ī**	**-ōrum**
DAT.	**-ō**	**-īs**
ACC.	-um	**-a**
ABL.	**-ō**	**-īs**

Now, sort the nouns from this week's Word List and put them in the proper columns below. The first one is done for you.

1st DECLENSION	2nd DECLENSION	2nd DECLENSION NEUTER
cēna	**dominus**	aedificium
epistula	**fīlius**	**forum**
fābula		
fēmina		
fīlia		
lingua		
mensa		
porta		
sella		
turba		

C. Decline the following nouns and answer the questions about them.

Decline *aedificium, -ī.*

	SINGULAR	PLURAL
NOM.	aedificium	aedificia
GEN.	aedificiī	aedificiōrum
DAT.	aedificiō	aedificiīs
ACC.	aedificium	aedificia
ABL.	aedificiō	aedificiīs

1. What is the *genitive singular* ending of all second declension nouns?

   a) -us   b) -ae   c) -ī

2. What is the *nominative singular* ending of all second declension neuter nouns?

   a) -um   b) -us   c) -ī

3. Which declension is *aedificium* in?

   a) second declension neuter   b) first declension   c) second conjugation

Decline *lingua, -ae.*

	SINGULAR	PLURAL
NOM.	lingua	linguae
GEN.	linguae	linguārum
DAT.	linguae	linguīs
ACC.	linguam	linguās
ABL.	linguā	linguīs

4. What is the *genitive singular* ending of all first declension nouns?

   a) -a   (b) -ae)   c) -ī

5. What is the gender of most first declension nouns?

   (a) feminine)   b) masculine   c) neuter

Decline *fīlius, -ī.*

	SINGULAR	PLURAL
NOM.	fīlius	fīliī
GEN.	fīliī	fīliōrum
DAT.	fīliō	fīliīs
ACC.	fīlium	fīliōs
ABL.	fīliō	fīliīs

6. What part of speech is *fīlius?*

   a) verb   b) adjective   (c) noun)

D. Fill in the blank with each noun's genitive singular ending. Then underline the correct definition for each word.

NOUN	GENITIVE	DEFINITION		
1. lingua	-ae	wheel	**language**	house
2. forum	-ī	door	stone	**marketplace**
3. dominus	-ī	stream	**lord**	walkway
4. fābula	-ae	dress	shoe	**story**
5. epistula	-ae	**letter**	tree	picture
6. pirum	-ī	grape	rabbit	**pear**

E. Answer the following questions about derivatives from this week's Word List. The derivatives are italicized.

1. The English word *bilingual* comes from the Latin word **lingua.**

2. If someone is *bilingual* he can speak two **languages.**

3. The English word *epistle* comes from the Latin word **epistula.**

4. The *epistles* of Paul are **letters** written to different churches.

List one derivative for each of these words. **Note: Answers may vary. Sample answers listed below.**

5. fābula **fable, fabulous**   6. probō **probation, probe, probable**

F. Give each noun's declension and gender. Then decline it by adding the endings to the base that is given. Each noun's nominative and genitive singular forms are provided.

DECLENSION ____**1**____ GENDER ____**F**____

	SINGULAR	PLURAL
NOM.	cēna	cēn**ae**
GEN.	cēnae	cēn**ārum**
DAT.	cēnae	cēn**īs**
ACC.	cēn**am**	cēn**ās**
ABL.	cēn**ā**	cēn**īs**

DECLENSION ____**2**____ GENDER ____**N**____

	SINGULAR	PLURAL
NOM.	pirum	pir**a**
GEN.	pirī	pir**ōrum**
DAT.	pir**ō**	pir**īs**
ACC.	pir**um**	pir**a**
ABL.	pir**ō**	pir**īs**

1. How do you find the base of a noun? **To find a noun's base, take its genitive singular form and remove the ending. What remains is the base.**

G. Translate these words from English into Latin. (Hint: Watch whether they're singular or plural!)

1. doors   **portae**   4. buildings **aedificia**

2. masters   **dominī**   5. apple   **mālum**

3. sailor   **nauta**   6. sea   **pontus**

Week 3 Quiz

name:

A. Derivatives

Draw a line to match each derivative with its Latin root.

1. epistle	exsultō
2. linguistics	nauta
3. ambulance	epistula
4. fabulous	equus
5. mesa	lingua
6. exult	ambulō
7. nautical	mensa
8. equestrian	fābula

B. Chants

Finish declining the words below, and answer the questions about the chants.

	SINGULAR	PLURAL
NOM.		
GEN.	foliī	
DAT.		foliīs
ACC.		
ABL.		

1. Which declension is this word? _____

2. What gender is this word? _____

3. What does this word mean in English? _____

	SINGULAR	PLURAL
NOM.	forum	
GEN.		
DAT.		
ACC.	forum	
ABL.		

4. Which declension is this word? _____

5. What gender is this word? _____

6. What does this word mean in English? _____

C. Vocabulary

Give each noun's genitive singular ending, gender (M, F, N), base, and declension (1 or 2).

	NOUN	GENITIVE	GENDER	BASE	DECLENSION
1.	turba				
2.	frāgum				
3.	dominus				
4.	aedificium				
5.	puer				

Week 3 Quiz: Answer Key

A. Derivatives

Draw a line to match each derivative with its Latin root.

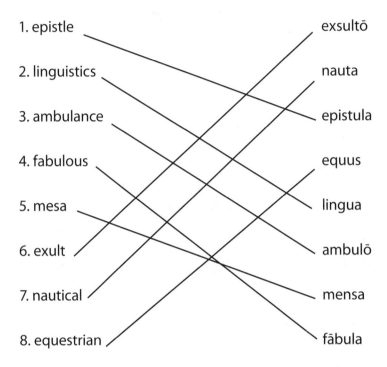

1. epistle
2. linguistics
3. ambulance
4. fabulous
5. mesa
6. exult
7. nautical
8. equestrian

exsultō

nauta

epistula

equus

lingua

ambulō

mensa

fābula

B. Chants

Finish declining the words below, and answer the questions about the chants.

	SINGULAR	PLURAL
NOM.	folium	folia
GEN.	foliī	foliōrum
DAT.	foliō	foliīs
ACC.	folium	folia
ABL.	foliō	foliīs

1. Which declension is this word? **second declension (neuter)**

2. What gender is this word? **neuter**

3. What does this word mean in English? **leaf**

	SINGULAR	PLURAL
NOM.	forum	**fora**
GEN.	**forī**	**forōrum**
DAT.	**forō**	**forīs**
ACC.	forum	**fora**
ABL.	**forō**	**forīs**

4. Which declension is this word? **second declension (neuter)**

5. What gender is this word? **neuter**

6. What does this word mean in English? **public square, marketplace**

C. Vocabulary

Give each noun's genitive singular ending, gender (M, F, N), base, and declension (1 or 2).

	NOUN	GENITIVE	GENDER	BASE	DECLENSION
1.	turba	**-ae**	**F**	**turb-**	**1**
2.	frāgum	**-ī**	**N**	**frāg-**	**2**
3.	dominus	**-ī**	**M**	**domin-**	**2**
4.	aedificium	**-ī**	**N**	**aedifici-**	**2**
5.	puer	**-ī**	**M**	**puer-**	**2**

Teaching Notes: Week 4

1. Word List: Introduce the Word List for Week 4. Review the new Word List regularly throughout the week.

2. Derivatives: Discuss the derivatives for this week's vocabulary:

1. coquus, *cook, chef:* cook
2. fungus, *mushroom, fungus:* fungus, fungal
3. nasus, *nose:* nasal
4. nucleus, *nut, kernel:* nucleus
5. porcus, *pig:* pork, porcini, porcine
6. radius, *staff, rod:* radius, ray
7. silva, *forest:* sylvan
8. ulmus, *elm tree:* elm
9. brūnus, *brown*
10. odōrātus, *sweet-smelling, fragrant*
11. perfectus, *perfect:* perfect
12. cumulō, *I pile up, fill up:* accumulate, cumulative
13. olefactō, *I smell, sniff:* olfactory
14. sub, *below, under:* subterranean, submarine, subarctic, subject, subordinate
15. suprā, *above*

Have the students write this week's derivatives in the Week 4 "Derivatives" section, which appears on the page after their Word List.

3. Chant: For the next three weeks, students will be reviewing verbs. This week, they'll be reintroduced to their first verb ending chant—the present active verb endings. (For more on stems and endings, refer back to the Latin Grammar Basics section on pages xii–xiv.)

It is very important that students remember that this is a chant of verb *endings*. Remind them that the endings can only function in a sentence when attached to a verb stem.

Ask students if they remember how to find a verb's stem. To find a verb's stem, take the second principal part of the verb (the infinitive) and remove the *-re* ending. For example, to find the stem of *cumulō, cumulāre,* you take *cumulāre* and remove *-re.* The stem of *cumulō* is *cumulā-.*

Next, refresh students on how to identify a verb's conjugation, or family. A verb conjugation is a group of verbs that share the same stem vowel. First conjugation, or "ā" family, verbs always have an "ā" at the end of their stem. Looking at the example of *cumulō,* we know that it is a first conjugation verb because its stem, *cumulā-,* ends in an "ā." So far, all of your Word List verbs have been from the first conjugation.

Once students have found the stem of a verb, they can add this week's endings to that stem to conjugate it. After completing the Latin conjugation, continue to the English translation. In the following example, the endings are in bold.

LATIN	SINGULAR	PLURAL		ENGLISH	SINGULAR	PLURAL
1ST	olefact**ō**	olefactā**mus**			I smell	we smell
2ND	olefactā**s**	olefactā**tis**			you smell	you all smell
3RD	olefacta**t**	olefacta**nt**			he/she/it smells	they smell

When translating in the present tense, it is equally correct to say "I *verb*" or "I am *verbing*" or "I do *verb*." For example, *cumulō* can be translated either "I pile up" or "I am piling up" or "I do pile up"; *olefactant* can be translated either "They sniff" or "They are sniffing" or "They do sniff." All of these translations faithfully reflect the present tense. However for the sake of space and clarity, only one translation will appear in the chant chart.

4. Quotation: Have the students write this week's quotation in the Week 4 "Quotation" section, which appears on the page after their Word List.

5. Worksheet: Follow the directions given on the worksheet.

6. Quiz: Administer Quiz 4 at the end of the week.

WEEK 4

Word List

NOUNS

1. coquus, -ī (m) . . . . cook, chef
2. fungus, -ī (m) . . . . mushroom, fungus
3. nasus, -ī (m) . . . . nose
4. nucleus, -ī (m) . . . . . . nut, kernel
5. porcus, -ī (m) . . . . pig
6. radius, -ī (m) . . . . staff, rod
7. silva, -ae (f) . . . . forest
8. ulmus, -ī (m) . . . . elm tree

ADJECTIVES

9. brūnus, -a, -um . . . . . . brown

10. odōrātus, -a, -um . . . . sweet-smelling, fragrant
11. perfectus, -a, um . . . . perfect

VERBS

12. cumulō, cumulāre . . . I pile up, fill up
13. olefactō, olefactāre . . I smell, sniff

ADVERBS

14. sub. . . . . below, under
15. suprā . . . . above

Chant:

Present Active Verb Endings

	LATIN			ENGLISH	
	SINGULAR	PLURAL		SINGULAR	PLURAL
1ST	-ō	-mus		I am *verbing*	we are *verbing*
2ND	-s	-tis		you are *verbing*	you all are *verbing*
3RD	-t	-nt		he/she/it is *verbing*	they are *verbing*

 Quotation:

porcī parvī trēs—"the three little pigs"

Weekly Worksheet 4: Answer Key

A. Answer the following questions about the verbs from this week's Word List.

1. A verb shows **action** or state of being.

2. How do you find a verb's stem? **To find a verb's stem, remove the -re ending from the**

second principal part.

3. What is the stem of *olefactō?* **olefactā-**

4. What is the stem of *cumulō?* **cumulā**

5. Are these "ā" family or "ē" family verbs? **"ā" family**

6. Which conjugation are these verbs in? **first conjugation**

B. Conjugate *cumulō* in the present tense and translate it.

LATIN

ENGLISH

	SINGULAR	PLURAL		SINGULAR	PLURAL
1ST	cumulō	**cumulāmus**		I pile up	**we pile up**
2ND	**cumulās**	**cumulātis**		**you pile up**	**you all pile up**
3RD	**cumulat**	**cumulant**		**he/she/it piles up**	**they pile up**

C. Latin's present tense can be translated into English in three different ways. For example, *olefactō* can be translated "I smell," "I do smell," or "I am smelling." Using *olefactō* as an example, write three translations for each verb.

1. cumulō **I pile up, I do pile up, I am piling up**

2. gustō **I taste, I do taste, I am tasting**

3. probant **they approve, they do approve, they are approving**

4. peccāmus **we sin, we do sin, we are sinning**

5. laudās **you praise, you do praise, you are praising**

6. astat **she stands by, she does stand by, she is standing by**

7. ambulātis **you all walk, you all do walk, you all are walking**

D. Underline the noun that goes with the verb and then translate the sentences.

NOUN	VERB	TRANSLATION
1. Porcus / **Porcī**	olefactant.	**Pigs are sniffing.**
2. **Puella** / Puellae	gustat.	**A girl tastes.**
3. Cunīculus / **Cunīculī**	occultant.	**The rabbits are hiding.**
4. Nauta / **Nautae**	astant.	**Sailors are standing near.**
5. **Coquus** / Coquī	exsultat.	**The cook rejoices.**

E. Each of the words below comes from a Latin root! Figure out which of your Latin words is the root, and then give its English meaning. The first one is done for you.

	ITALIAN	SPANISH	FRENCH	LATIN	ENGLISH
1.	fragola	fresa	fraise	**frāgum**	**strawberry**
2.	perfetto	perfecto	parfait	**perfectus**	**perfect**
3.	terra	tierra	terre	**terra**	**land**
4.	lingua	lengua	langue	**lingua**	**language**
5.	naso	nariz	nez	**nasus**	**nose**

F. Underline the ending for each verb and translate it.

1. gustā**tis**   **you all are tasting**   4. astā**s**   **you are standing near**

2. olefactā**mus**   **we sniff**   5. pecca**t**   **he does sin**

3. laud**ō**   **I am praising**   6. ambulā**tis**   **you all walk**

G. Give the following forms of *silva*.

    1. nominative singular **silva**

    2. genitive singular **silvae**

    3. nominative plural **silvae**

Give these forms of *nucleus*.

    4. genitive singular **nucleī**

    5. nominative plural **nucleī**

H. For each English word, circle the nominative plural in Latin.

	ENGLISH	LATIN		
1.	walls	mūra	mūrae	(mūrī)
2.	elm trees	ulmus	(ulmī)	ulmōs
3.	chairs	sellās	(sellae)	sella
4.	seas	pontae	pontuses	(pontī)
5.	letters	(epistulae)	epistula	epistulī
6.	kernels	nucleuī	(nucleī)	nucleum
7.	friends	(amicī)	amicae	amica
8.	pears	(pira)	pirī	pirum
9.	sons	fīlius	fīlium	(fīliī)
10.	forests	silva	(silvae)	silvī

I. Translate these Latin sentences into English. See if you can remember how to translate the last one!

    1. Fīlia ambulat. **The daughter is walking.**

2. Turba exsultat. **The crowd is rejoicing.**

3. Dominus amat. **The Lord loves.**

4. Nasī olefactant. **Noses are sniffing.**

5. Fēminae probant. **The women approve.**

6. Puer occultat. **A boy is hiding.**

7. Amīcī ambulant. **Friends are walking.**

8. Fīliī exsultant. **The sons are dancing.**

9. Fēmina cumulat. **The woman piles up.**

10. Poēta gustābit. **The poet will taste.**

J. Answer the questions about this week's quotation.

1. How would you say "the three little pigs" in Latin? **porcī parvī trēs**

2. Which word means "three"? **trēs**

3. Which declension is the Latin word for "pigs"? **second declension**

K. The chart below is missing its labels! Fill in the blanks, then decline *sella*.

	SINGULAR	PLURAL
NOMINATIVE	sella	sellae
GENITIVE	sellae	sellārum
DATIVE	sellae	sellīs
ACCUSATIVE	sellam	sellās
ABLATIVE	sellā	sellīs

Week 4 Quiz

name:

A. Chant

Underline the sentences that have verbs in the present tense.

1. The trees are losing their leaves.

2. The sun will rise at 6:30.

3. Fido was chewing Spot's bone.

4. Tom had done his homework.

5. Jessie bakes cookies every day.

6. Luke does like malted milk balls.

7. The crowd at the observatory will see the comet.

8. Sarah is laughing.

9. Will the mail come soon?

10. I know her.

Fill in the present tense endings. Then conjugate *olefactō* in the present tense and translate it.

	SINGULAR	PLURAL
1ST		
2ND	-s	
3RD		

LATIN

ENGLISH

	SINGULAR	PLURAL		SINGULAR	PLURAL
1ST					
2ND	olefactās				
3RD					

B. Vocabulary

Complete the story using the Latin words below. Each word will be used once.

brūnus   *nucleus*   *odōrātus*   *sub*   *ulmus*   *coquus*

1. A little _____ squirrel was preparing for winter.

2. He lived in a tall old _____ in the forest with his wife and children.

3. All day long, whenever he found a _____, he would hide it in the dirt.

4. _____ the dirt, the nuts would stay fresh and cold, like in a refrigerator.

5. His wife was a wonderful _____ and would make them acorn soup, pecan pie,

and roasted chestnuts during the winter.

6. And their cozy little tree always smelled _____, especially at Christmas.

Translate these sentences into English.

7. Colōnī astant. _____

8. Porcus gustat. _____

9. Occultātis. _____

10. Cunīculus exsultat. _____

C. Quotation

Write out this week's quotation, then answer the questions about it.

_____

1. Which word means "pigs"? _____

2. Which word means "little"? _____

3. What part of speech is the word "little"? _____

Week 4 Quiz: Answer Key

A. Chant

Underline the sentences that have verbs in the present tense.

1. **The trees are losing their leaves.**

2. The sun will rise at 6:30.

3. Fido was chewing Spot's bone.

4. Tom had done his homework.

5. **Jessie bakes cookies every day.**

6. **Luke does like malted milk balls.**

7. The crowd at the observatory will see the comet.

8. **Sarah is laughing.**

9. Will the mail come soon?

10. **I know her.**

Fill in the present tense endings. Then conjugate *olefactō* in the present tense and translate it.

	SINGULAR	PLURAL
1ST	**-ō**	**-mus**
2ND	-s	**-tis**
3RD	**-t**	**-nt**

LATIN

	SINGULAR	PLURAL
1ST	**olefactō**	**olefactāmus**
2ND	olefactās	**olefactātis**
3RD	**olefactat**	**olefactant**

ENGLISH

	SINGULAR	PLURAL
1ST	**I smell**	**we smell**
2ND	**you smell**	**you all smell**
3RD	**he/she/it smells**	**they smell**

B. Vocabulary

Complete the story using the Latin words below. Each word will be used once.

brūnus   *nucleus*   *odōrātus*   *sub*   *ulmus*   *coquus*

1. A little **brūnus** squirrel was preparing for winter.

2. He lived in a tall old **ulmus** in the forest with his wife and children.

3. All day long, whenever he found a **nucleus**, he would hide it in the dirt.

4. **Sub** the dirt, the nuts would stay fresh and cold, like in a refrigerator.

5. His wife was a wonderful **coquus** and would make them acorn soup, pecan pie, and roasted

chestnuts during the winter.

6. And their cozy little tree always smelled **odōrātus**, especially at Christmas.

Translate these sentences into English.

7. Colōnī astant. **The settlers are standing near.**

8. Porcus gustat. **A pig is tasting.**

9. Occultātis. **You all are hiding.**

10. Cunīculus exsultat. **A rabbit leaps up.**

C. Quotation

Write out this week's quotation, then answer the questions about it.

porcī parvī trēs

1. Which word means "pigs"? **porcī**

2. Which word means "little"? **parvī**

3. What part of speech is the word "little"? **adjective**

Teaching Notes: Week 5

1. Word List: Introduce the Word List for Week 5. Review the new Word List throughout the week on a regular basis. Continue to review older vocabulary as well.

2. Derivatives: Discuss the derivatives for this week's vocabulary:

1. agricola, *farmer*
2. aquila, *eagle:* aquiline
3. armentum, *herd*
4. cervus, *stag, deer:* cervine
5. coma, *hair, leaves, wool, mane:* Coma Berenices (constellation)
6. lūna, *moon:* lunar, lunatic
7. lupus, *wolf:* lupus, lupine
8. nuntius, *message, messenger:* nuncio
9. rīpa, *riverbank*
10. saxum, *rock*
11. appāreō, *I appear:* apparition, appear

12. clāmō, *I shout:* clamor
13. errō, *I wander:* error, err, erratic, aberration
14. labōrō, *I work, toil:* labor, collaborate, elaborate, belabor
15. lībō, *I sip, taste:* libation
16. lūceō, *I shine, am bright:* translucent
17. properō, *I hurry, rush*
18. spīrō, *I breathe:* aspiration, conspiracy, respiration, transpire
19. ululō, *I howl, scream:* ululate
20. volō, *I fly:* volley, volatile

Have the students write this week's derivatives in the Week 5 "Derivatives" section, which appears on the page after their Word List.

3. Chant: This week's chant is the future active verb endings. Have students compare this week's chant with last week's, noting the similarities. Practice this chant throughout the week.

This week, you'll be refreshing students on the second conjugation, or "ē" family, verbs. Second conjugation verbs always have an "ē" at the end of their stem. Remember, to find the stem of a verb, take its second principal part and remove the *-re*.

Let's look at *appāreō,* the first verb in this week's list. We know that it's a second conjugation verb because its stem, *appāre-,* ends in an "ē." This week, there are only two second conjugation verbs in your Word List, but many more will follow in the weeks ahead.

Once students have found the stem of a verb, they can add this week's endings to that stem to conjugate it. In the following example, the endings are in bold.

LATIN

	SINGULAR	PLURAL
1ST	appāre**bō**	appāre**bimus**
2ND	appāre**bis**	appāre**bitis**
3RD	appāre**bit**	appāre**bunt**

ENGLISH

	SINGULAR	PLURAL
1ST	I will appear	we will appear
2ND	you will appear	you all will appear
3RD	he/she/it will appear	they will appear

Remind students to use the terms first, second, and third person when referring to verbs. For example, *appārebis* is in the "second person singular" in the future tense. (Refer to page xi for more regarding the use of person.)

4. Quotation: With last week's quotation being "the three little pigs," this week's quotation is extra fun. The quote is an ancient proverb, which appears in a Roman comedy called *Phormio,* written by the playwright Terence during the second century B.C. It refers to being in a situation you do not enjoy but cannot escape without more disastrous consequences. The quote is also reminiscent of Proverbs 26:17.

Have the students write this week's quotation in the Week 5 "Quotation" section, which appears on the page after their Word List.

5. Worksheet: Follow the directions given to complete the worksheet.

6. Quiz: Administer Quiz 5 at the end of the week.

WEEK 5

Word List

NOUNS

1. agricola, -ae (m) . . . . . farmer
2. aquila, -ae (m/f) . . . . . eagle
3. armentum, -ī (n) . . . . . herd
4. cervus, -ī (m) . . . . stag, deer
5. coma, -ae (f) . . . . hair, leaves, wool, mane
6. lūna, -ae (f) . . . . moon
7. lupus, -ī (m) . . . . wolf
8. nuntius, -ī (m) . . . . . . message, messenger
9. rīpa, -ae (f) . . . . riverbank
10. saxum, -ī (n) . . . . rock

VERBS

11. appāreō, appārēre . . . I appear
12. clāmō, clāmāre . . . . . I shout
13. errō, errāre . . . . I wander
14. labōrō, labōrāre . . . . . I work, toil
15. lībō, lībāre . . . . I sip, taste
16. lūceō, lūcēre . . . . I shine, am bright
17. properō, properāre . . . I hurry, rush
18. spīrō, spīrāre . . . . I breathe
19. ululō, ululāre . . . . I howl, scream
20. volō, volāre . . . . I fly

Chant:

Future Active Verb Endings

	LATIN			ENGLISH	
	SINGULAR	PLURAL		SINGULAR	PLURAL
1ST	-bō	-bimus		I will *verb*	we will *verb*
2ND	-bis	-bitis		you will *verb*	you all will *verb*
3RD	-bit	-bunt		he/she/it will *verb*	they will *verb*

Quotation:
Auribus teneō lupum—"I hold a wolf by the ears"

Weekly Worksheet 5: Answer Key

A. Fill in the blank with each verb's stem.

1. clāmō, clāmāre **clāmā-**

2. spīrō, spīrāre **spīrā-**

3. appāreō, appārēre **appārē-**

4. ululō, ululāre **ululā-**

5. lībō, lībāre **lībā-**

B. Answer the following questions about the verb *lūceō*.

1. What is the stem of *lūceō, lūcēre?* **lūcē-**

2. Which verb family is *lūceō* in? **the "ē" family**

3. Which conjugation is it in? **second conjugation**

Fill in the future tense endings. Then conjugate *lūceō* in the future tense and translate it.

	SINGULAR	PLURAL
1ST	-bō	**-bimus**
2ND	**-bis**	**-bitis**
3RD	**-bit**	**-bunt**

LATIN

	SINGULAR	PLURAL
1ST	**lūcēbō**	**lūcēbimus**
2ND	**lūcēbis**	**lūcēbitis**
3RD	**lūcēbit**	**lūcēbunt**

ENGLISH

	SINGULAR	PLURAL
1ST	**I will shine**	**we will shine**
2ND	**you will shine**	**you all will shine**
3RD	**he/she/it will shine**	**they will shine**

C. Give the English meaning of these Latin quotations.

1. Auribus teneō lupum **I hold a wolf by the ears**

2. Dominus vōbīscum **The Lord be with you**

3. Amīcus verus est rara avis **A true friend is a rare bird**

4. Magna Carta **Great Charter**

5. Porcī parvī trēs **the three little pigs**

D. Underline the ending of each verb. Then translate the verb and state whether it is first, second, or third person. The first one is done for you!

	VERB	TRANSLATION	PERSON
1.	errā**mus**	we are wandering	first
2.	propera**t**	**he is rushing**	**third**
3.	ululā**bitis**	**you all will scream**	**second**
4.	lībō	**I sip**	**first**
5.	vola**nt**	**they are flying**	**third**
6.	spīrā**bis**	**you will breathe**	**second**

E. Translate these Latin sentences into English.

1. Coma lūcet. **The hair is shining.**

2. Cervī properābunt. **The deer will hurry.**

3. Dominus probat. **The lord approves.**

4. Lupī ululant. **Wolves are howling.**

5. Armentum errābunt. **The herd will wander.**

6. Porcī cumulābunt. **The pigs will sniff.**

7. Nuntius clamat. **A messenger is shouting.**

8. Nautae astant. **The sailors stand near.**

9. Fēmina peccat. **The woman sins.**

10. Poēta probābit. **The poet will approve.**

F. Here are some interesting English words derived from this week's Word List! Look them up in an English dictionary and write their definitions on the lines. In the parentheses next to each word, write the word's Latin root.

1. aquiline: **of or like an eagle; curved or hooked like an eagle's beak** (**aquila**)

2. lupine: **a type of flower; of or like a wolf** (**lupus**)

3. libation: **the ritual of pouring out wine or oil on the ground as a sacrifice** (**lībō**)

4. translucent: **allowing light to shine through, but diffusing it so that objects are not seen**

clearly; shining through (**lūceō**)

5. spiracle: **an air hole** (**spīrō**)

G. Answer the following questions about nouns.

1. What is the definition of a noun? **A noun names a person, place, or thing.**

2. What case does a Latin subject noun take? **nominative**

3. Find and circle all the nouns below!

(cēna)	exsultō	(lingua)	apricus	(fungus)
malus	perfectus	(folium)	volō	(puer)
(dominus)	(radius)	(ariēna)	odōrātus	suprā
ambulō	brūnus	(latebra)	(nucleus)	amō
(mūrus)	(agricola)	(virga)	(nasus)	(cervus)

H. First, label the noun cases in the gray boxes to the left, then decline *saxum, -ī*.

	SINGULAR	PLURAL
NOMINATIVE	saxum	saxa
GENITIVE	saxī	saxōrum
DATIVE	saxō	saxīs
ACCUSATIVE	saxum	saxa
ABLATIVE	saxō	saxīs

I. Give the Latin plural, gender (M, F, N), declension (1 or 2), and singular translation of each noun.

	NOUN	PLURAL	GENDER	DECLENSION	TRANSLATION
1.	nauta, -ae	nautae	F	1	sailor
2.	caelum, -ī	caelī	N	2	sky, heaven
3.	cibus, -ī	cibī	M	2	food
4.	poēta, -ae	poētae	F	1	poet
5.	amīcus, -ī	amīcī	M	2	friend

Week 5 Quiz

name:

A. Chant

Complete the chant, then answer the questions about it.

	SINGULAR	PLURAL
1ST	-bō	
2ND		
3RD		

1. Is this a verb ending chant or a noun ending chant? _____

2. Are the *-bō* endings for the present or future tense? _____

Conjugate *appāreō* in the future tense and translate it.

LATIN			ENGLISH		
	SINGULAR	**PLURAL**		**SINGULAR**	**PLURAL**
1ST					
2ND					
3RD					

3. What conjugation is *appāreō* a part of? _____

4. Which verb family is it in? _____

5. How do you find the stem of a verb? _____

_____

B. Review

For each noun, write its declension and gender on the line above. Then decline each noun by adding the endings to the base that is given. Each noun's nominative and genitive singular forms are provided.

DECLENSION _____ GENDER _____

	SINGULAR	PLURAL
NOM.	armentum	arment
GEN.	armentī	arment
DAT.	arment	arment
ACC.	arment	arment
ABL.	arment	arment

DECLENSION _____ GENDER _____

	SINGULAR	PLURAL
NOM.	agricola	agricol
GEN.	agricolae	agricol
DAT.	agricol	agricol
ACC.	agricol	agricol
ABL.	agricol	agricol

C. Vocabulary

Give the stem of each verb.

1. labōrō, labōrāre _____

2. errō, errāre _____

3. lūceō, lūcēre _____

4. volō, volāre _____

5. astō, astāre _____

6. clāmō, clāmāre _____

Translate these sentences into English.

1. Luna lūcet. _____

2. Nuntiī properābunt. _____

3. Stellae appārent. _____

4. Lupī ululābunt. _____

5. Filiī exsultant. _____

6. Armenta errant. _____

Week 5 Quiz: Answer Key

A. Chant

Complete the chant, then answer the questions about it.

	SINGULAR	PLURAL
1ST	-bō	-bimus
2ND	-bis	-bitis
3RD	-bit	-bunt

1. Is this a verb ending chant or a noun ending chant? **verb ending chant**

2. Are the *-bō* endings for the present or future tense? **future**

Conjugate *appāreō* in the future tense and translate it.

LATIN

ENGLISH

	SINGULAR	PLURAL			SINGULAR	PLURAL
1ST	appārēbō	appārēbimus			I will appear	we will appear
2ND	appārēbis	appārēbitis			you will appear	you all will appear
3RD	appārēbit	appārēbunt			he/she/it will appear	they will appear

3. What conjugation is *appāreō* a part of? **second conjugation**

4. Which verb family is it in? **the "ē" family**

5. How do you find the stem of a verb? **Take the second principal part and remove the *-re*.**

B. Review

For each noun, write its declension and gender on the line above. Then decline each noun by adding the endings to the base that is given. Each noun's nominative and genitive singular forms are provided.

DECLENSION ___2___ GENDER ___N___

	SINGULAR	PLURAL
NOM.	armentum	armenta
GEN.	armentī	armentōrum
DAT.	armentō	armentīs
ACC.	armentum	armenta
ABL.	armentō	armentīs

DECLENSION ___1___ GENDER ___M___

	SINGULAR	PLURAL
NOM.	agricola	agricolae
GEN.	agricolae	agricolārum
DAT.	agricolae	agricolīs
ACC.	agricolam	agricolās
ABL.	agricolā	agricolīs

C. Vocabulary

Give the stem of each verb.

1. labōrō, labōrāre **labōrā-**

2. errō, errāre **errā-**

3. lūceō, lūcēre **lūcē-**

4. volō, volāre **volā-**

5. astō, astāre **astā-**

6. clāmō, clāmāre **clāmā-**

Translate these sentences into English.

1. Luna lūcet. **The moon is bright.**

2. Nuntiī properābunt. **The messengers will hurry.**

3. Stellae appārent. **Stars are appearing.**

4. Lupī ululābunt. **Wolves will howl.**

5. Filiī exsultant. **The sons leap up.**

6. Armenta errant. **The herds are wandering.**

Teaching Notes: Week 6

1. Word List: Introduce the Word List for Week 6. Review the new Word List throughout the week on a regular basis. Continue to review older vocabulary as well.

2. Derivatives: Discuss the derivatives for this week's vocabulary:

1. alga, *seaweed:* algae
2. bālaena, *whale:* baleen
3. delphīnus, *dolphin:* dolphin
4. fuscina, *harpoon, trident*
5. harēna, *sand*
6. hydrus, *sea serpent*
7. nausea, *nausea, seasickness:* nausea
8. ōceanus, *ocean:* ocean
9. aequus, *level, even, calm:* equal, equable, equate, equator, equity, equilateral, equivalent, equivocal, egalitarian, equinox
10. albus, *white:* albino, albumen, auburn
11. āridus, *dry:* arid, aridity
12. salsus, *salty, witty:* sauce, salsa, saucy
13. ūmidus, *wet:* humid, humidity, humidifier
14. et, *and:* et cetera
15. instō, *I pursue eagerly, follow closely:* instant
16. rīdeō, *I laugh:* deride, ridicule, ridiculous
17. statim, *immediately:* stat

Have the students write this week's derivatives in the Week 6 "Derivatives" section, which appears on the page after their Word List.

3. Chant: This week's chant is the imperfect active endings. The imperfect tense is a type of past tense (there are several in Latin). Have students compare this week's chant with last week's, noting again the similarities. Practice this chant throughout the week.

Once students have found a verb's stem, they can add this week's endings to that stem to conjugate the verb. In the following example, the endings are in bold.

LATIN

	SINGULAR	PLURAL
1ST	appārē**bam**	appārē**bāmus**
2ND	appārē**bās**	appārē**bātis**
3RD	appārē**bat**	appārē**bant**

ENGLISH

	SINGULAR	PLURAL
	I was appearing	we were appearing
	you were appearing	you all were appearing
	he/she/it was appearing	they were appearing

4. Quotation: This week's quotation is one students may have encountered before, and is almost always used metaphorically, as in, "She explained each detail ad nauseam."

Have the students write this week's quotation in the Week 6 "Quotation" section of their student book.

5. Worksheet: This week, there are two sentences given in Exercise B which use adjectives. Students may remember from last year how to translate using adjectives, but if not, a quick refresher will be in order. Refer to the the section on Adjectives in the Basic Grammar section of this book, on page xvi.

They will also begin translating with adverbs again, starting with *statim* this week in Exercise B. Latin adverbs will generally appear before the verb they modify. Adjective and adverb use will be reviewed more during Unit 2. Follow the directions given to complete the worksheet.

6. Quiz: Administer Quiz 6 at the end of the week.

WEEK 6

Word List

NOUNS

1. alga, -ae (f). . . . . seaweed
2. bālaena, -ae (f) . . . . . whale
3. delphīnus, -ī (m) . . . . dolphin
4. fuscina, -ae (f). . . . . . harpoon, trident
5. harēna, -ae (f). . . . . . sand
6. hydrus, -ī (m) . . . . . . sea serpent
7. nausea, -ae (f) . . . . . . nausea, seasickness
8. ōceanus, -ī (m) . . . . . ocean

ADJECTIVES

9. aequus, -a, -um . . . . . level, even, calm
10. albus, -a, -um . . . . . white
11. āridus, -a, -um . . . . . dry

12. salsus, -a, -um . . . . . salty, witty
13. ūmidus, -a, -um . . . . wet

CONJUNCTIONS

14. et. . . . . and

VERBS

15. instō, instāre. . . . . . I pursue eagerly, follow closely
16. rīdeō, rīdēre . . . . . . I laugh

ADVERBS

17. statim . . . . immediately

Chant:

Imperfect Active Verb Endings

	LATIN			ENGLISH	
	SINGULAR	**PLURAL**		**SINGULAR**	**PLURAL**
1ST	-bam	-bāmus		I was *verbing*	we were *verbing*
2ND	-bās	-bātis		you were *verbing*	you all were *verbing*
3RD	-bat	-bant		he/she/it was *verbing*	they were *verbing*

 Quotation:

ad nauseam—"to the point of sickness"

Weekly Worksheet 6: Answer Key

A. Fill in the imperfect tense endings. Then conjugate *rīdeō* in the imperfect tense and translate it.

	SINGULAR	PLURAL
1ST	-bam	-bāmus
2ND	-bās	-bātis
3RD	-bat	-bant

LATIN

	SINGULAR	PLURAL
1ST	rīdēbam	rīdēbāmus
2ND	rīdēbās	rīdēbātis
3RD	rīdēbat	rīdēbant

ENGLISH

	SINGULAR	PLURAL
1ST	I was laughing	we were laughing
2ND	you were laughing	you all were laughing
3RD	he/she/it was laughing	they were laughing

Answer the following questions about this week's verbs.

1. What conjugation is *rīdeō?* **second**

2. What conjugation is *īnstō?* **first**

3. What is the stem of *īnstō?* **īnstā-**

B. Translate the following sentences into English. Watch out—a few include adjectives! Do you remember how to translate using them?

1. Delphīnī exsultant et rīdent. **Dolphins are leaping and laughing**.

2. Bālaena alba appāret. **The white whale appears**.

3. Nautae clāmant. **The sailors shout.**

4. Fuscinae volābunt! **Harpoons will fly!**

5. Statim occultat. **Immediately, he [the whale] hides**.

6. Ōceanus salus lūcet. **The salty ocean shines**.

C. For each verb, first underline its ending. Then fill in the blanks to tell whether it's first, second, or third person and whether it's singular or plural. Finally, translate the verb into English. The first one is done for you.

	VERB	PERSON	NUMBER	TRANSLATION
1.	ulula<u>t</u>	3rd	singular	he/she/it howls
2.	instā**s**	**2nd**	**singular**	**you follow closely**
3.	spirā**mus**	**1st**	**plural**	**we are breathing**
4.	appārē**tis**	**2nd**	**plural**	**you all appear**
5.	properā**bis**	**2nd**	**singular**	**you will hurry**
6.	lūce**nt**	**3rd**	**plural**	**they are bright**
7.	clamā**bō**	**1st**	**singular**	**I will shout**
8.	volā**bant**	**3rd**	**plural**	**they were flying**

D. Draw a line to match each derivative with its Latin root.

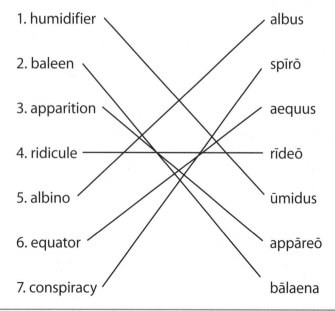

1. humidifier — albus
2. baleen — spīrō
3. apparition — aequus
4. ridicule — rīdeō
5. albino — ūmidus
6. equator — appāreō
7. conspiracy — bālaena

E. For each sentence, underline the Latin noun and verb that match the English sentence.

ENGLISH	NOUN	VERB
1. A sea serpent is hiding.	<u>Hydrus</u> / Hydrī	<u>occultat</u> / occultātis.
2. The cooks were laughing.	Coquus / <u>Coquī</u>	rīdēbās / rīdēbunt / <u>rīdēbant</u>.
3. The herd hurries.	<u>Armentum</u> / Armenta	<u>properat</u> / properant.
4. The dolphins will follow closely.	Delphīnus / <u>Delphīnī</u>	instābant / <u>instābunt</u> / instant.
5. The rabbit was dancing.	<u>Cunīculus</u> / Cunīculī	exsultābam / <u>exsultābat</u>.

F. Decline the following nouns and write which declension each one is in. Then answer the questions.

1st DECLENSION

	SINGULAR	PLURAL
NOM.	harēna	harēnae
GEN.	harēnae	harēnārum
DAT.	harēnae	harēnīs
ACC.	harēnam	harēnās
ABL.	harēnā	harēnīs

2nd DECLENSION

	SINGULAR	PLURAL
NOM.	cibus	cibī
GEN.	cibī	cibōrum
DAT.	cibō	cibīs
ACC.	cibum	cibōs
ABL.	cibō	cibīs

1. Which case is used for subjects? **nominative**

2. What is the gender of *cibus?* **masculine**

3. What is the gender of *harēna?* **feminine**

G. Answer the following questions about this week's quotation.

1. If you talk on and on and on about something, you are talking **ad nauseam**.

2. What does that phrase mean in English? **"to the point of sickness"**

H. Give the genitive singular ending of each noun, then write whether it is first declension (1), second declension (2), or second declension neuter (2N). The first one is done for you.

1. fuscina ___-ae___ ___1___

2. radius ___-ī___ ___2___

3. pontus ___-ī___ ___2___

4. alga ___-ae___ ___1___

5. aedificium ___-ī___ ___2N___

6. fungus ___-ī___ ___2___

7. rīpa ___-ae___ ___1___

8. ulmus ___-ī___ ___2___

9. pirum ___-ī___ ___2N___

10. cēna ___-ae___ ___1___

I. Find and circle the hidden vocabulary words!

statim	albus	odoratus	latebra	pecco
hortus	gusto	supra	puella	aequus
salsus	turba	ululo	mensa	deliciosus

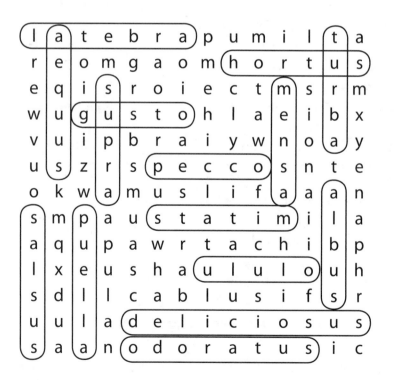

Week 6 Quiz

name: _____

A. Review

Complete the chart and conjugate *ululō* in the present tense. Give the translation of each word, then answer the questions.

	LATIN			ENGLISH	
	SINGULAR	PLURAL		SINGULAR	PLURAL
1ST	ululō				
2ND					
3RD					

1. In the chart, what do 1st, 2nd, and 3rd refer to? _____

2. What conjugation is *ululō?* _____

3. What family is *ululō* in? _____

4. How do you find the stem of a verb? _____

_____

B. Vocabulary

On the lines below, give the Latin word for each image.

1. _____   2. _____   3. _____

4. _____   5. _____   6. _____

Translate these sentences into English.

1. Saxa appārent. _____

2. Nautae rīdēbant. _____

3. Delphīnus instābat. _____

4. Harēna alba lucet. _____

C. Chant

Fill in the imperfect tense endings. Then conjugate *instō* in the imperfect tense and translate it.

	SINGULAR	PLURAL
1ST	-bam	
2ND		
3RD		

LATIN

	SINGULAR	PLURAL
1ST		
2ND		
3RD		

ENGLISH

	SINGULAR	PLURAL
1ST		
2ND		
3RD		

Week 6 Quiz: Answer Key

A. Review

Complete the chart and conjugate *ululō* in the present tense. Give the translation of each word, then answer the questions.

LATIN

	SINGULAR	PLURAL
1ST	ululō	ululāmus
2ND	ululās	ululātis
3RD	ululat	ululant

ENGLISH

	SINGULAR	PLURAL
1ST	I howl	we howl
2ND	you howl	you all howl
3RD	he/she/it howls	they howl

1. In the chart, what do 1st, 2nd, and 3rd refer to? **person**

2. What conjugation is *ululō?* **first conjugation**

3. What family is *ululō* in? **"ā" family**

4. How do you find the stem of a verb? **Take the second principal part and remove the -re.**

B. Vocabulary

On the lines below, give the Latin word for each image.

1. **hydrus**

2. **mālum**

3. **lupus**

4. **nimbus**

5. **delphīnus**

6. **taurus**

Translate these sentences into English.

1. Saxa appārent. **Rocks appear**.

2. Nautae rīdēbant. **The sailors were laughing**.

3. Delphīnus instābat. **A dolphin was following closely**.

4. Harēna alba lucet. **The white sand is bright**.

C. Chant

Fill in the imperfect tense endings. Then conjugate *instō* in the imperfect tense and translate it.

	SINGULAR	PLURAL
1ST	-bam	-bāmus
2ND	-bās	-bātis
3RD	-bat	-bant

LATIN

	SINGULAR	PLURAL
1ST	instābam	instābāmus
2ND	instābās	instābātis
3RD	instābat	instābant

ENGLISH

	SINGULAR	PLURAL
1ST	I was following closely	we were following closely
2ND	you were following closely	you all were following closely
3RD	he/she/it was following closely	they were following closely

Teaching Notes: Week 7

1. Word List: Introduce the Word List for Week 7. It may help students if you point out that an *inimīcus* (Word #1) is the opposite of an *amīcus!*

Review the new Word List throughout the week on a regular basis. Continue to review older vocabulary as well.

2. Derivatives: Discuss the derivatives for this week's vocabulary:

1. inimīcus, *personal enemy:* enemy, inimical
2. morbus, *sickness, disease:* morbid
3. opera, *effort, service:* operate, operation
4. pharetra, *quiver*
5. sagitta, *arrow:* Sagittarius
6. venēnum, *poison:* venom, venomous
7. ventus, *wind:* vent
8. augeō, *I increase:* augment, auction
9. censeō, *I estimate:* census, censor
10. cibō, *I feed*
11. exanimō, *I kill*
12. oppugnō, *I attack*
13. parō, *I prepare:* prepare, pare, repair
14. pugnō, *I fight:* impugn, pugilist, pugnacious, repugnant
15. significō, *I indicate, point out:* significant, signify
16. superō, *I defeat, conquer:* insuperable, superable

Have the students write this week's derivatives in the Week 7 "Derivatives" section, which appears on the page after their Word List.

3. Chant: There is no new chant this week. Take this opportunity to review the chants from the last six weeks. Check that students are comfortable finding noun bases and verb stems, and have them practice conjugating verbs and declining nouns.

4. Quotation: This week's quotation is taken from Proverbs 25:21. Have the students write this week's quotation in the Week 7 "Quotation" section, which appears on the page after their Word List.

5. Worksheet: Follow the directions given to complete the worksheet.

6. Quiz: Administer Quiz 7 at the end of the week.

WEEK 7

Word List

NOUNS

1. inimīcus, -ī (m) . . . . . . personal enemy
2. morbus, -ī (m). . . . . . . sickness, disease
3. opera, -ae (f) . . . . effort, services
4. pharetra, -ae (f). . . . . . quiver
5. sagitta, -ae (f) . . . . . . arrow
6. venēnum, -ī (n) . . . . . . poison
7. ventus, -ī (m) . . . . wind

VERBS

8. augeō, augēre . . . . . . I increase
9. censeō, censēre . . . . . I estimate
10. cibō, cibāre . . . . I feed
11. exanimō, exanimāre . . I kill
12. oppugnō, oppugnāre . I attack
13. parō, parāre . . . . I prepare
14. pugnō, pugnāre . . . . I fight
15. significō, significāre . . I indicate, point out
16. superō, superāre . . . . I defeat, conquer

Chant:

No new chant this week.

> ## Quotation:
>
>
> *Sī ēsurierit inimīcus tuus, ciba illum.*
>
> "If your enemy is hungry, give him bread to eat." [Prov. 25:21a]

Weekly Worksheet 7: Answer Key

A. Write the nominative plural of these nouns from this week's Word List.

1. morbus   **morbī**   4. opera   **operae**

2. sagitta   **saggitae**   5. venēnum   **venēna**

3. pharetra   **pharetrae**   6. inimīcus   **inimīcī**

B. Answer the questions, then conjugate *pugnō* in the present, future, and imperfect tenses and translate it.

1. What is the stem of *pugnō*? **pugnā-**

2. Which conjugation is *pugnō*? **first conjugation**

Present Active

LATIN			ENGLISH		
	SINGULAR	PLURAL		SINGULAR	PLURAL
1ST	**pugnō**	**pugnāmus**		**I fight**	**we fight**
2ND	**pugnās**	**pugnātis**		**you fight**	**you all fight**
3RD	**pugnat**	**pugnant**		**he/she/it fights**	**they fight**

Future Active

LATIN			ENGLISH		
	SINGULAR	PLURAL		SINGULAR	PLURAL
1ST	**pugnābō**	**pugnābimus**		**I will fight**	**we will fight**
2ND	**pugnābis**	**pugnābitis**		**you will fight**	**you all will fight**
3RD	**pugnābit**	**pugnābunt**		**he/she/it will fight**	**they will fight**

Imperfect Active

| | LATIN | | | ENGLISH | |
	SINGULAR	PLURAL		SINGULAR	PLURAL
1ST	**pugnābam**	**pugnābāmus**		**I was fighting**	**we were fighting**
2ND	**pugnābās**	**pugnābātis**		**you were fighting**	**you all were fighting**
3RD	**pugnābat**	**pugnābant**		**he/she/it was fighting**	**they were fighting**

C. For each sentence, underline the Latin noun and verb that match the English sentence.

ENGLISH	NOUN	VERB
1. The farmers estimate.	Agricola / **Agricolae**	censet / **censent**.
2. The enemies are increasing.	Inimīcus / **Inimīcī**	auget / **augent**.
3. An arrow flies.	**Sagitta** / Sagittae	**volat** / volant.
4. The stags will fight.	Cervus / **Cervī**	pugnat / pugnābatis / **pugnābunt**.
5. An eagle was hiding.	**Aquila** / Aquilae	occultābam / **occultābat** / occultābit.

D. On the lines below, label what each animal is called in Latin.

1. **porcus**   2. **aquila**   3. **bālaena**

4. **cervus**   5. **delphīnus**   6. **cunīculus**

E. For each verb, first underline its ending. Then fill in the blanks to tell whether it's first, second, or third person and whether it's singular or plural. Finally, translate the verb into English. The first one is done for you.

	VERB	PERSON	NUMBER	TRANSLATION
1.	parant	3rd	plural	they prepare
2.	lūcētis	**2nd**	**plural**	**you all shine**
3.	spīrat	**3rd**	**singular**	**it is breathing**
4.	significābimus	**1st**	**plural**	**we will point out**
5.	superant	**3rd**	**plural**	**they conquer**
6.	censeō	**1st**	**singular**	**I estimate**
7.	cibābam	**1st**	**singular**	**I was feeding**
8.	augēbitis	**2nd**	**plural**	**you all will increase**

F. In some of these sentences, the noun and verb don't match in number. Cross out the incorrect sentences and translate the rest.

1. Nimbī apparent. **Clouds are appearing**.

2. ~~Agricolae significābat.~~ _____

3. Cervus properat. **The deer is hurrying**.

4. Venēna exanimābunt. **The poisons will kill**.

5. ~~Lūpus ululant.~~ _____

G. Fill in the blanks to complete these Latin quotations.

1. ad **nauseam**

2. Auribus teneō **lupum**

3. **Sī** ēsurierit **inimīcus** tuus, **ciba** illum.

H. Each of these verbs is in the present tense. Translate each one in three different ways.

1. censent **they estimate, they are estimating, they do estimate**

2. augēs **you increase, you are increasing, you do increase**

3. significāmus **we indicate, we are indicating, we do indicate**

4. parō **I prepare, I am preparing, I do prepare**

I. List the verbs from this week on the blank lines below, then circle the verbs in the second conjugation, or "ē" family. When you have finished, answer the questions below.

1. **augeō**　　　　6. **parō**

2. **censeō**　　　　7. **pugnō**

3. **cibō**　　　　　8. **significō**

4. **exanimō**　　　9. **superō**

5. **oppugnō**

10. The uncircled verbs are in the **first** conjugation.

11. Another name for the uncircled verbs is the **"ā"** family.

J. Each of the words below comes from a Latin root! Figure out which of your Latin words is the root, and then give its English meaning.

	ITALIAN	SPANISH	FRENCH	LATIN	ENGLISH
1.	lupo	lobo	loup	**lupus**	**wolf**
2.	vento	viento	vent	**ventus**	**wind**
3.	balena	ballena	baleine	**bālaena**	**whale**
4.	luna	luna	lune	**luna**	**moon**

Week 7 Quiz   *name:*

A. *Vocabulary*

Write the declensions in the blanks, then complete the chants.

	SINGULAR	PLURAL
NOM.		
GEN.		
DAT.		
ACC.	-am	
ABL.	-ā	

	SINGULAR	PLURAL
NOM.		-ī
GEN.	-ī	
DAT.		
ACC.		
ABL.		

	SINGULAR	PLURAL
NOM.		-a
GEN.	-ī	
DAT.		
ACC.		
ABL.		

In the first blank, give the genitive singular ending for each noun. In the second blank, write the noun's gender (M, F, or N). And in the third blank, give the English meaning of each word.

	NOUN	GENITIVE	GENDER	TRANSLATION
1.	venēnum			
2.	morbus			
3.	puer			
4.	frāgum			
5.	opera			
6.	poēta			
7.	saxum			
8.	nasus			

B. Chant

Answer the questions, then conjugate *censeō* in the present, future, and imperfect tenses and translate it.

1. What is the stem of *censeō?* _____

2. Which conjugation is *censeō?* _____

Present Active

LATIN

	SINGULAR	PLURAL
1ST		
2ND		
3RD		

ENGLISH

	SINGULAR	PLURAL
1ST		
2ND		
3RD		

Future Active

LATIN

	SINGULAR	PLURAL
1ST		
2ND		
3RD		

ENGLISH

	SINGULAR	PLURAL
1ST		
2ND		
3RD		

Imperfect Active

LATIN

	SINGULAR	PLURAL
1ST		
2ND		
3RD		

ENGLISH

	SINGULAR	PLURAL
1ST		
2ND		
3RD		

Week 7 Quiz: Answer Key

A. Vocabulary

Write the declensions in the blanks, then complete the chants.

1st Declension

	SINGULAR	PLURAL
NOM.	-a	-ae
GEN.	-ae	-ārum
DAT.	-ae	-īs
ACC.	-am	-ās
ABL.	-ā	-īs

2nd Declension

	SINGULAR	PLURAL
NOM.	-us	-ī
GEN.	-ī	-ōrum
DAT.	-ō	-īs
ACC.	-um	-ōs
ABL.	-ō	-īs

2nd Declension Neuter

	SINGULAR	PLURAL
NOM.	-um	-a
GEN.	-ī	-ōrum
DAT.	-ō	-īs
ACC.	-um	-a
ABL.	-ō	-īs

In the first blank, give the genitive singular ending for each noun. In the second blank, write the noun's gender (M, F, or N). And in the third blank, give the English meaning of each word.

	NOUN	GENITIVE	GENDER	TRANSLATION
1.	venēnum	-ī	N	poison
2.	morbus	-ī	M	sickness, disease
3.	puer	-ī	M	boy
4.	frāgum	-ī	N	strawberry
5.	opera	-ae	F	effort, services
6.	poēta	-ae	M	poet
7.	saxum	-ī	N	rock
8.	nasus	-ī	M	nose

B. Chant

Answer the questions, then conjugate *censeō* in the present, future, and imperfect tenses and translate it.

1. What is the stem of *censeō*? **censē-**

2. Which conjugation is *censeō*? **second conjugation**

Present Active

	LATIN			ENGLISH	
	SINGULAR	PLURAL		SINGULAR	PLURAL
1ST	censeō	censēmus		I estimate	we estimate
2ND	censēs	censētis		you estimate	you all estimate
3RD	censēt	censēnt		he/she/it estimates	they estimate

Future Active

	LATIN			ENGLISH	
	SINGULAR	PLURAL		SINGULAR	PLURAL
1ST	censēbō	censēbimus		I will estimate	we will estimate
2ND	censēbis	censēbitis		you will estimate	you all will estimate
3RD	censēbit	censēbunt		he/she/it will estimate	they will estimate

Imperfect Active

	LATIN			ENGLISH	
	SINGULAR	PLURAL		SINGULAR	PLURAL
1ST	censēbam	censēbāmus		I was estimating	we were estimating
2ND	censēbās	censēbātis		you were estimating	you all were estimating
3RD	censēbat	censēbant		he/she/it was estimating	they were estimating

Teaching Notes: Week 8

1. Word List: Introduce the Word List for Week 8. Review the new Word List throughout the week. Continue to review older vocabulary as well. Check that students are memorizing the gender of nouns; noun gender will become increasingly important when translating with adjectives in the next unit.

2. Derivatives: Discuss the derivatives for this week's vocabulary:

1. noctua, *owl*
2. sciūrus, *squirrel:* squirrel, squirrely
3. audeō, *I dare:* audacious, audacity
4. occupō, *I seize:* occupy, occupation, preoccupied
5. valeō, *I am well:* ambivalent, avail, prevail, convalescent, valor, value, valedictorian
6. maneō, *I remain, stay:* remain, permanent, mansion

Have the students write this week's derivatives in the Week 8 "Derivatives" section, which appears on the page after their Word List. Look over previous derivatives from Unit 1.

3. Chant: There is no new chant this week. Use this week to review the chants from the first six weeks. Do students find it easy to distinguish between first and second conjugation verbs? Are they proficient in identifying which declension a noun is in?

4. Quotation: There is no quotation this week. Look over quotations from previous weeks and test the students' memory of the translations.

5. Worksheet: Follow the directions given to complete the worksheet.

6. Quiz: Since there is a test at the end of the week, this week's quiz is optional. Feel free to use it as practice for the test.

7. Test: The Unit 1 Test should be given at the end of this week.

WEEK 8

Word List

NOUNS

1. noctua, -ae (f) . . . . owl
2. sciūrus, -ī (m) . . . . squirrel

VERBS

3. audeō, audēre . . . . . . I dare
4. occupō, occupāre . . . . I seize
5. valeō, valēre. . . . . I am well
6. maneō, manēre . . . . . I remain, stay

Chant:

No new chant this week.

Quotation:

No quotation this week.

Weekly Worksheet 8: Answer Key

A. The verbs below are all **third** person verbs. After each verb, write the subject and whether it is singular or plural. The first one is done for you.

VERB	SUBJECT	SINGULAR/PLURAL
1. libant	they	plural
2. properābant	**they**	**plural**
3. occupant	**they**	**plural**
4. exanimābit	**he/she/it**	**singular**
5. censet	**he/she/it**	**singular**
6. oppugnābunt	**they**	**plural**
7. audēt	**he/she/it**	**singular**

B. Use each of the verbs above to write your own Latin sentences! Match a noun with each verb. Remember, the noun needs to match the verb in number (singular/plural). Then translate your sentences into English. **Note: Student answers will vary and will need to be checked individually. Sample answers are provided below.**

1. **Coquī libant.** *The cooks are sipping.*

2. **Sciūrī properābant.** *The squirrels were hurrying.*

3. **Lupī occupant.** *Wolves are seizing.*

4. **Morbus exanimābat.** *The disease was killing.*

5. **Agricola censet.** *A farmer does estimate.*

6. **Inimīcī oppugnābunt.** *The enemies will attack.*

7. **Armentum audēt.** *The herd dares.*

C. Conjugate *valeō* and *occupō* in the present tense. Above each box, write the verb's conjugation.

2nd CONJUGATION

	SINGULAR	PLURAL
1ST	valeō	valēmus
2ND	valēs	valētis
3RD	valet	valent

1st CONJUGATION

	SINGULAR	PLURAL
	occupō	occupāmus
	occupās	occupātis
	occupat	occupant

D. These sentences change a little at a time. See how quickly and accurately you can translate them.

1. Parō. **I prepare**.

2. Parāmus. **We prepare**.

3. Parat. **He/she/it prepares**.

4. Agricola parat. **The farmer prepares**.

5. Agricolae parant. **The farmers prepare**.

6. Inimīcī parant. **The enemies prepare**.

7. Inimīcī oppugnant. **The enemies attack**.

8. Inimīcus clamat. **The enemy shouts**.

9. Nuntius clamat. **The messenger shouts**.

10. Nuntius properat. **The messenger hurries**.

11. Lūpus properat. **The wolf is hurrying**.

12. Lūpī ululant. **The wolves are howling**.

13. Lūpī augent. **The wolves are increasing**.

14. Armenia augent. **The herds are increasing**.

15. Armentum errat. **The herd wanders**.

16. Noctua errat. **An owl wanders**.

17. Noctua volat. **An owl is flying**.

18. Sagitta volat. **An arrow is flying**.

19. Sagittae volant. **Arrows are flying**.

20. Sagitta apparet. **An arrow appears**.

21. Lūna apparet. **The moon appears**.

22. Lūna lūcet. **The moon shines**.

23. Saxum lucet. **The rock shines**.

24. Saxa manent. **The rocks remain**.

25. Cervi manent. **The deer remain**.

E. Decline *sciūrus,* and then answer the questions about it.

	SINGULAR	PLURAL
NOM.	sciūrus	**sciūrī**
GEN.	**sciūrī**	**sciūrōrum**
DAT.	**sciūrō**	**sciūrīs**
ACC.	**sciūrum**	**sciūrōs**
ABL.	**sciūrō**	**sciūrīs**

Circle the answer.

1. What is the *genitive singular* ending of all second declension nouns?

a) -us   b) -īs   c) -ī

2. Which case does a subject noun always take?

a) nominative   b) neuter   c) plural

3. What is the gender of *sciūrus?*

a) neuter   b) feminine   c) masculine

F. Give a definition for these parts of speech.

1. Noun: **A noun names a person, place, or thing.**

2. Verb: **A verb shows action or state of being.**

G. Draw a line to match each derivative with its Latin root.

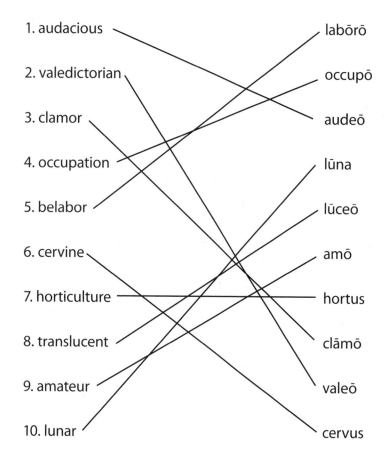

1. audacious   labōrō

2. valedictorian   occupō

3. clamor   audeō

4. occupation   lūna

5. belabor   lūceō

6. cervine   amō

7. horticulture   hortus

8. translucent   clāmō

9. amateur   valeō

10. lunar   cervus

Week 8 Quiz

name:

A. Vocabulary

In the first blank, write the second principal part for each verb. In the second blank, write the verb's conjugation (1 or 2). And in the third blank, give the English translation of each verb.

	VERB	SECOND PRINCIPAL PART	CONJUGATION	TRANSLATION
1.	maneō			
2.	occultō			
3.	cibō			
4.	rīdeō			
5.	occupō			
6.	audeō			
7.	valeō			
8.	significō			

Underline the noun that goes with the verb and then translate the sentences.

NOUN	VERB	TRANSLATION
9. Ventus / Ventī	augēbat.	_____
10. Noctua / Noctuae	occupābit.	_____
11. Cervus / Cervī	lībat.	_____
12. Sciūrus / Sciūrī	rīdent.	_____
13. Agricola / Agricolae	manēbunt.	_____
14. Hydrus / Hydrī	pugnābit.	_____

B. Chant

For each noun, write its declension in the blank, then decline it.

DECLENSION _____ GENDER _____

	SINGULAR	PLURAL
NOM.	venēnum	
GEN.		
DAT.		
ACC.		
ABL.		

DECLENSION _____ GENDER _____

	SINGULAR	PLURAL
NOM.	noctua	
GEN.		
DAT.		
ACC.		
ABL.		

Fill in the missing verb endings to complete the chants.

Present Active

	SINGULAR	PLURAL
1ST		
2ND	-s	
3RD		

Future Active

	SINGULAR	PLURAL
	-bit	

Imperfect Active

	SINGULAR	PLURAL
		-bamus

C. Derivatives

Read each sentence. Then circle which Latin word the italicized derivative comes from.

1. The teacher decided to make the class seating arrangement *permanent*.

   a) maneō   b) pharetra   c) mensa

2. Our cat had the *audacity* to sneak on the table and eat part of the Thanksgiving turkey!

   a) aquila   b) augeō   c) audeō

3. The white part of an egg is called *albumen*, and the yellow part is called the yolk.

   a) audeō   b) alga   c) albus

Week 8 Quiz: Answer Key

A. Vocabulary

In the first blank, write the second principal part for each verb. In the second blank, write the verb's conjugation (1 or 2). And in the third blank, give the English translation of each verb.

	VERB	SECOND PRINCIPAL PART	CONJUGATION	TRANSLATION
1.	maneō	**manēre**	2	**I remain, stay**
2.	occultō	**occultāre**	1	**I hide, conceal**
3.	cibō	**cibāre**	1	**I feed**
4.	rīdeō	**rīdēre**	2	**I laugh**
5.	occupō	**occupāre**	1	**I seize**
6.	audeō	**audēre**	2	**I dare**
7.	valeō	**valēre**	2	**I am well**
8.	significō	**significāre**	1	**I defeat, conquer**

Underline the noun that goes with the verb and then translate the sentences.

NOUN	VERB	TRANSLATION
9. **Ventus** / Ventī	augēbat.	**The wind was increasing.**
10. **Noctua** / Noctuae	occupābit.	**An owl will seize.**
11. **Cervus** / Cervī	lībat.	**The deer drinks.**
12. Sciūrus / **Sciūrī**	rīdent.	**Squirrels are laughing.**
13. Agricola / **Agricolae**	manēbunt.	**The farmers will stay.**
14. **Hydrus** / Hydrī	pugnābit.	**The sea serpent will fight.**

B. Chant

For each noun, write its declension and gender in the blank, then decline it.

DECLENSION __2__ GENDER __N__

	SINGULAR	PLURAL
NOM.	venēnum	venēna
GEN.	venēnī	venēnōrum
DAT.	venēnō	venēnīs
ACC.	venēnum	venēna
ABL.	venēnō	venēnīs

DECLENSION __1__ GENDER __F__

	SINGULAR	PLURAL
NOM.	noctua	noctuae
GEN.	noctuae	noctuārum
DAT.	noctuae	noctuīs
ACC.	noctuam	noctuās
ABL.	noctuā	noctuīs

Fill in the missing verb endings to complete the chants.

Present Active

	SINGULAR	PLURAL
1ST	-ō	-mus
2ND	-s	-tis
3RD	-t	-nt

Future Active

	SINGULAR	PLURAL
1ST	-bō	-bimus
2ND	-bis	-bitis
3RD	-bit	-bunt

Imperfect Active

	SINGULAR	PLURAL
1ST	-bam	-bāmus
2ND	-bās	-bātis
3RD	-bat	-bant

C. Derivatives

Read each sentence. Then circle which Latin word the italicized derivatives comes from.

1. The teacher decided to make the class seating arrangement *permanent*.

   a) maneō (circled)   b) pharetra   c) mensa

2. Our cat had the *audacity* to sneak on the table and eat part of the Thanksgiving turkey!

   a) aquila   b) augeō   c) audeō (circled)

3. The white part of an egg is called *albumen,* and the yellow part is called the yolk.

   a) audeō   b) alga   c) albus (circled)

Unit 1 Test

name: _____

Chants

A. Complete these sentences.

1. A *noun* _____ a _____ , _____ , or _____ .

2. A *verb* shows _____ or _____ of being.

3. In Latin, the *subject* always takes the _____ case.

4. To find the *base* of a noun, you remove its _____ singular ending.

5. To find the *stem* of a verb, you remove the _____ from the _____
principal part.

B. Fill in the missing verb endings to complete the chants.

Present Active

	SINGULAR	PLURAL
1ST		-mus
2ND		
3RD		

Future Active

	SINGULAR	PLURAL
		-bimus

Imperfect Active

	SINGULAR	PLURAL
		-bāmus

C. Give the stem of each verb, and write whether it's a first (1) or second (2) conjugation verb. (Hint: You
will need to remember each verb's second principal part!)

1. peccō _____

2. probō _____

3. lūceō _____

4. olefactō _____

5. appāreō _____

6. maneō _____

7. instō _____

8. censeō _____

D. For each noun, write its declension and gender in the blank, then decline it.

DECLENSION _____ GENDER _____

	SINGULAR	PLURAL
NOM.	venēnum	
GEN.		
DAT.		
ACC.		
ABL.		

DECLENSION _____ GENDER _____

	SINGULAR	PLURAL
NOM.	turba	
GEN.		
DAT.		
ACC.		
ABL.		

E. Give each verb's person (1, 2, or 3) and number (singular or plural). Then translate each verb.

	VERB	PERSON	NUMBER	TRANSLATION
1.	exanimābimus			
2.	lūcent			
3.	lībō			
4.	significās			
5.	augēbātis			

E. Conjugate *maneō* in the future tense, then translate it.

LATIN

	SINGULAR	PLURAL
1ST		
2ND		
3RD		

ENGLISH

	SINGULAR	PLURAL
1ST		
2ND		
3RD		

1. Which conjugation is *maneō* in? _____

Vocabulary

F. For each noun, give its genitive singular ending, gender (M, F, or N), declension (1 or 2), and its English translation.

	NOUN	GENITIVE	GENDER	DECLENSION	TRANSLATION
1.	ulmus				
2.	inimīcus				
3.	saxum				
4.	fuscina				
5.	pharetra				
6.	coma				
7.	mālum				
8.	colōnus				
9.	virga				
10.	nucleus				

G. Underline the noun that goes with the verb and then translate the sentences.

NOUN	VERB	TRANSLATION
1. Aquila / Aquilae	ululant.	_____
2. Nuntius / Nuntiī	significābat.	_____
3. Sagitta / Sagittae	volābunt.	_____
4. Bālaena / Bālaenae	spīrant.	_____
5. Saxum / Saxa	augēbant.	_____
6. Puer / Puerī	valēbat.	_____

H. Translate these sentences into English.

1. Amīcus astat. _____

2. Nausea oppugnābit. _____

3. Fēminae et puellae parābunt. _____

Quotations

I. Translate each of these English sentences and phrases into Latin.

1. If your enemy is hungry, give him bread to eat. _____

_____

2. the three little pigs _____

3. Great Charter _____

Derivatives

J. Each sentence below uses a derivative (in italics). Use your knowledge of Latin vocabulary to finish each sentence by circling the correct answer!

1. *Venomous* snakes use _____ to kill their prey.

   a) strength   b) poison   c) arrows

2. A *pugilist* is someone who enjoys _____.

   a) dogs   b) harpoons   c) fighting

3. Many _____ have *baleen* in their mouths, which they use to eat tiny sea creatures.

   a) whales   b) dolphins   c) sea monsters

4. A *perambulator* is an old-fashioned stroller, used to take a baby on a _____.

   a) walk   b) train   c) boat

5. A *lunatic* is a person who is driven crazy by the _____.

   a) ocean   b) moon   c) sun

Unit 1 Test: Answer Key

Chants

A. Complete these sentences.

1. A *noun* **names** a **person**, **place**, or **thing**.

2. A *verb* shows **action** or **state** of being.

3. In Latin, the *subject* always takes the **nominative** case.

4. To find the *base* of a noun, you remove its **genitive** singular ending.

5. To find the *stem* of a verb, you remove the **-re** from the **second** principal part.

B. Fill in the missing verb endings to complete the chants.

Present Active

	SINGULAR	PLURAL
1ST	**-ō**	-mus
2ND	**-s**	-tis
3RD	**-t**	-nt

Future Active

	SINGULAR	PLURAL
1ST	**-bō**	-bimus
2ND	**-bis**	**-bitis**
3RD	**-bit**	**-bunt**

Imperfect Active

	SINGULAR	PLURAL
1ST	**-bam**	-bāmus
2ND	**-bās**	**-bātis**
3RD	**-bat**	**-bant**

C. Give the stem of each verb, and write whether it's a first (1) or second (2) conjugation verb. (Hint: You will need to remember each verb's second principal part!)

1. peccō   **peccā-**   **1**

2. probō   **probā-**   **1**

3. lūceō   **lūcē-**   **2**

4. olefactō   **olefactā-**   **1**

5. appāreō   **appārē-**   **2**

6. maneō   **manē-**   **2**

7. instō   **instā-**   **1**

8. censeō   **censē-**   **2**

D. For each noun, write its declension and gender in the blank, then decline it.

DECLENSION __2__ GENDER __N__

	SINGULAR	PLURAL
NOM.	venēnum	**venēna**
GEN.	**venēnī**	**venēnōrum**
DAT.	**venēnō**	**venēnīs**
ACC.	**venēnum**	**venēna**
ABL.	**venēnō**	**venēnīs**

DECLENSION __1__ GENDER __F__

	SINGULAR	PLURAL
NOM.	turba	**turbae**
GEN.	**turbae**	**turbārum**
DAT.	**turbae**	**turbīs**
ACC.	**turbam**	**turbās**
ABL.	**turbā**	**turbīs**

E. Give each verb's person (1, 2, or 3) and number (singular or plural). Then translate each verb.

	VERB	PERSON	NUMBER	TRANSLATION
1.	exanimābimus	**1**	**plural**	**we will kill**
2.	lūcent	**3**	**plural**	**they shine**
3.	lībō	**1**	**singular**	**I sip**
4.	significās	**2**	**singular**	**you are indicating**
5.	augēbātis	**2**	**plural**	**you all were increasing**

E. Conjugate *maneō* in the future tense, then translate it.

LATIN

	SINGULAR	PLURAL
1ST	**manēbō**	**manēbimus**
2ND	**manēbis**	**manēbitis**
3RD	**manēbit**	**manēbunt**

ENGLISH

	SINGULAR	PLURAL
1ST	**I will stay**	**we will stay**
2ND	**you will stay**	**you all will stay**
3RD	**he/she/it will stay**	**they will stay**

1. Which conjugation is *maneō* in? **second conjugation**

Vocabulary

F. For each noun, give its genitive singular ending, gender (M, F, or N), declension (1 or 2), and its English translation.

	NOUN	GENITIVE	GENDER	DECLENSION	TRANSLATION
1.	ulmus	**-ī**	**M**	**2**	**elm tree**
2.	inimīcus	**-ī**	**M**	**2**	**personal enemy**
3.	saxum	**-ī**	**N**	**2**	**rock**
4.	fuscina	**-ae**	**F**	**1**	**harpoon, trident**
5.	pharetra	**-ae**	**F**	**1**	**quiver**
6.	coma	**-ae**	**F**	**1**	**hair, leaves, wool, mane**
7.	mālum	**-ī**	**N**	**2**	**apple**
8.	colōnus	**-ae**	**M**	**2**	**settler**
9.	virga	**-ae**	**F**	**1**	**branch, twig**
10.	nucleus	**-ī**	**M**	**2**	**nut, kernel**

G. Underline the noun that goes with the verb and then translate the sentences.

NOUN	VERB	TRANSLATION

1. Aquila / **Aquilae**   ululant.   **Eagles scream.**

2. **Nuntius** / Nuntiī   significābat.   **A messenger was indicating.**

3. Sagitta / **Sagittae**   volābunt.   **The arrows will fly.**

4. Bālaena / **Bālaenae**   spīrant.   **The whales are breathing.**

5. Saxum / **Saxa**   augēbant.   **The rocks were increasing.**

6. **Puer** / Puerī   valēbat.   **The boy was well.**

H. Translate these sentences into English.

1. Amīcus astat. **A friend is standing by**.

2. Nausea oppugnābit. **Seasickness will attack**.

3. Fēminae et puellae parābunt. **The women and girls were preparing**.

Quotations

I. Translate each of these English sentences and phrases into Latin.

1. If your enemy is hungry, give him bread to eat. **Sī ēsurierit inimīcus tuus, ciba illum.**

2. the three little pigs **porcī parvī trēs**

3. Great Charter **Magna Carta**

Derivatives

J. Each sentence below uses a derivative (in italics). Use your knowledge of Latin vocabulary to finish each sentence by circling the correct answer!

1. *Venomous* snakes use _____ to kill their prey.

   a) strength   (b) poison)   c) arrows

2. A *pugilist* is someone who enjoys _____.

   a) dogs   b) harpoons   (c) fighting)

3. Many _____ have *baleen* in their mouths, which they use to eat tiny sea creatures.

   (a) whales)   b) dolphins   c) sea monsters

4. A *perambulator* is an old-fashioned stroller, used to take a baby on a _____.

   (a) walk)   b) train   c) boat

5. A *lunatic* is a person who is driven crazy by the _____.

   a) ocean   (b) moon)   c) sun

2 UNIT TWO

UNIT 2: GOALS

By the end of Week 16, students should be able to . . .

- Recognize and conjugate third conjugation verbs in the present, future, and imperfect tenses
- Decline adjectives in their masculine, feminine, and neuter forms
- Recognize and translate predicate adjectives and predicate nouns
- Recognize and decline third declension nouns
- Conjugate *sum* in the present and future tenses

Unit 2 Overview (Weeks 9–16)

In the first half of Unit 2, you'll delve into third conjugation verbs—the "e" family—represented by *dūcō*. Beginning in Week 13, students will be introduced to nouns of the third declension. The *sum* verb chant and adjective use will also be reviewed, in preparation for the end of the Unit, when you'll learn the future chant for *sum—erō*. Like any language, Latin is a cumulative study, so be sure that students stay current with previously learned chants and vocabulary. Week 14 is a review week.

Teaching Notes: Week 9

1. Word List: Introduce the Word List for Week 9. Review the new Word List throughout the week. Continue to review older vocabulary as well.

2. Derivatives: Discuss the derivatives for this week's vocabulary:

1. āla, *wing:* aisle, aileron
2. ancora, *anchor:* anchor
3. astrum, *star, constellation:* astral
4. aurōra, *dawn:* Aurora Borealis and Australis
5. fluvius, *river, stream*
6. prōra, *prow (of a ship):* prow
7. rēmus, *oar*
8. unda, *wave:* undulate, inundate, redundant
9. vēlum, *sail, curtain:* velum, veil
10. aliēnus, *foreign:* alien
11. aptus, *suitable, fit, ready:* apt
12. gelidus, *cold, icy:* gelid
13. lātus, *wide, broad:* latitude
14. mīrus, *strange, wonderful*
15. serēnus, *calm, bright, clear:* serene
16. dūcō, *I lead:* deduct, induce, reduction
17. hiemō, *I spend the winter*
18. nāvigō, *I sail:* navigate, navigable
19. spectō, *I look at, watch:* spectacles, spectacle, spectator, spectacular, expect

Have the students write this week's derivatives in the Week 9 "Derivatives" section of their student book.

3. Chant: This week, you'll introduce third conjugation or "e" family verbs. Third conjugation verbs all share a short "e" in their stem.

Dūcō—Third Conjugation or "e" Family

First, how do you identify a third conjugation verb? Exactly the same as you would a first or second conjugation verb—check the stem! All third conjugation verbs share a short "e" in their stem. Let's look at *dūcō*. To find the stem of *dūcō*, look at its second principal part—*dūcere*. Take the second principal part and remove the *-re* ending. This will leave you with the stem, *dūce-*. The "e" is short, so you know *dūcō* is in the third conjugation.

Now, once you know a verb is in the third conjugation, you can expect it to act a little oddly. First and second conjugation verbs are very predictable, but third conjugation verbs like to show off a little bit. Let's take a closer look.

All verbs in the third conjugation, or "e" family, follow the example of *dūcō* when they are conjugated. In the following example, *dūcō* has been conjugated in the present tense and the endings are bold.

	SINGULAR	PLURAL
1ST	dūcō	dūcimus
2ND	dūcis	dūcitis
3RD	dūcit	dūcunt

Where is the "e" we would expect to see in the stem? Nowhere to be found! Though the short "e" will *identify* a third conjugation verb, it will never appear in the present tense. Third conjugation verbs are quite bohemian in this way, casting off the "traditional" stem approach and doing their own thing! Students will need to memorize the *dūcō* paradigm, rather than just the endings, in order to be able to conjugate third conjugation verbs.

Student learned last year that first conjugation verbs follow the pattern of *amō* and second conjugation verbs follow the pattern of *videō*. In the same way, all third conjugation verbs follow the pattern of *dūcō*.

4. Quotation: *Ālīs volat propriīs* is the motto of the state of Oregon. The Oregon Laws explain that before becoming a state, Oregon was torn as to "whether their future lay beneath the wing" of Britain or the United States. The settlers wound up deciding that their government would be local, and not dependent on either Britain or the U.S., and thus the motto was born. In later years, Oregon decided to keep the motto as they felt it aptly related the independent, visionary spirit of the state.

Have the students write this week's quotation in the Week 9 "Quotation" section of their student book.

5. Worksheet: This week, students will begin reviewing adjective use. They may need to be reminded that an adjective describes a noun or a pronoun, and answers the questions *what kind? which one?* and *how many?* For example, a *bright* night, the *spotted* dog, the *three* curtains.

As students may remember from last year, many adjectives have a special trait: they come with three different endings! This gives them the ability to match the gender of any noun. Adjectives must *always* match the noun they describe in gender, number, and case.

And, unlike English, Latin adjectives usually come after the nouns they modify. (For more on adjective use, refer to page xvi.)

Follow the directions given to complete the worksheet.

6. Quiz: Administer Quiz 9 at the end of the week.

WEEK 9

Word List

NOUNS

1. āla, -ae (f) . . . . wing
2. ancora, -ae (f) . . . . . . anchor
3. astrum, -ī (n) . . . . star, constellation
4. aurōra, -ae (f) . . . . . . dawn
5. fluvius, -ī (m) . . . . . . river, stream
6. prōra, -ae (f) . . . . prow (of a ship)
7. rēmus, -ī (m) . . . . oar
8. unda, -ae (f) . . . . wave
9. vēlum, -ī (n) . . . . sail, curtain

ADJECTIVES

10. aliēnus, -a, -um . . . . . foreign
11. aptus, -a, -um . . . . . . suitable, fit, ready

NOUNS (continued)

12. gelidus, -a, -um . . . . . cold, icy
13. lātus, -a, -um . . . . wide, broad
14. mīrus, -a, -um . . . . . . strange, wonderful
15. serēnus, -a, -um . . . . . calm, bright, clear

VERBS

16. dūcō, dūcere . . . . I lead
17. hiemō, hiemāre . . . . . I spend the winter
18. nāvigō, nāvigāre . . . . I sail
19. spectō, spectāre . . . . I look at, watch

Chant:

Dūcō, *I lead*—Present Active

Third Conjugation or "e" Family Verb

| | LATIN | | | ENGLISH | |
	SINGULAR	PLURAL		SINGULAR	PLURAL
1ST	dūcō	dūcimus		I lead	we lead
2ND	dūcis	dūcitis		you lead	you all lead
3RD	dūcit	dūcunt		he/she/it leads	they lead

> ## Quotation:
> *Ālīs volat propriīs*—"She flies on her own wings"
> (Motto for the state of Oregon)

Weekly Worksheet 9: Answer Key

A. Conjugate and translate this week's verb chant, then answer the questions about it.

	LATIN			ENGLISH	
	SINGULAR	PLURAL		SINGULAR	PLURAL
1ST	dūcō	**dūcimus**		I lead	**we lead**
2ND	**dūcis**	dūcitis		**you lead**	**you all lead**
3RD	**dūcit**	dūcunt		**he/she/it leads**	**they lead**

1. Which conjugation is *dūcō, dūcere* in? **third conjugation**

2. Which family is it in? **"e" family**

3. How do you find the stem of *dūcō* and other verbs in this conjugation? **Just like any other verb—take the second principal part and remove the -re.**

4. Do verbs in this conjugation act just like the other conjugations you've learned? **no**

B. Below is a list of *singular* adjectives. As you learned last year, adjectives can have masculine, feminine, or neuter endings. Decide which ending each adjective has, and then write in the blank M (masculine), F (feminine), or N (neuter).

1. serēnus __**M**__   4. mīrum __**N**__   7. apta __**F**__

2. aliēna __**F**__   5. gelidum __**N**__   8. lātus __**M**__

All of these adjectives are *plural*. Like you did above, fill in the blank with whether they are M (masculine), F (feminine), or N (neuter).

10. aliēna __**N**__   13. mīra __**N**__   16. lātī __**M**__

11. aptae __**F**__   14. gelidī __**M**__   17. serēnae __**F**__

C. Fill in the blanks.

1. An adjective describes a **noun** or a **pronoun**.

2. In Latin, adjectives must match the **noun** they describe in **gender**, **number**, and **case**.

D. Below are noun and adjective phrases in Latin. For each phrase, underline the noun's ending and circle the adjective's ending. Then translate each phrase. (Hint: The last two phrases are plural.)

1. āl**a** lāt**a**   **a broad wing**

2. fluvi**us** lāt**us**   **the wide river**

3. aurōr**a** gelid**a**   **a chilly dawn**

4. vēl**um** mīr**um**   **the strange curtain**

5. harēn**a** serēn**a**   **the bright beach**

6. astr**a** aliēn**a**   **foreign constellations**

7. rēm**ī** apt**ī**   **suitable oars**

E. Fill in the blanks with five English words that are derivatives of this week's vocabulary. Write the derivative, then write its Latin root in parentheses. The first one is done for you. **Answers will vary.**

1. _____ undulate (unda) _____   4. _____ **latitude (lātus)** _____

2. _____ **anchor (ancora)** _____   5. _____ **serene (serēnus)** _____

3. _____ **veil (vēlum)** _____   6. _____ **spectacles (spectō)** _____

F. Label each declension and complete the chants.

1st DECLENSION

	SINGULAR	PLURAL
NOM.	-a	**-ae**
GEN.	**-ae**	**-ārum**
DAT.	**-ae**	**-īs**
ACC.	**-am**	**-ās**
ABL.	**-ā**	**-īs**

2nd DECLENSION

	SINGULAR	PLURAL
NOM.	-us	**-ī**
GEN.	**-ī**	**-ōrum**
DAT.	**-ō**	**-īs**
ACC.	**-um**	**-ōs**
ABL.	**-ō**	**-īs**

2ND DECLENSION **Neuter**

	SINGULAR	PLURAL
NOM.	-um	**-a**
GEN.	**-ī**	**-ōrum**
DAT.	**-ō**	**-īs**
ACC.	**-um**	**-a**
ABL.	**-ō**	**-īs**

Choose one noun from each declension from this week's list and decline them below. **Note: Answers will vary, and will need to be checked on an individual basis.**

FIRST DECLENSION

	SINGULAR	PLURAL
NOM.	āl<u>a</u>	āl<u>ae</u>
GEN.	āl<u>ae</u>	āl<u>ā</u>rum
DAT.	āl<u>ae</u>	āl<u>ī</u>s
ACC.	āl<u>am</u>	āl<u>ā</u>s
ABL.	āl<u>ā</u>	āl<u>ī</u>s

SECOND DECLENSION

	SINGULAR	PLURAL
NOM.	fluvi<u>us</u>	fluvi<u>ī</u>
GEN.	fluvi<u>ī</u>	fluvi<u>ō</u>rum
DAT.	fluvi<u>ō</u>	fluvi<u>ī</u>s
ACC.	fluvi<u>um</u>	fluvi<u>ō</u>s
ABL.	fluvi<u>ō</u>	fluvi<u>ī</u>s

SECOND DECLENSION NEUTER

	SINGULAR	PLURAL
NOM.	astr<u>um</u>	astr<u>a</u>
GEN.	astr<u>ī</u>	astr<u>ō</u>rum
DAT.	astr<u>ō</u>	astr<u>ī</u>s
ACC.	astr<u>um</u>	astr<u>a</u>
ABL.	astr<u>ō</u>	astr<u>ī</u>s

Now, go back to the nouns you've just declined and underline all of the endings. (Remember, the part of the noun that doesn't change is called the *base*.)

G. Look up these words in a Latin dictionary. For each word, give it's genitive singular ending, gender (M, F, or N), base, and declension (1 or 2).

NOUN	GENITIVE	GENDER	BASE	DECLENSION
1. diēcula	-ae	F	diēcul-	1
2. rubus	-ī	M	rub-	2
3. ientāculum	-ī	N	ientācul-	2
4. scriptūra	-ae	F	scriptūr-	1
5. fīliolus	-ī	M	fīliol-	2
6. columbus	-ī	M	columb-	2
7. sūdārium	-ī	N	sūdāri-	2
8. Narnia	-ae	F	Narni-	1

H. All the words listed below are in French, but all of them are related to words you've learned this week. Use your Word List to figure out what each word means in English!

1. aile   **wing**

2. astre   **star**

3. serein   **serene**

4. fleuve   **river**

5. ancre   **anchor**

I. Answer the questions about this week's quotation.

1. What does *Ālīs volat propriīs* mean? **She flies on her own wings**

2. Which state uses this as their motto? **Oregon**

Week 9 Quiz   *name:*

A. Chant

Conjugate and translate *dūcō, dūcere* in the present tense, then answer the questions about it.

LATIN

	SINGULAR	PLURAL
1ST		
2ND		
3RD		

ENGLISH

	SINGULAR	PLURAL

1. Which conjugation is *dūcō, dūcere* in? _____

2. Which family is it in? _____

3. How do you find the stem of *dūcō* and other verbs in this conjugation? _____

_____

4. Do verbs in this conjugation act just like the other conjugations you've learned? _____

Conjugate and translate *audeō, audēre* in the present tense, then answer the questions about it.

LATIN

	SINGULAR	PLURAL
1ST		
2ND		
3RD		

ENGLISH

	SINGULAR	PLURAL

5. Which conjugation is *audeō* in? _____

6. Which family is it in? _____

B. Vocabulary

In the first blank, give the genitive singular ending. In the second blank, write the noun's base. And in the third blank, tell which declension each noun is in.

	NOUN	GENITIVE	BASE	DECLENSION
1.	aurōra			
2.	rēmus			
3.	vēlum			
4.	nuntius			
5.	nausea			

Give the masculine, feminine, and neuter singular forms of these adjectives in Latin.

	ADJECTIVE	MASCULINE	FEMININE	NEUTER
6.	wide			
7.	strange			
8.	ready			

Below are noun and adjective phrases in Latin. For each phrase, underline the noun's ending and circle the adjective's ending. Then translate each phrase.

9. sciūrus mīrus _____

10. noctua serēna _____

11. morbī aliēnī _____

12. saxa gelida _____

13. unda ūmida _____

Week 9 Quiz: Answer Key

A. Chant

Conjugate and translate *dūcō, dūcere,* then answer the questions about it.

LATIN

ENGLISH

	SINGULAR	PLURAL		SINGULAR	PLURAL
1ST	dūcō	dūcimus		I lead	we lead
2ND	dūcis	dūcitis		you lead	you all lead
3RD	dūcit	dūcunt		he/she/it leads	they lead

1. Which conjugation is *dūcō, dūcere* in? **third conjugation**

2. Which family is it in? **"e" family**

3. How do you find the stem of *dūcō* and other verbs in this conjugation? **Just like any other**

verb—take the second principal part and remove the -re.

4. Do verbs in this conjugation act just like the other conjugations you've learned? **no**

Conjugate and translate *audeō, audēre* in the present tense, then answer the questions about it.

LATIN

ENGLISH

	SINGULAR	PLURAL		SINGULAR	PLURAL
1ST	audeō	audēmus		I dare	we dare
2ND	audēs	audētis		you dare	you all dare
3RD	audet	audent		he/she/it dares	they dare

5. Which conjugation is *audeō* in? **second conjugation**

6. Which family is it in? **"ē" family**

B. Vocabulary

In the first blank, give the genitive singular ending. In the second blank, write the noun's base. And in the third blank, tell which declension each noun is in.

	NOUN	GENITIVE	BASE	DECLENSION
1.	aurōra	-ae	aurōr-	1
2.	rēmus	-ī	rēm-	2
3.	vēlum	-ī	vēl-	2N
4.	nuntius	-ī	nunti-	2
5.	nausea	-ae	nause-	1

Give the masculine, feminine, and neuter singular forms of these adjectives in Latin.

	ADJECTIVE	MASCULINE	FEMININE	NEUTER
6.	wide	lātus	lāta	lātum
7.	strange	mīrus	mīra	mīrum
8.	ready	aptus	apta	aptum

Below are noun and adjective phrases in Latin. For each phrase, underline the noun's ending and circle the adjective's ending. Then translate each phrase.

9. sciūr**us** mīr**us** __the wonderful squirrel__

10. noctu**a** serēn**a** __a calm owl__

11. morb**ī** aliēn**ī** __foreign diseases__

12. sax**a** gelid**a** __the icy rocks__

13. und**a** ūmid**a** __a wet wave__

Teaching Notes: Week 10

1. Word List: Introduce the Word List for Week 10. Review the list throughout the week. Continue to review older vocabulary as well.

2. Derivatives: Discuss the derivatives for this week's vocabulary:

1. pulvīnus, *pillow, cushion:* pillow
2. somnus, *sleep:* insomnia, somnambulist
3. antīquus, *ancient:* antiquity, antique, antiquated
4. beātus, *happy, blessed:* beatitude, beatific
5. famēlicus, *hungry*
6. foedus, *horrible, ugly*
7. maculōsus, *spotted, stained*
8. pulcher, *beautiful:* pulchritude
9. pūrpureus, *purple*
10. pūrus, *pure, clean:* pure, purity, purify, purely, impure, purblind
11. quiētus, *quiet, sleeping:* quiet, quietly
12. rīdiculus, *funny, amusing:* ridiculous
13. tardus, *slow:* tardy, retard
14. crescō, *I grow, arise:* crescendo, crescent
15. somniō, *I dream*
16. sum, *I am*

Have the students write this week's derivatives in the Week 10 "Derivatives" section of their student book.

3. Chant: This week, you'll be reintroducing the chant for the Latin verb, *sum. Sum* is the verb of "being" in the present tense. It's irregular and doesn't follow the pattern of any conjugation.

Say this chant reading down the left column, then down the right: *sum, es, est, sumus, estis, sunt.* Chant it a few times, until students recall the rhythm and are comfortable saying it. Then chant through the English translation. Continue to review the chant each day during the week.

Once students are comfortable with the chant, move on to reviewing the use of *sum* in sentence translation. Last year, they learned to translate sentences using adjectives paired with *sum,* like *Mālum est dēliciōsus* (The apple is delicious). The name for an adjective used in this way is **predicate adjective.** A predicate adjective is *an adjective that follows a linking verb, like sum, and describes the subject noun.*

Though the verb often comes at the end of a Latin sentence, in sentences like these, *sum* will usually appear in the middle, like an "equals" sign, linking the subject and the predicate adjective. Here are a few sample sentences:

Sum apta.	*I am ready.*
Fluvius est gelidus.	*The stream is icy.*
Pulvīnī sunt pulchrī.	*The pillows are beautiful.*
Astrum est serēnum.	*The constellation is bright.*

Remember, all adjectives must match the noun they describe in gender, number, and case.

4. Quotation: To repeat something verbatim is to quote it exactly, or word for word. Have the students write this week's quotation in the Week 10 "Quotation" section of their student book.

5. Worksheet: Students will continue to review the use of adjectives this week, and starting in this lesson, they will begin declining adjectives. Declining adjectives is very simple—they decline exactly like nouns! Take a look at the following examples. The endings have been bolded.

FIRST DECLENSION

	SINGULAR	PLURAL
NOM.	beāt**a**	beāt**ae**
GEN.	beāt**ae**	beāt**ārum**
DAT.	beāt**ae**	beāt**īs**
ACC.	beāt**am**	beāt**ās**
ABL.	beāt**ā**	beāt**īs**

SECOND DECLENSION

	SINGULAR	PLURAL
NOM.	beāt**us**	beāt**ī**
GEN.	beāt**ī**	beāt**ōrum**
DAT.	beāt**ō**	beāt**īs**
ACC.	beāt**um**	beāt**ōs**
ABL.	beāt**ō**	beāt**īs**

SECOND DECLENSION NEUTER

	SINGULAR	PLURAL
NOM.	beāt**um**	beāt**a**
GEN.	beāt**ī**	beāt**ōrum**
DAT.	beāt**ō**	beāt**īs**
ACC.	beāt**um**	beāt**a**
ABL.	beāt**ō**	beāt**īs**

Once students are comfortable declining adjectives, you may want to challenge them by having them decline adjective/noun combinations out loud! A couple of examples are listed below. Remember, **the adjective must always match the noun's gender, number, and case.**

	SINGULAR	PLURAL
NOM.	pulvīnus pūrus	pulvīnī pūrī
GEN.	pulvīnī pūrī	pulvīnōrum pūrōrum
DAT.	pulvīnō pūrō	pulvīnīs pūrīs
ACC.	pulvīnum pūrum	pulvīnōs pūrōs
ABL.	pulvīnō pūrō	pulvīnīs pūrīs

	SINGULAR	PLURAL
NOM.	aurōra pulchra	aurōrae pulchrae
GEN.	aurōrae pulchrae	aurōrārum pulchrārum
DAT.	aurōrae pulchrae	aurōrīs pulchrīs
ACC.	aurōram pulchram	aurōrās pulchrās
ABL.	aurōrā pulchrā	aurōrīs pulchrīs

Follow the directions given to complete the worksheet.

6. Quiz: Administer Quiz 10 at the end of the week.

WEEK 10

Word List

NOUNS

1. pulvīnus, -ī (m) . . . . pillow, cushion

2. somnus, -ī (m) . . . . sleep

ADJECTIVES

3. antīquus, -a, -um . . . . . . ancient

4. beātus, -a, -um . . . . happy, blessed

5. famēlicus, -a, -um . . . . . hungry

6. foedus, -a, -um . . . . horrible, ugly

7. maculōsus, -a, -um . . . . . spotted, stained

8. pulcher, -chra, -chrum . . . beautiful

9. pūrpureus, -a, -um . . . . . purple

10. pūrus, -a, -um . . . . pure, clean

11. quiētus, -a, -um . . . . . . quiet, sleeping

12. rīdiculus, -a, -um . . . . . funny, amusing

13. tardus, -a, -um . . . . . . slow

VERBS

14. crescō, crescere . . . . . . I grow, arise

15. somniō, somniāre . . . . . I dream

16. sum . . . . I am

Chant:

Sum, *I am*—Present Active
Irregular Verb

	LATIN			ENGLISH	
	SINGULAR	**PLURAL**		**SINGULAR**	**PLURAL**
1ST	sum	sumus		I am	we are
2ND	es	estis		you are	you all are
3RD	est	sunt		he/she/it is	they are

 Quotation:
verbātim—"word for word"

Weekly Worksheet 10: Answer Key

A. Fill in the blanks.

1. An adjective modifies a **noun** or **pronoun**.

2. An adjective answers the questions **what** kind? **which** one? or how **many**?

3. In Latin, a **predicate adjective** follows a linking verb and describes a subject noun.

4. It matches the subject noun in **gender**, number, and **case**.

5. Give an example in Latin of a linking verb: **sum**

6. In Latin sentences with predicate adjectives, does the verb usually appear at the beginning, in the middle, or at the end of the sentence? **in the middle**

B. Translate each English adjective into Latin, in the gender given. Use the *nominative singular* form. The first one is done for you.

1. feminine: *wonderful* _____ mīra _____   4. masculine: *happy* _____ **beātus** _____

2. masculine: *hungry* _____ **famēlicus** _____   5. neuter: *horrible* _____ **foedum** _____

3. feminine: *purple* _____ **pūrpurea** _____   6. neuter: *amusing* _____ **rīdiculum** _____

C. Give the base for each of these nouns.

1. ancora   **ancor-**   4. prōra   **prōr-**

2. fluvius   **fluvi-**   5. astrum   **astr-**

3. pulvīnus   **pulvīn-**   6. āla   **āl-**

D. Underline the adjective that goes with the noun and then translate the phrase.

NOUN	ADJECTIVE	TRANSLATION
1. Pulvīnus	**pulcher** / pulchrum	**the beautiful pillow**

2. Somnus   quiētum / **quiētus**   **a quiet sleep**

3. Ancora   **antīqua** / antīquae   **an ancient anchor**

4. Sciūrī   rīdicula / **rīdiculī**   **the funny squirrels**

5. Vēla   **maculōsa** / maculōsae   **spotted sails**

6. Coma   **ūmida** / ūmidum   **the wet wool**

E. Answer the following questions about *crescō, crescere.*

1. Which conjugation is *crescō* in?   **third conjugation**

2. Which family is it in?   **"e" family**

3. What is the stem of *crescō?*   **cresce-**

4. Does *crescō* conjugate like *amō, videō,* or *ducō?*   **ducō**

Conjugate and translate *crescō* in the present tense.

LATIN   ENGLISH

	SINGULAR	PLURAL		SINGULAR	PLURAL
1ST	**crescō**	**crescimus**		**I grow**	**we grow**
2ND	**crescis**	**crescitis**		**you grow**	**you all grow**
3RD	**crescit**	**crescunt**		**he/she/it grows**	**they grow**

F. Conjugate and translate *sum* in the present tense, then answer the questions.

LATIN   ENGLISH

	SINGULAR	PLURAL		SINGULAR	PLURAL
1ST	**sum**	**sumus**		**I am**	**we are**
2ND	**es**	**estis**		**you are**	**you all are**
3RD	**est**	**sunt**		**he/she/it is**	**they are**

1. Does *sum* conjugate regularly or irregularly? **irregularly**

G. Each sentence below uses an adjective and a form of *sum*. Translate each sentence, then write in the parentheses whether the adjective is masculine (M), feminine (F), or neuter (N). The first one is done for you.

1. Est dēliciōsus! _____ It is delicious! (M)

2. Sum famēlica. _____ **I am hungry.** (**F**)

3. Es famēlicus. _____ **You are hungry.** (**M**)

4. Sunt rīdiculī. _____ **They are amusing.** (**M**)

5. Est foedum! _____ **It is horrible!** (**N**)

6. Sumus pūrae. _____ **We are clean.** (**F**)

7. Sunt pūrpurea. _____ **They are purple.** (**N**)

H. Translate these sentences. (Hint: It's best to start by finding the verb!)

1. Equus gelidus nat. **The cold horse is swimming.**

2. Estis serēnae et aptae. **You all are calm and ready.**

3. Venēnum pūrpureum exanimābit. **The purple poison will kill.**

4. Astrum est serēnum. **The constellation is bright.**

5. Sciūrus maculōsus somniābat. **A spotted squirrel was dreaming.**

6. Ōceanī sunt antīquī. **The oceans are ancient.**

7. Harēnae sunt apricae. **The beaches are sunny.**

8. Fēmina pulchra dūcit. **A beautiful woman is leading.**

9. Cunīculī quiētī olefactānt. **The quiet rabbits are sniffing.**

10. Coquus est famēlicus. **The cook is hungry.**

11. Nucleī sunt brūnī. **The nuts are brown.**

12. Saxum est āridum. **The rock is dry.**

13. Parvus ulmus crescit. **A little elm tree is growing.**

I. Adjectives decline just like the nouns they modify. Below, decline *tardus* in the masculine and *beātus* in the feminine.

	SINGULAR	PLURAL
NOM.	tardus	**tardī**
GEN.	**tardī**	tardōrum
DAT.	**tardō**	tardīs
ACC.	**tardum**	tardōs
ABL.	**tardō**	tardīs

	SINGULAR	PLURAL
NOM.	beata	**beatae**
GEN.	**beatae**	beatārum
DAT.	**beatae**	**beatīs**
ACC.	**beatam**	**beatās**
ABL.	**beatā**	**beatīs**

Now, decline the phrase below.

	SINGULAR	PLURAL
NOM.	**quiēta noctua**	quiētae noctuae
GEN.	**quiētae noctuae**	**quiētārum noctuārum**
DAT.	**quiētae noctuae**	**quiētīs noctuīs**
ACC.	**quiētam noctuam**	**quiētās noctuās**
ABL.	**quiētā noctuā**	**quiētīs noctuīs**

J. Give the stems for the following verbs.

1. somniō, somniāre   **somniā-**

2. augeō, augēre   **augē-**

3. hiemō, hiemāre   **hiemā-**

4. dūcō, dūcere   **dūce-**

5. valeō, valēre   **valē-**

6. instō, instāre   **instā-**

Week 10 Quiz

name: _____

A. Vocabulary

Underline the adjective that goes with the noun and then translate the phrase.

NOUN	ADJECTIVE	TRANSLATION
1. Inimīcus	quiētum / quiētus	_____
2. Alga	pūrpurea / pūrpureae	_____
3. Delphīnī	famēlicī / famēlicae	_____
4. Frāgum	pulchrus / pulchrum	_____
5. Folia	maculōsa / maculōsae	_____
6. Silvae	magna / magnae	_____
7. Nuntius	tardum / tardus	_____
8. Vēla	foedum / foeda	_____

Translate these sentences.

9. Hortus crescit. _____

10. Sunt quiētī. _____

11. Noctua maculōsa somniat. _____

12. Lūna suprā lūcēbat. _____

13. Somnus est bonus. _____

14. Pulvinī sunt pūrī. _____

15. Āla est alba. _____

16. Aptī estis. _____

B. Chant

Conjugate and translate *sum* in the present tense.

LATIN

	SINGULAR	PLURAL
1ST		
2ND		
3RD		

ENGLISH

SINGULAR	PLURAL

Decline *pūrus* in the neuter and *foedus* in the feminine.

	SINGULAR	PLURAL
NOM.		
GEN.		
DAT.		
ACC.		
ABL.		

SINGULAR	PLURAL

C. Review

Translate each of these verbs in three different ways.

1. significat _____

2. errās _____

3. augent _____

4. What tense are all of these verbs in? _____

5. *Significant* and *errās* are _____ conjugation verbs.

6. *Augent* is a _____ conjugation verb.

Week 10 Quiz: Answer Key

A. Vocabulary

Underline the adjective that goes with the noun and then translate the phrase.

NOUN	ADJECTIVE	TRANSLATION
1. Inimīcus	quiētum / **quiētus**	**a sleeping enemy**
2. Alga	**pūrpurea** / pūrpureae	**purple seaweed**
3. Delphīnī	**famēlicī** / famēlicae	**the hungry dolphins**
4. Frāgum	pulchrus / **pulchrum**	**a beautiful strawberry**
5. Folia	**maculōsa** / maculōsae	**spotted leaves**
6. Silvae	magna / **magnae**	**the large forests**
7. Nuntius	tardum / **tardus**	**a slow messenger**
8. Vēla	foedum / **foeda**	**horrible curtains**

Translate these sentences.

9. Hortus crescit. **The garden is growing.**

10. Sunt quiētī. **They are quiet.**

11. Noctua maculōsa somniat. **The spotted owl is dreaming.**

12. Lūna suprā lūcēbat. **The moon was shining above.**

13. Somnus est mīrus. **Sleep is wonderful.**

14. Pulvinī sunt pūrī. **The pillows are clean.**

15. Āla est alba. **The wing is white.**

16. Aptī estis. **You all are ready.**

B. Chant

Conjugate and translate *sum* in the present tense.

LATIN   ENGLISH

	SINGULAR	PLURAL
1ST	sum	sumus
2ND	es	estis
3RD	est	sunt

	SINGULAR	PLURAL
1ST	I am	we are
2ND	you are	you all are
3RD	he/she/it is	they are

Decline *pūrus* in the neuter and *foedus* in the feminine.

	SINGULAR	PLURAL
NOM.	pūrum	pūra
GEN.	pūrī	pūrōrum
DAT.	pūrō	pūrīs
ACC.	pūrum	pūra
ABL.	pūrō	pūrīs

	SINGULAR	PLURAL
foeda	foedae
foedae	foedārum
foedae	foedīs
foedam	foedās
foedā	foedīs

C. Review

Translate each of these verbs in three different ways.

1. significant **he/she/it points out, he/she/it does point out, he/she/it is pointing out**

2. errās **you wander, you do wander, you are wandering**

3. augent **they increase, they do increase, they are increasing**

4. What tense are all of these verbs in? **present tense**

5. *Significant* and *errās* are **first** conjugation verbs.

6. *Augent* is a **second** conjugation verb.

Teaching Notes: Week 11

1. Word List: Introduce the Word List for Week 11. Review this list throughout the week and continue to review vocabulary from previous weeks.

2. Derivatives: Discuss the derivatives for this week's vocabulary:

1. Deus, *God:* adieu, deity, deify, deism
2. familia, *family, household:* family, familial, familiar
3. germāna, *sister:* germane
4. germānus, *brother:* germane
5. liber, *book:* library, libretto, librarian
6. verbum, *word:* verb, adverb, proverb, verve
7. vir, *man:* triumvirate, virtue
8. aeternus, *eternal:* eternal
9. bonus, *good:* bonbon, bonanza, boon, debonair, bounteous, bonus
10. caecus, *blind*

11. iūstus, *just, righteous:* just
12. laetus, *happy, joyful*
13. cōgitō, *I think:* cogitate
14. dēclārō, *I declare, explain:* declare, declaration
15. flō, *I blow, breathe*
16. gaudeō, *I rejoice*
17. iūdicō, *I judge:* judge, adjudicate, judiciary, judicial
18. lūgeō, *I grieve, mourn*
19. mūtō, *I change:* mutant, mutable, immutable, mutate
20. spērō, *I hope:* despair, sperable

Have the students write this week's derivatives in the Week 11 "Derivatives" section of their student book.

3. Chant: As you learned in Week 9, all verbs in the third conjugation, or "e" family, follow the example of *dūcō* when they are conjugated. Week 9 introduced the *present* active form for third conjugation. This week, you'll be learning the *future* active form—again illustrated by the example of *dūcō*.

As before, since "e" family verbs conjugate so oddly, students will need to memorize the "e" family future chant, rather than just the endings. Below, *dūcō* has been conjugated in the future tense and the endings are bold.

LATIN

	SINGULAR	PLURAL
1ST	dūca**m**	dūcē**mus**
2ND	dūcē**s**	dūcē**tis**
3RD	dūce**t**	dūce**nt**

ENGLISH

	SINGULAR	PLURAL
	I will lead	we will lead
	you will lead	you all will lead
	he/she/it will lead	they will lead

Notice how similar this chant is to second conjugation verb in the present tense! How can you tell them apart? By recalling the verb's conjugation. For example:

Does *gaudēs* mean "You are rejoicing" (2nd conj., present tense), or does it mean "You will rejoice" (3rd conj., present tense)? Judging just by appearances, it could go either way!

First, determine what the first principal part of the word is—*gaudēs* is a form of *gaudeō* (Word 16 in this week's list). The second principal part of *gaudeō* is *gaudēre*. Since *gaudēre* has a long "e" in it's stem, you know it has to be a second conjugation verb. Therefore, the correct translation is "You are rejoicing."

Let's try it again. Does *crescēmus* mean "We are arising" (2nd conj., present tense), or does it mean "We will arise" (3rd conj., future tense)?

First, we know *crescēmus* comes from *crescō*. The second principal part of *crescō* is *crescere*. Since *crescere* has a short "e" in it's stem, we know it's a third conjugation verb. So the correct translation is "We will arise."

4. Quotation: *Ipsissima verba* is a Latin phrase often used in legal settings. It typically refers to authoritative materials (for example, a Supreme Court precedent) which are being quoted by the speaker.

Have the students write this week's quotation in the Week 11 "Quotation" section of their student book.

5. Worksheet: Follow the directions given to complete the worksheet.

6. Quiz: Administer Quiz 11 at the end of the week.

WEEK 11

Word List

NOUNS

1. Deus, -ī (m) . . . . God
2. familia, -ae (f) . . . . . . family, household
3. germāna, -ae (f) . . . . sister
4. germānus, -ī (m) . . . . brother
5. liber, librī (m) . . . . . . book
6. verbum, -ī (n) . . . . . . word
7. vir, virī (m) . . . . man

ADJECTIVES

8. aeternus, -a, -um . . . . . eternal
9. bonus, -a, -um . . . . . good
10. caecus, -a, -um . . . . blind

11. iūstus, -a, -um . . . . . just, righteous
12. laetus, -a, -um . . . . . happy, joyful

VERBS

13. cōgitō, cōgitāre . . . . I think
14. dēclārō, dēclārāre . . . I declare, explain
15. flō, flāre . . . . I blow, breathe
16. gaudeō, gaudēre . . . . I rejoice
17. iūdicō, iūdicāre . . . . . I judge
18. lūgeō, lūgēre . . . . . . I grieve, mourn
19. mūtō, mūtāre . . . . . . I change
20. spērō, spērāre . . . . . . I hope

Chant:

Dūcam, *I will lead*—Future Active
Third Conjugation or "e" Family Verb

	LATIN			ENGLISH	
	SINGULAR	**PLURAL**		**SINGULAR**	**PLURAL**
1ST	dūcam	dūcēmus		I will lead	we will lead
2ND	dūcēs	dūcētis		you will lead	you all will lead
3RD	dūcet	dūcent		he/she/it will lead	they will lead

 Quotation:

ipsissima verba—"the very words"

Weekly Worksheet 11: Answer Key

A. Conjugate and translate this week's verb chant, then answer the questions about it.

	LATIN			ENGLISH	
	SINGULAR	**PLURAL**		**SINGULAR**	**PLURAL**
1ST	dūcam	**dūcēmus**		I will lead	**we will lead**
2ND	**dūcēs**	**dūcētis**		**you will lead**	**you all will lead**
3RD	**dūcet**	**dūcent**		**he/she/it will lead**	**they will lead**

1. Which conjugation is *dūcō, ducere* in? **third conjugation**

2. Which family is it in? **"e" family**

3. How do you find the stem of *dūcō*? **Remove -re from the second principal part**

4. What is the stem of *dūcō, dūcere*? **duce-**

B. Translate these review words from memory!

1. virga	**branch, twig**		10. cēna	**dinner, meal**
2. peccō	**I sin**		11. ambulō	**I walk**
3. latebra	**hiding place**		12. sella	**seat, chair**
4. pontus	**sea, seawater**		13. epistula	**letter**
5. poēta	**poet**		14. armentum	**herd**
6. mālum	**apple**		15. censeō	**I estimate**
7. turba	**crowd, mob**		16. ūva	**grape**
8. inimīcus	**personal enemy**		17. brūnus	**brown**
9. fuscina	**harpoon, trident**		18. valeō	**I am well**

C. Using this week's Word List, look at the genitive forms of these nouns and give the base for each.

1. familia — **famili-**

2. germana — **german-**

3. liber — **libr-**

4. verbum — **verb-**

5. germanus — **german-**

6. vir — **vir-**

D. For each word, give the nominative singular and plural forms, then tell which declension each word is in (1, 2, or 2N). The first one is done for you.

	ENGLISH	LATIN SINGULAR	LATIN PLURAL	DECLENSION
1.	cushion	pulvīnus	pulvīnī	2
2.	sister	germāna	germānae	1
3.	brother	germānus	germānī	2
4.	household	familia	familiae	1
5.	word	verbum	verba	2N
6.	man	vir	virī	2
7.	book	liber	librī	2
8.	star	astrum	astra	2N
9.	owl	noctua	noctuae	1

E. Give the masculine, feminine, and neuter singular forms of these adjectives in Latin.

	ADJECTIVE	MASCULINE	FEMININE	NEUTER
1.	happy	beātus	beāta	beātum
2.	blind	caecus	caeca	caecum
3.	eternal	aeternus	aeterna	aeternum

F. Decline *bonus liber.*

	SINGULAR	PLURAL
NOM.	bonus liber	bonī librī
GEN.	bonī librī	bonōrum librōrum
DAT.	bonō librō	bonīs librīs
ACC.	bonum librum	bonōs librōs
ABL.	bonō librō	bonīs librīs

G. Below are seven English derivatives. Draw a line to match each word to its Latin root!

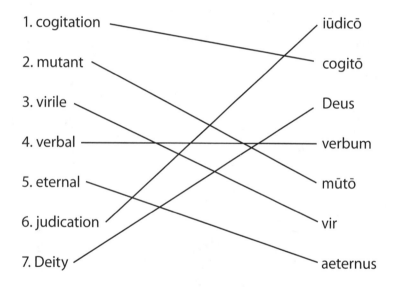

1. cogitation   iūdicō

2. mutant   cogitō

3. virile   Deus

4. verbal   verbum

5. eternal   mūtō

6. judication   vir

7. Deity   aeternus

H. Underline the ending of each verb and translate it.

1. cogitā**tis** **you all think**   2. fl**ō** **I blow**

3. gaude**nt** **they are rejoicing** 5. declārā**mus** **we are declaring**

4. iūdica**t** **he/she/it judges** 6. mūta**t** **he/she/it is changing**

I. Translate these sentences into English.

1. Germānus bonus gaudet. **A good brother rejoices.**

2. Virī laetī sperant. **The happy men are hoping.**

3. Puella caeca dūcet. **The blind girl will lead.**

4. Germānae salsae dēclārābunt. **The witty sisters will explain.**

5. Pulvīnī sunt maculōsī. **The pillows are stained.**

6. Deus est iūstus et bonus. **God is just and good.**

7. Fluvius gelidus properat. **The cold river is rushing.**

8. Fīliī iūstī exsultant. **The just sons rejoice.**

9. Pontus est serēnus. **The sea is calm.**

10. Vir est caecus. **The man is blind.**

J. Conjugate and translate each word in the tense given.

crescō, crescere—Future Active

	SINGULAR	PLURAL		SINGULAR	PLURAL
LATIN			ENGLISH		
1ST	crescam	crescēmus		I will grow	we will grow
2ND	crescēs	crescētis		you will grow	you all will grow
3RD	crescet	crescent		he/she/it will grow	they will grow

gaudeō, gaudēre—Present Active

	SINGULAR	PLURAL		SINGULAR	PLURAL
LATIN			ENGLISH		
1ST	gaudeō	gaudēmus		I rejoice	we rejoice
2ND	gaudēs	gaudētis		you rejoice	you all rejoice
3RD	gaudet	gaudent		he/she/it rejoice	they rejoice

Week 11 Quiz

name:

A. Chants

Conjugate and translate *ducō* in the present tense.

LATIN

	SINGULAR	PLURAL
1ST		
2ND		
3RD		

ENGLISH

	SINGULAR	PLURAL
1ST		
2ND		
3RD		

Conjugate and translate *ducō* in the future tense.

LATIN

	SINGULAR	PLURAL
1ST		
2ND		
3RD		

ENGLISH

	SINGULAR	PLURAL
1ST		
2ND		
3RD		

1. Which conjugation is *dūcō* in? _____

2. Which family is it in? _____

B. Quotations

Answer the following questions about this week's quotation.

1. How do you say "the very words" in Latin?_____

2. Which word means "words?" _____

3. What is its gender? _____

C. Vocabulary

Give the masculine, feminine, and neuter singular forms of these adjectives in Latin.

	ADJECTIVE	MASCULINE	FEMININE	NEUTER
1.	just			
2.	joyful			
3.	purple			

Underline the adjective that goes with the noun and then translate the phrase.

NOUN	ADJECTIVE	TRANSLATION
4. Verbum	bonus / bonum	_____
5. Deus	aeternus / aeternum	_____
6. Librī	parvus / parvī	_____
7. Turba	laetum / laeta	_____
8. Forum	iūstum / iūstus	_____

Translate these sentences into English.

9. Familia crescet. _____

10. Coquī tardī lūgēnt. _____

11. Noctua est caeca. _____

12. Ventus flat. _____

13. Vir malus dūcet. _____

14. Verba sunt bona. _____

15. Statim dūcimus. _____

Week 11 Quiz: Answer Key

A. Chants

Conjugate and translate *ducō* in the present tense.

LATIN

	SINGULAR	PLURAL
1ST	dūcō	dūcimus
2ND	dūcis	dūcitis
3RD	dūcit	dūcunt

ENGLISH

	SINGULAR	PLURAL
1ST	I lead	we lead
2ND	you lead	you all lead
3RD	he/she/it leads	they lead

Conjugate and translate *ducō* in the future tense.

LATIN

	SINGULAR	PLURAL
1ST	dūcam	dūcēmus
2ND	dūcēs	dūcētis
3RD	dūcet	dūcent

ENGLISH

	SINGULAR	PLURAL
1ST	I will lead	we will lead
2ND	you will lead	you all will lead
3RD	he/she/it will lead	they will lead

1. Which conjugation is *dūcō* in? **third conjugation**

2. Which family is it in? **"e" family**

B. Quotations

Answer the following questions about this week's quotation.

1. How do you say "the very words" in Latin? **ipsissima verba**

2. Which word means "words?" **verba**

3. What is its gender? **neuter**

C. *Vocabulary*

Give the masculine, feminine, and neuter singular forms of these adjectives in Latin.

	ADJECTIVE	MASCULINE	FEMININE	NEUTER
1.	just	**iūstus**	**iūsta**	**iūstum**
2.	joyful	**laetus**	**laeta**	**laetum**
3.	purple	**pūrpureus**	**pūrpurea**	**pūrpureum**

Underline the adjective that goes with the noun and then translate the phrase.

NOUN	ADJECTIVE	TRANSLATION
4. Verbum	bonus / **bonum**	**a good word**
5. Deus	**aeternus** / aeternum	**eternal God**
6. Librī	parvus / **parvī**	**little books**
7. Turba	laetum / **laeta**	**the joyful crowd**
8. Forum	**iūstum** / iūstus	**a just marketplace**

Translate these sentences into English.

9. Familia crescet. **The family will grow.**

10. Coquī tardī lūgēnt. **The slow cooks are grieving.**

11. Noctua est caeca. **The owl is blind.**

12. Ventus flat. **The wind is blowing.**

13. Vir malus dūcet. **An evil man will lead.**

14. Verba sunt bona. **The words are good.**

15. Statim dūcimus. **We lead immediately.**

Teaching Notes: Week 12

1. Word List: Introduce the Word List for Week 12. Review this list throughout the week and continue to review vocabulary from previous weeks.

2. Derivatives: Discuss the derivatives for this week's vocabulary:

1. avia, *grandmother*
2. avus, *grandfather*
3. littera, *letter of the alphabet:* letter, alliteration, illiterate, literal, obliterate, transliterate
4. matrimonium, *marriage:* matrimony
5. certātim, *eagerly*
6. crās, *tomorrow:* procrastinate
7. herī, *yesterday*
8. hodiē, *today*
9. minūtātim, *gradually, bit by bit*
10. nōn, *not:* nonsense, noncombatant
11. satis, *enough:* satiate, insatiable
12. semper, *always*
13. simul, *at the same time:* simultaneous
14. agō, *I do, act:* agent, agenda, agitate, act, agile
15. scribō, *I write:* ascribe, circumscribe, conscription, inscription, nondescript, postscript, prescribe, scribe, superscript, transcribe
16. serō, *I sow, plant*
17. vīvō, *I live:* convivial, revive, survive, victuals, vivacious, vivify, vivid

Have the students write this week's derivatives in the Week 12 "Derivatives" section of their student book.

3. Chant: You've been learning that all verbs in the third conjugation, or "e" family, follow the example of *dūcō* when they are conjugated. This week, you'll be learning the *imperfect* active form.

"E" family verbs conjugate oddly, as you now know, but hopefully this week's chant will seem slightly less bizarre. However, as before, students will need to memorize the chant, rather than just the endings. Below, *dūcō* has been conjugated in the imperfect tense and the endings are bold.

LATIN

	SINGULAR	PLURAL
1ST	dūcē**bam**	dūcē**bāmus**
2ND	dūcē**bās**	dūcē**bātis**
3RD	dūcē**bat**	dūcē**bant**

ENGLISH

	SINGULAR	PLURAL
1ST	I was leading	we were leading
2ND	you were leading	you all were leading
3RD	he/she/it was leading	they were leading

Notice that in the imperfect tense, a third conjugation acts exactly like a second conjugation verb, right down to the ē in the stem!

4. Quotation: *Iam satis est* is a quotation from Horace's *Epistles*. Horace was a Roman poet who lived from 65 to 8 B.C. The quotation in its original context refers to a man who is refusing pears from an over-generous friend; but students will probably find it to be a fun and versatile quote for everyday use. The only word in the quote which they haven't learned is *iam*, which means "already" or "now."

Have the students write this week's quotation in the Week 12 "Quotation" section of their student book.

5. Worksheet: This week, students will begin reviewing adverb use. Adverbs can modify verbs, adjectives, or other adverbs. An adverb answers the question *how?, where?, when?,* or *to what extent?* For example:

How?	The dog barked *eagerly.*
Where?	A bird flew *above* our heads.
When?	Let's swim *today.*
To what extent?	I never drink *enough* water.

Latin adverbs do not decline or conjugate. In a typical Latin sentence, they will come right before the verb, and they are very easy to translate! Take a look at these examples.

Germānae salsae dēclārābit.	*The witty sisters will explain.*
Germānae salsae **certātim** dēclārābit.	*The witty sisters will explain **eagerly.***
Pulvīnī sunt maculōsī.	*The pillows are stained.*
Pulvīnī **nōn** sunt maculōsī.	*The pillows are **not** stained.*
Deus est iūstus et bonus.	*God is just and good.*
Deus **semper** est iūstus et bonus.	*God is **always** just and good.*
Fīliī iūstī exsultant.	*The just sons rejoice.*
Fīliī iūstī **simul** exsultant.	*The just sons rejoice **at the same time.***

Feel free to practice using adverbs in sentences from previous weeks! Follow the directions given to complete the worksheet.

6. Quiz: Administer Quiz 12 at the end of the week.

WEEK 12

Word List

NOUNS

1. avia, -ae (f) . . . . grandmother
2. avus, -ī (m) . . . . grandfather
3. littera, -ae (f) . . . . letter of the alphabet
   PLURAL: litterae, -ārum . . letter, epistle
4. matrimonium, -ī (n) . . . marriage

ADVERBS

5. certātim . . . . eagerly
6. crās . . . . tomorrow
7. herī . . . . yesterday
8. hodiē . . . . today

9. minūtātim . . . . gradually, bit by bit
10. nōn . . . . not
11. satis . . . . enough
12. semper . . . . always
13. simul . . . . at the same time

VERBS

14. agō, agere . . . . I do, act
15. scrībō, scribere . . . . . I write
16. serō, serere . . . . I sow, plant
17. vīvō, vīvere . . . . I live

Chant:

Dūcēbam, *I was leading*—Imperfect Active
Third Conjugation or "e" Family Verb

	LATIN			ENGLISH	
	SINGULAR	PLURAL		SINGULAR	PLURAL
1ST	dūcēbam	dūcēbāmus		I was leading	we were leading
2ND	dūcēbās	dūcēbātis		you were leading	you all were leading
3RD	dūcēbat	dūcēbant		he/she/it was leading	they were leading

 Quotation:

Iam satis est!—"That's enough already!"

Weekly Worksheet 12: Answer Key

A. Conjugate and translate this week's verb chant, then answer the questions about it.

LATIN

	SINGULAR	PLURAL
1ST	**dūcēbam**	**dūcēbāmus**
2ND	dūcēbās	**dūcēbātis**
3RD	**dūcēbat**	**dūcēbant**

ENGLISH

	SINGULAR	PLURAL
1ST	**I was leading**	**we were leading**
2ND	**you were leading**	**you all were leading**
3RD	**he/she/it was leading**	**they were leading**

1. What is the tense of this chant? **imperfect**

2. Which conjugation is *dūcō, ducere* in? **third conjugation**

3. Which family is it in? **"e" family**

B. Fill in the imperfect tense endings. Then conjugate *flō, flāre* in the imperfect tense and translate it.

	SINGULAR	PLURAL
1ST	**-bam**	**-bāmus**
2ND	-bās	**-bātis**
3RD	**-bat**	**-bant**

LATIN

	SINGULAR	PLURAL
1ST	**flābam**	**flābāmus**
2ND	**flābās**	**flābātis**
3RD	**flābat**	**flābant**

ENGLISH

	SINGULAR	PLURAL
1ST	**I was breathing**	**we were breathing**
2ND	**you were breathing**	**you all were breathing**
3RD	**he/she/it was breathing**	**they were breathing**

C. Fill in the blanks.

1. An adverb can modify a **verb**, an **adjective**, or another **adverb**.

2. An adverb answers the questions **how**? **when**? **where**? or to what extent?

D. Translate these sentences.

1. Germāna caeca certātim sperat. **The blind sister eagerly hopes.**

2. Deus semper est bonus. **God is always good.**

3. Germānī crās serent. **The brothers will plant tomorrow.**

4. Fābula est mīra. **The legend is strange.**

5. Sumus aptī. **We are ready.**

6. Avus herī scribēbat. **The grandfather was writing yesterday.**

7. Astrum nōn est serēnum. **The constellation is not bright.**

8. Avus et avia simul ridēbant. **The grandfather and grandmother were laughing at the same time.**

9. Estis laetī. **You all are joyful.**

10. Satis agis. **You are doing enough.**

E. Fill in the chart's missing labels, then look up the word *puer* in Word List 1. Using the information given there, decline *puer* below.

	SINGULAR	PLURAL
NOMINATIVE	puer	puerī
GENITIVE	puerī	puerōrum
DATIVE	puerō	puerīs
ACCUSATIVE	puerum	puerōs
ABLATIVE	puerō	puerīs

F. Fill in the blank with the correct form of each word.

1. Nominative singular for *grandfather* **avus**

2. Base of the noun that means *anchor* **ancor-**

3. Base of the noun that means *book* **libr-**

4. First principle part of the verb that means *I live* **vivō**

5. The verb form that means *he lives* **vivit**

6. Masculine form of the adjective meaning *eternal* **aeternus**

7. Feminine form of the adjective meaning *blind* **caeca**

8. Neuter form of the adjective that means *calm* **serēnum**

9. Base of the adjective that means *suitable* **apt-**

G. Translate each verb and give its stem and conjugation (1, 2, or 3). The first one is done for you.

	VERB	TRANSLATION	STEM	CONJUGATION
1.	peccāmus	we sin	peccā-	1
2.	gaudet	he/she/it rejoices	gaudē-	2
3.	crescitis	you all are growing	cresce-	3
4.	lūgēs	you are grieving	lugē-	2
5.	somniābō	I will dream	somniā-	1
6.	scribēbātis	you all were writing	scribe-	3
7.	agō	I act	age-	3
8.	flābant	they were blowing	flā-	1

H. Give the base for each of these nouns.

1. liber   **libr-**   4. avia   **avi-**

2. matrimonium   **matrimoni-**   5. pulvīnus   **pulvīn-**

3. vir   **vir-**   6. astrum   **astr-**

I. Conjugate the following words in the present, future, and imperfect tenses.

Present Active

FIRST CONJUGATION			SECOND CONJUGATION			THIRD CONJUGATION		
	SINGULAR	PLURAL		SINGULAR	PLURAL		SINGULAR	PLURAL
1ST	mūtō	mūtāmus		lūgeō	lūgēmus		vīvō	vīvimus
2ND	mūtās	mūtātis		lūgēs	lūgētis		vīvis	vīvitis
3RD	mūtat	mūtant		lūget	lūgent		vīvit	vīvunt

Future Active

FIRST CONJUGATION			SECOND CONJUGATION			THIRD CONJUGATION		
	SINGULAR	PLURAL		SINGULAR	PLURAL		SINGULAR	PLURAL
1ST	mūtābō	mūtābimus		lūgēbō	lūgēbimus		vīvam	vīvēmus
2ND	mūtābis	mūtābitis		lūgēbis	lūgēbitis		vīvēs	vīvētis
3RD	mūtābit	mūtābunt		lūgēbit	lūgēbunt		vīvet	vīvent

Imperfect Active

FIRST CONJUGATION			SECOND CONJUGATION			THIRD CONJUGATION		
	SINGULAR	PLURAL		SINGULAR	PLURAL		SINGULAR	PLURAL
1ST	mūtābam	mūtābāmus		lūgēbam	lūgēbāmus		vīvēbam	vīvēbāmus
2ND	mūtābās	mūtābātis		lūgēbās	lūgēbātis		vīvēbās	vīvēbātis
3RD	mūtābat	mūtābant		lūgēbat	lūgēbant		vīvēbat	vīvēbant

Week 12 Quiz

name:

A. Chants

Conjugate the following words in the present, future, and imperfect tenses.

Present Active

FIRST CONJUGATION

	SINGULAR	PLURAL
1ST	spērō	
2ND		
3RD		

SECOND CONJUGATION

	SINGULAR	PLURAL
1ST	valeō	
2ND		
3RD		

THIRD CONJUGATION

	SINGULAR	PLURAL
1ST	scrībō	
2ND		
3RD		

Future Active

FIRST CONJUGATION

	SINGULAR	PLURAL
1ST		
2ND		
3RD		

SECOND CONJUGATION

	SINGULAR	PLURAL
1ST		
2ND		
3RD		

THIRD CONJUGATION

	SINGULAR	PLURAL
1ST		
2ND		
3RD		

Imperfect Active

FIRST CONJUGATION

	SINGULAR	PLURAL
1ST		
2ND		
3RD		

SECOND CONJUGATION

	SINGULAR	PLURAL
1ST		
2ND		
3RD		

THIRD CONJUGATION

	SINGULAR	PLURAL
1ST		
2ND		
3RD		

B. Vocabulary

Translate these sentences.

1. Avī certātim dēclārābant. _____

2. Germānus et germāna errābant. _____

3. Agricola herī serēbat. _____

4. Nuntius semper parat. _____

5. Crās scribam. _____

6. Nōn semper manēmus. _____

7. Minūtātim crescētis. _____

8. Ulmus antīquus vivēbat. _____

For each noun, list its genitive singular ending, gender, declension, and English translation. The first one is done for you.

	NOUN	GENITIVE	GENDER	DECLENSION	ENGLISH
1.	colōnus	-ī	M	2	settler
2.	aurōra				
3.	avus				
4.	littera				
5.	somnus				
6.	matrimonium				
7.	rēmus				
8.	avia				
9.	vēlum				

Week 12 Quiz: Answer Key

A. Chants

Conjugate the following words in the present, future, and imperfect tenses.

Present Active

FIRST CONJUGATION

	SINGULAR	PLURAL
1ST	spērō	spērāmus
2ND	spērās	spērātis
3RD	spērat	spērant

SECOND CONJUGATION

	SINGULAR	PLURAL
1ST	valeō	valēmus
2ND	valēs	valētis
3RD	valet	valent

THIRD CONJUGATION

	SINGULAR	PLURAL
1ST	scribō	scribimus
2ND	scribis	scribitis
3RD	scribit	scribunt

Future Active

FIRST CONJUGATION

	SINGULAR	PLURAL
1ST	spērābō	spērābimus
2ND	spērābis	spērābitis
3RD	spērābit	spērābunt

SECOND CONJUGATION

	SINGULAR	PLURAL
1ST	valēbō	valēbimus
2ND	valēbis	valēbitis
3RD	valēbit	valēbunt

THIRD CONJUGATION

	SINGULAR	PLURAL
1ST	scribam	scribēmus
2ND	scribēs	scribētis
3RD	scribet	scribent

Imperfect Active

FIRST CONJUGATION

	SINGULAR	PLURAL
1ST	spērābam	spērābāmus
2ND	spērābās	spērābātis
3RD	spērābat	spērābant

SECOND CONJUGATION

	SINGULAR	PLURAL
1ST	valēbam	valēbāmus
2ND	valēbās	valēbātis
3RD	valēbat	valēbant

THIRD CONJUGATION

	SINGULAR	PLURAL
1ST	scribēbam	scribēbāmus
2ND	scribēbās	scribēbātis
3RD	scribēbat	scribēbant

B. Vocabulary

Translate these sentences.

1. Avī certātim dēclārābant. **The grandfathers were eagerly explaining.**

2. Germānus et germāna errābant. **The brother and sister were wandering.**

3. Agricola herī serēbat. **The famer was planting yesterday.**

4. Nuntius semper parat. **A sailor always prepares.**

5. Crās scrībam. **I will write tomorrow.**

6. Nōn semper manēmus. **We do not always stay.**

7. Minūtātim crescētis. **You all will grow bit by bit.**

8. Ulmus antīquus vivēbat. **The ancient elm tree was living.**

For each noun, list its genitive singular ending, gender, declension, and English translation. The first one is done for you.

	NOUN	GENITIVE	GENDER	DECLENSION	ENGLISH
1.	colōnus	-ī	M	2	settler
2.	aurōra	**-ae**	**F**	**1**	**dawn**
3.	avus	**-ī**	**M**	**2**	**grandfather**
4.	littera	**-ae**	**F**	**1**	**letter of the alphabet**
5.	somnus	**-ī**	**M**	**2**	**sleep**
6.	matrimonium	**-ī**	**N**	**2**	**marriage**
7.	rēmus	**-ī**	**M**	**2**	**oar**
8.	avia	**-ae**	**F**	**1**	**grandmother**
9.	vēlum	**-ī**	**N**	**2**	**sail, curtain**

Teaching Notes: Week 13

1. Word List: Introduce the Word List for Week 13. This week, students will be learning a new noun declension, the third declension (see more under the "Chant" notes below). In most dictionaries, and in this book, the genitive singular ending of third declension nouns appears in its full form. This is due to the wide variance of third declension noun bases.

Also notice that Word 11, *tigris,* can be either masculine or feminine. This is the first noun like this that students have learned, but it won't change how the word declines. In the third declension, both masculine and feminine nouns use the same endings.

Review the list throughout the week and continue to review older vocabulary.

2. Derivatives: Discuss the derivatives for this week's vocabulary:

1. ariēs, *ram*

2. balatrō, *jester, clown*

3. caper, *billy goat:* caper

4. cauda, *tail:* coda

5. cavea, *cage, animal den:* cajole

6. circus, *circle, racecourse:* circus, circle

7. elephantus, *elephant:* elephant, elephantitis

8. flagellum, *whip:* flagellum, flagella

9. mannus, *pony*

10. pābulum, *fodder, food for animals:* pabulum

11. tigris, *tiger:* tiger, tigrine, tigress

12. trochus, *hoop for games*

13. currō, *I run:* curriculum, current, currency, cursive, cursory, concourse, concur, concurrent, discourse, incur, precursor, recur, succor

14. pāreō, *I obey*

15. rudō, *I roar, bellow, bray*

Have the students write this week's derivatives in the Week 13 "Derivatives" section of their student book.

3. Chant: This week you'll be introducing third declension noun endings. This chant will work in exactly the same way as the first and second declension chants you've already learned.

However, the one difference to note is the "x" in the nominative singular. This is *not* an ending. Third declension nouns have no fixed nominative singular ending, so the "x" in the chant functions as a place-holder. The "x" is chanted (*x, is, ī, em, e . . .*), but students must understand that it is not an ending.

Run through the chant several times with the students to familiarize them with it.

Third Declension Noun Endings

The first thing to remember as you learn a new declension is that **a noun's genitive ending will tell you which declension that noun is in**. Third declension nouns will *always* have *-īs* as their genitive singular ending. Once you see the *-īs* genitive ending following a noun, you can be sure you are working with a noun in the third declension.

Third declension nouns can be either masculine, feminine, or neuter in gender. For the next two weeks, you'll only be working with masculine and feminine nouns. (In Week 15, you'll learn the third declension neuter chant.)

Let's work with an example. Which declension is the word *ariēs* in? If we look in this week's Word List, we can see that its genitive singular ends in *-īs*. Only third declension nouns have an *-īs* genitive ending, therefore we know *ariēs* is in the third declension.

In the chart below, *ariēs* has been declined. The endings, shown in bold, have been applied to the base of *ariēs*. Remember, to find a noun's base, simply remove the genitive ending from the word. What remains is the base.

LATIN   ENGLISH

	SINGULAR	PLURAL		SINGULAR	PLURAL
NOM.	ariēs	arietēs		a, the *ram*	the *rams*
GEN.	arietis	arietum		of the *ram*, the *ram's*	of the *rams*, the *rams'*
DAT.	arietī	arietibus		to, for the *ram*	to, for the *rams*
ACC.	arietem	arietēs		the *ram*	the *rams*
ABL.	ariete	arietibus		by, with, from the *ram*	by, with, from the *rams*

Once students have gotten into the rhythm of chanting these endings, begin applying the endings to whole nouns. Having visible examples of declined nouns as they are recited often makes the connection easier.

Example:

	SINGULAR	PLURAL
NOM.	balatrō	balatrōnēs
GEN.	balatrōnis	balatrōnum
DAT.	balatrōnī	balatrōnibus
ACC.	balatrōnem	balatrōnēs
ABL.	balatrōne	balatrōnibus

	SINGULAR	PLURAL
	tigris	tigridēs
	tigridis	tigridum
	tigridī	tigridibus
	tigridem	tigridēs
	tigride	tigridibus

4. Quotation: The Circus Maximus was a giant arena in the heart of Rome. Though our word "circus" comes from the Latin word *circus*, the two mean very different things. There were no ringmasters or acrobats in the Roman circus. The Roman circus usually involved very competitive chariot racing, and the Circus Maximus was large enough for twelve chariots to race at the same time.

Have the students write this week's quotation in the Week 13 "Quotation" section of their student book.

5. Worksheet: Follow the directions given to complete the worksheet.

6. Quiz: Administer Quiz 13 at the end of the week.

WEEK 13

Word List

NOUNS

1. ariēs, arietis (m) . . . . . . ram

2. balatrō, balatrōnis (m) . jester, clown

3. caper, caprī (m) . . . . . billy goat

4. cauda, -ae (f) . . . . . . tail

5. cavea, -ae (f) . . . . . . cage, animal den

6. circus, -ī (m) . . . . circle, racecourse

7. elephantus, -ī (m) . . . . elephant

8. flagellum, -ī (n) . . . . . whip

9. mannus, -ī (m) . . . . . . pony

10. pābulum, -ī (n) . . . . . fodder, food for animals

11. tigris, tigridis (m/f) . . . tiger

12. trochus, -ī (m) . . . . . . hoop for games

VERBS

13. currō, currere . . . . . . I run

14. pāreō, pārēre . . . . . . I obey

15. rudō, rudere . . . . I roar, bellow, bray

Chant:

Third Declension Noun Endings

	LATIN			ENGLISH	
	SINGULAR	PLURAL		SINGULAR	PLURAL
NOM.	x	-ēs		a, the *noun*	the *nouns*
GEN.	-is	-um		of the *noun*, the *noun's*	of the *nouns*, the *nouns'*
DAT.	-ī	-ibus		to, for the *noun*	to, for the *nouns*
ACC.	-em	-ēs		the *noun*	the *nouns*
ABL.	-e	-ibus		by, with, from the *noun*	by, with, from the *nouns*

Quotation:
Circus Maximus—"Greatest Circus"

Weekly Worksheet 13: Answer Key

A. Complete the chant for this week and answer the questions about it.

	SINGULAR	PLURAL
NOMINATIVE	x	-ēs
GENITIVE	-is	-um
DATIVE	-ī	-ibus
ACCUSATIVE	-em	-ēs
ABLATIVE	-e	-ibus

1. Which ending tells you a noun's declension? **genitive singular**

2. The genitive ending for the third declension is **-is.**

3. The genitive ending for the second declension is **-ī.**

4. The genitive ending for the first declension is **-ae.**

B. Decline *ariēs* and *tigris* in the chart below, then answer the questions.

	SINGULAR	PLURAL		SINGULAR	PLURAL
NOM.	ariēs	**arietēs**		tigris	**tigridēs**
GEN.	**arietis**	**arietum**		**tigridis**	**tigridum**
DAT.	**arietī**	**arietibus**		**tigridī**	**tigridibus**
ACC.	**arietem**	**arietēs**		**tigridem**	**tigridēs**
ABL.	**ariete**	**arietibus**		**tigride**	**tigridibus**

1. Which declension are *ariēs* and *tigris* in? **third declension**

2. How can you tell? **The genitive singular ending of both words is *-is.***

C. Translate these sentences into English.

1. Elephantus albus certātim ambulābit. **The white elephant will walk eagerly.**

2. Est magnus. **He is large.**

3. Mannus brunus appāret. **A brown pony appears.**

4. Statim pāret et currit. **He immediately obeys and runs.**

5. Puerī et puellae exsultant. **Boys and girls dance.**

6. Simul rīdēmus. **We laugh at the same time.**

7. Caper maculōsus est famēlicus. **A spotted billy goat is hungry.**

8. Tigrēs spectant et rudunt. **The tigers watch and roar.**

9. Balatrōnēs salsī semper clāmant. **The witty clowns are always shouting.**

10. Semper sunt rīdiculī. **They are always funny.**

D. Give the masculine, feminine, and neuter nominative singular of these adjectives in Latin.

	ADJECTIVE	MASCULINE	FEMININE	NEUTER
1.	quiet	**quiētus**	**quiēta**	**quiētum**
2.	joyful	**laetus**	**laeta**	**laetum**
3.	horrible	**foedus**	**foeda**	**foedum**
4.	sunny	**apricus**	**aprica**	**apricum**
5.	cold	**gelidus**	**gelida**	**gelidum**

E. For each noun, write in the blank whether it is in the first declension (1), second declension (2), second declension neuter (2N), or third declension (3).

1. pābulum, -ī _____**2N**_____

2. circus, -ī _____**2**_____

3. ariēs, arietis _____**3**_____

4. cauda, -ae _____**1**_____

147

5. tigris, tigridis _____**3**_____

6. caper, caprī _____**2**_____

7. cavea, -ae _____**1**_____

8. balatrō, balatrōnis _____**3**_____

9. matrimonium, -ī _____**2N**_____

10. liber, librī _____**2**_____

F. Label the picture using the words below. All of the words should be used once. (Hint: Some of them are review words from last year.)

puer	leō	ursa	elephantus	circus
trochus	equus	tigris	puella	

G. Conjugate and translate *currō* in the present, future, and imperfect tenses.

Present Active

	LATIN		ENGLISH	
	SINGULAR	PLURAL	SINGULAR	PLURAL
1ST	currō	currimus	I run	we run
2ND	curris	curritis	you run	you all run
3RD	currit	currunt	he/she/it runs	they run

Future Active

	LATIN		ENGLISH	
	SINGULAR	PLURAL	SINGULAR	PLURAL
1ST	curram	currēmus	I will run	we will run
2ND	currēs	currētis	you will run	you all will run
3RD	curret	current	he/she/it will run	they will run

Imperfect Active

	LATIN		ENGLISH	
	SINGULAR	PLURAL	SINGULAR	PLURAL
1ST	currēbam	currēbāmus	I was running	we were running
2ND	currēbās	currēbātis	you were running	you all were running
3RD	currēbat	currēbant	he/she/it was running	they were running

H. Answer the questions about this week's quotation.

1. What Latin phrase means "the greatest circus"? **Circus Maximus**

2. Which word means "greatest"? **maximus**

3. Was the Roman circus like our circuses today? **no**

Week 13 Quiz

name:

A. Vocabulary

Decline *balatrō* and *ariēs* in the chart below, then answer the questions.

	SINGULAR	PLURAL
NOM.	balatrō	
GEN.		
DAT.		
ACC.		
ABL.		

	SINGULAR	PLURAL
NOM.	ariēs	
GEN.		
DAT.		
ACC.		
ABL.		

1. Which declension is *balatrō* in? _____

2. What does *balatrō* mean? _____

3. Which declension is *ariēs* in? _____

4. What does *ariēs* mean? _____

Translate these sentences into English.

5. Mannus maculōsus est tardus. _____

6. Elephantī simul rudēbant._____

7. Germānae crās current. _____

8. Pābulum est aptum. _____

9. Balatrō nōn lūget. _____

10. Circī sunt magnī et aequī. _____

B. Chants

Conjugate and translate *rudō* in the present and future tenses.

Present Active

	LATIN			ENGLISH	
	SINGULAR	PLURAL		SINGULAR	PLURAL
1ST					
2ND					
3RD					

Future Active

	LATIN			ENGLISH	
	SINGULAR	PLURAL		SINGULAR	PLURAL
1ST					
2ND					
3RD					

C. Review

Conjugate and translate *sum* in the present tense.

	LATIN			ENGLISH	
	SINGULAR	PLURAL		SINGULAR	PLURAL
1ST					
2ND					
3RD					

1. Does *sum* conjugate regularly, like other verbs? _____

Week 13 Quiz: Answer Key

A. Vocabulary

Decline *balatrō* and *ariēs* in the chart below, then answer the questions.

	SINGULAR	PLURAL
NOM.	balatrō	**balatrōnēs**
GEN.	**balatrōnis**	**balatrōnum**
DAT.	**balatrōnī**	**balatrōnibus**
ACC.	**balatrōnem**	**balatrōnēs**
ABL.	**balatrōne**	**balatrōnibus**

	SINGULAR	PLURAL
ariēs	**arietēs**
arietis	**arietum**
arietī	**arietibus**
arietem	**arietēs**
ariete	**arietibus**

1. Which declension is *balatrō* in? **third declension**

2. What does *balatrō* mean? **jester, clown**

3. Which declension is *ariēs* in? **third declension**

4. What does *ariēs* mean? **ram**

Translate these sentences into English.

5. Mannus maculōsus est tardus. **The spotted pony is slow.**

6. Elephantī simul rudēbant. **Elephants were bellowing at the same time.**

7. Germānae crās current. **The sisters will run tomorrow.**

8. Pābulum est aptum. **The fodder is suitable.**

9. Balatrō nōn lūget. **A jester does not grieve.**

10. Circī sunt magnī et aequī. **The racecourses are large and level.**

B. Chants

Conjugate and translate *rudō* in the present and future tenses.

Present Active

	LATIN			ENGLISH	
	SINGULAR	PLURAL		SINGULAR	PLURAL
1ST	rudō	rudimus		I roar	we roar
2ND	rudis	ruditis		you roar	you all roar
3RD	rudit	rudunt		he/she/it roars	they roar

Future Active

	LATIN			ENGLISH	
	SINGULAR	PLURAL		SINGULAR	PLURAL
1ST	rudam	rudēmus		I will roar	we will roar
2ND	rudēs	rudētis		you will roar	you all will roar
3RD	rudet	rudent		he/she/it will roar	they will roar

C. Review

Conjugate and translate *sum* in the present tense.

	LATIN			ENGLISH	
	SINGULAR	PLURAL		SINGULAR	PLURAL
1ST	sum	sumus		I am	we are
2ND	es	estis		you are	you all are
3RD	est	sunt		he/she/it is	they are

1. Does *sum* conjugate regularly, like other verbs? **No, it conjugates irregularly.**

Teaching Notes: Week 14

1. Word List: Introduce the Word List for Week 14. Review this list throughout the week and continue to review vocabulary from previous weeks.

2. Derivatives: Discuss the derivatives for this week's vocabulary:

1. insidiae, *ambush, trap, plot:* insidious
2. rēgīna, *queen*
3. rēx, *king:* regal, regalia
4. servus, *slave, servant:* serf, serve, service, servile, servitude
5. honestus, *honorable:* honest
6. improbus, *wicked*
7. accūsō, *I accuse, blame:* accuse
8. administrō, *I help, manage:* administration, administrate
9. arō, *I plow:* arable
10. dubitō, *I doubt, hesitate:* doubt, indubitable
11. explōrō, *I find out, explore:* explore
12. intrō, *I enter:* introspection, introduce
13. līberō, *I set free:* liberate
14. narrō, *I tell, relate, recount:* narrate, narrator
15. nuntiō, *I announce, declare:* Annunciation, denounce, renunciation
16. obsecrō, *I beg, implore*
17. recuperō, *I recover:* recuperate
18. regnō, *I rule, govern, reign*
19. rogō, *I ask:* abrogate, arrogance, interrogation, prerogative, surrogate
20. vocō, *I call, summon, invite:* vocation, vocative, invoke, invocation, revoke, avocation, evoke, vouch, advocate, provoke, convocation

Have the students write this week's derivatives in the Week 14 "Derivatives" section of their student book.

3. Chant: There is no new chant this week. Use this week to review the chants from previous weeks. Are students able to easily distinguish between second and third conjugation verbs? Are they comfortable identifying which declension a noun is in?

4. Quotation: The phrase *Vīvat rēx!* was shouted by the congregation at the coronation of William the Conqueror on Christmas Day, 1066:

> In terms of the law of blood descent the Duke of Normandy knew that his claim to the throne was slight, so he introduced a new element into the Anglo-Saxon coronation ceremony—a call for the people's consent to his rule. Questioned in both English and French as to whether they freely accepted William as their lord, the assembled congregation obediently burst into shouts of *"Vivat rex!"* (Robert Lacey, *Great Tales from English History* [New York: Little, Brown and Co., 2003], 100).

Have the students write this week's quotation in the Week 14 "Quotation" section of their student book.

5. Worksheet: Follow the directions given to complete the worksheet.

6. Quiz: Administer Quiz 14 at the end of the week.

WEEK 14

Word List

NOUNS

1. insidiae, -ārum (f) . . . . . .ambush, trap, plot
2. rēgīna, -ae (f) . . . . .queen
3. rēx, rēgis (m) . . . . .king
4. servus, -ī (m) . . . . .slave, servant

ADJECTIVES

5. honestus, -a, -um . . . . . .honorable
6. improbus, -a, -um . . . . . .wicked

VERBS

7. accūsō, accūsāre . . . . . . .I accuse, blame
8. administrō, administrāre . .I help, manage

9. arō, arāre. . . . . I plow
10. dubitō, dubitāre . . . . I doubt, hesitate
11. explōrō, explōrāre . . . I find out, explore
12. intrō, intrāre . . . . . . I enter
13. līberō, līberāre. . . . . . I set free
14. narrō, narrāre . . . . . . I tell, relate, recount
15. nuntiō, nuntiāre. . . . . I announce, declare
16. obsecrō, obsecrāre. . . I beg, implore
17. recuperō, recuperāre. . I recover
18. regnō, regnāre . . . . . I rule, govern, reign
19. rogō, rogāre . . . . . . I ask
20. vocō, vocāre. . . . . . I call, summon, invite

Chant:

No new chant this week.

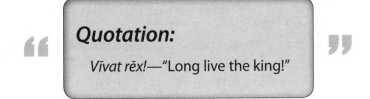

Quotation:

Vīvat rēx!—"Long live the king!"

Weekly Worksheet 14: Answer Key

A. Conjugate the following words in the present, future, and imperfect tenses.

Present Active

FIRST CONJUGATION

	SINGULAR	PLURAL
1ST	arō	**arāmus**
2ND	**arās**	**arātis**
3RD	**arat**	**arant**

SECOND CONJUGATION

SINGULAR	PLURAL
audeō	**audēmus**
audēs	**audētis**
audet	audent

THIRD CONJUGATION

SINGULAR	PLURAL
rudō	**rudimus**
rudis	**ruditis**
rudit	**rudunt**

Future Active

FIRST CONJUGATION

	SINGULAR	PLURAL
1ST	**arābō**	**arābimus**
2ND	**arābis**	**arābitis**
3RD	**arābit**	**arābunt**

SECOND CONJUGATION

SINGULAR	PLURAL
audēbō	**audēbimus**
audēbis	**audēbitis**
audēbit	**audēbunt**

THIRD CONJUGATION

SINGULAR	PLURAL
rudam	**rudēmus**
rudēs	**rudētis**
rudet	**rudent**

Imperfect Active

FIRST CONJUGATION

	SINGULAR	PLURAL
1ST	**arābam**	**arābāmus**
2ND	**arābās**	**arābātis**
3RD	**arābat**	**arābant**

SECOND CONJUGATION

SINGULAR	PLURAL
audēbam	**audēbāmus**
audēbās	**audēbātis**
audēbat	**audēbant**

THIRD CONJUGATION

SINGULAR	PLURAL
rudēbam	**rudēbāmus**
rudēbās	**rudēbātis**
rudēbat	**rudēbant**

B. Circle the subject noun, underline the verb, and draw a box around adjectives; leave adverbs unmarked. Then translate these sentences.

1. (Servus) minūtātim <u>recuperābit</u>. **The slave will recover bit by bit.**

2. (Rex) certātim <u>intrābit</u>. **The king will enter eagerly.**

3. (Amicī) aliēnī <u>dubitant</u>. **The foreign friends doubt.**

4. (Balatrō) rīdiculus <u>nuntiābit</u>. **A ridiculous clown will announce.**

5. (Avus) improbus <u>accūsābat</u>. **The wicked grandfather was accusing.**

6. (Tigris) nōn <u>est</u> contentus. **The tiger is not satisfied.**

7. (Rēx) nōn <u>arat</u>. **The king does not plow.**

8. (Nuntius) aptus <u>ambulābit</u>. **The fit messenger will walk.**

9. (Rēx) iūstus nōn <u>peccābit</u>. **The just king will not sin.**

10. (Lupus) salsus <u>rogāt</u>. **A witty wolf is asking.**

C. Circle the correct meaning of these English words by considering their Latin sources, all of which are words on your current list.

1. *Arable* land is land that _____.

   (a) can be cultivated   b) belongs to many people   c) can be inherited

2. A *narrator* in a play _____.

   a) is the lead actor   b) is a starving stagehand   (c) tells of events instead of acting them out)

3. If Sally is *recuperating,* she is _____.

   a) planning   b) pouring more tea   (c) getting well after being sick)

4. If something is *indubitable,* it is _____.

   (a) so clear it cannot be doubted)   b) impossible to believe   c) wicked

5. If someone is being *interrogated,* it means they're being _____ .

   a) followed   (b) questioned)   c) set free

D. For each noun, write in the blank whether it is in the first declension (1), second declension (2), second declension neuter (2N), or third declension (3).

1. insidiae, -ārum **1**

2. trochus, -ī **2**

3. rēgīna, -ae **1**

4. pābulum, -ī **2N**

5. ariēs, arietis **3**

6. servus, -ī **2**

7. rēx, rēgis **3**

8. flagellum, -ī **2N**

9. littera, -ae **1**

10. avus, -ī **2**

E. Answer the following questions.

ITALIAN	SPANISH	FRENCH
re e regina	rey y reina	roi et reine

1. The phrases above say the same thing in different Romance languages. Use your knowledge of

Latin to guess what they mean! **king and queen**

2. How would you write this phrase in Latin? **rēx et rēgīna**

F. *Pēs* and *mater* are words you learned last year. Find their genitive forms in a Latin dictionary and decline them below. Include their gender and declension.

DECLENSION **3** GENDER **M**

	SINGULAR	PLURAL
NOM.	pēs	**pedēs**
GEN.	**pedis**	**pedum**
DAT.	**pedī**	**pedibus**
ACC.	**pedem**	**pedēs**
ABL.	**pede**	**pedibus**

DECLENSION **3** GENDER **F**

	SINGULAR	PLURAL
NOM.	mater	**matrēs**
GEN.	**matris**	**matrum**
DAT.	**matrī**	**matribus**
ACC.	**matrem**	**matrēs**
ABL.	**matre**	**matribus**

G. Translate these phrases and sentences from English into Latin.

1. the wicked trap **insidiae improbae**

2. horse and pony **equus et mannus**

3. The king will reign. **Rēx regnābit.**

4. The queen is not recovering. **Rēgīna nōn recuperat.**

5. An honorable slave is plowing. **Servus honestus arat.**

6. The billy goat is exploring eagerly. **Caper certātim explōrat.**

H. Give the stem of each verb and which conjugation it's in. The first one is done for you.

	VERB	STEM	CONJUGATION
1.	accūsō, accūsāre	accūsā-	1
2.	obsecrō, obsecrāre	**obsecrā-**	**1**
3.	rudō, rudere	**rude-**	**3**
4.	pāreō, pārēre	**pārē-**	**2**
5.	nuntiō, nuntiāre	**nuntiā-**	**1**
6.	intrō, intrāre	**intrā-**	**1**
7.	currō, currere	**curre-**	**3**
8.	gaudeō, gaudēre	**gaudē-**	**2**

I. Answer the following questions about this week's quotation.

1. How do you say "Long live the king!" in Latin? **Vīvat rēx!**

2. Which word means "king"? **rēx**

Week 14 Quiz

name:

A. Vocabulary

Fill in the blank with the correct translation. For Latin words, give the English. For English words, give the Latin.

1. I invite _____

2. administrō _____

3. tail _____

4. cavea _____

5. matrimonium _____

6. gradually _____

7. intrō _____

8. obsecrō _____

9. plot _____

10. accūsō _____

11. trochus _____

12. whip _____

13. hodiē _____

14. nuntiō _____

15. foedus _____

16. I think _____

Give the genitive singular form, gender, declension, and English translation for each Latin noun. The first one is done for you.

	NOUN	GENITIVE	GENDER	DECLENSION	TRANSLATION
1.	caelum	caelī	N	2	sky, heaven
2.	insidiae				
3.	balatrō				
4.	servus				
5.	pābulum				
6.	ariēs				

B. Chants

Decline *rēx* and *servus* in the chart below, then answer the questions.

	SINGULAR	PLURAL
NOM.	rēx	
GEN.		
DAT.		
ACC.		
ABL.		

	SINGULAR	PLURAL
NOM.	servus	
GEN.		
DAT.		
ACC.		
ABL.		

1. Which declension is *rēx* in? _____

2. Which declension is *servus* in? _____

3. Which ending do you use to find a noun's declension? _____

Conjugate and translate *ducō* in the future tense.

LATIN

	SINGULAR	PLURAL
1ST		
2ND		
3RD		

ENGLISH

	SINGULAR	PLURAL

4. Which conjugation is *ducō* in? _____

5. What family is it in? _____

C. Quotations

1. What does *Vīvat rēx!* mean? _____

Week 14 Quiz: Answer Key

A. Vocabulary

Fill in the blank with the correct translation. For Latin words, give the English. For English words, give the Latin.

1. I invite	**vocō**	9. plot	**insidiae**	
2. administrō	**I help, manage**	10. accūsō	**I accuse, blame**	
3. tail	**cauda**	11. trochus	**hoop for games**	
4. cavea	**cage, animal den**	12. whip	**flagellum**	
5. matrimonium	**marriage**	13. hodiē	**today**	
6. gradually	**minūtātim**	14. nuntiō	**I announce**	
7. intrō	**I enter**	15. foedus	**horrible, ugly**	
8. obsecrō	**I beg, implore**	16. I think	**cōgitō**	

Give the genitive singular form, gender, declension, and English translation for each Latin noun. The first one is done for you.

	NOUN	GENITIVE SINGULAR	GENDER	DECLENSION	TRANSLATION
1.	caelum	caelī	N	2	sky, heaven
2.	insidiae	**insidiārum**	**F**	**1**	**ambush, trap, plot**
3.	balatrō	**balatrōnis**	**M**	**3**	**jester, clown**
4.	servus	**servī**	**M**	**2**	**slave, servant**
5.	pābulum	**pābulī**	**N**	**2N**	**fodder**
6.	ariēs	**arietis**	**M**	**3**	**ram**

B. Chants

Decline *rēx* and *servus* in the chart below, then answer the questions.

	SINGULAR	PLURAL
NOM.	rēx	**rēgēs**
GEN.	**rēgis**	**rēgum**
DAT.	**rēgī**	**rēgibus**
ACC.	**rēgem**	**rēgēs**
ABL.	**rēge**	**rēgibus**

	SINGULAR	PLURAL
NOM.	servus	**servī**
GEN.	**servī**	**servōrum**
DAT.	**servō**	**servīs**
ACC.	**servum**	**servōs**
ABL.	**servō**	**servīs**

1. Which declension is *rēx* in? **third declension**

2. Which declension is *servus* in? **second declension**

3. Which ending do you use to find a noun's declension? **genitive singular**

Conjugate and translate *ducō* in the future tense.

LATIN

	SINGULAR	PLURAL
1ST	**dūcam**	**dūcēmus**
2ND	**dūcēs**	**dūcētis**
3RD	**dūcet**	**dūcent**

ENGLISH

	SINGULAR	PLURAL
1ST	**I will lead**	**we will lead**
2ND	**you will lead**	**you all will lead**
3RD	**he/she/it will lead**	**they will lead**

4. Which conjugation is *ducō* in? **third conjugation**

5. What family is it in? **the "e" family**

C. Quotations

1. What does *Vīvat rēx!* mean? **Long live the king!**

Teaching Notes: Week 15

1. Word List: Introduce the Word List for Week 15. Review this list throughout the week and continue to review vocabulary from previous weeks.

2. Derivatives: Discuss the derivatives for this week's vocabulary:

1. aranea, *spider*

2. bestiola, *insect*

3. caput, *head:* cap, captain, chapter, capital, capitalism, cape, recapitulate

4. cornix, *crow:* cornice

5. corpus, *body:* corpse, corporeal, corpulence, corporate, incorporation

6. crūs, *leg*

7. musca, *fly:* mosquito

8. pinna, *feather, wing:* pin, pinnacle, pinnate

9. vulnus, *wound:* vulnerable

10. caeruleus, *blue:* cerulean

11. flavus, *yellow, blond:* flavin

12. fīgō, *I fasten, attach, make firm:* affix, fixate

13. mittō, *I send, let go:* commissary, demise, emissary, missive, emit, intermittent, remint, noncommital, premise, remission, surmise

14. reptō, *I crawl, creep:* reptile

15. scalpō, *I carve, scratch:* scalpel

Have the students write this week's derivatives in the Week 15 "Derivatives" section of their student book.

3. Chant: This week, you'll be introducing the noun ending chant for the third declension *neuter* endings. Just like it sounds, the third declension neuter is a variation on the third declension endings that you learned in Week 13. It functions in exactly the same way; the difference is that this week's chant is specifically for nouns of the third declension that are *neuter* in gender.

Third Declension Neuter Noun Endings

Always remember: **a noun's genitive singular ending will tell you which declension that noun is in.** Third declension nouns, regardless of their gender, will *always* have -*īs* as their genitive singular ending. Once you see the -*īs* genitive ending following a noun, you can be sure you are working with a noun in the third declension.

However, knowing a noun's declension doesn't always tell you its gender. With second declension neuter nouns, you learned a trick that told you the noun's gender—the nominative singular ending is always -*um*. But there is no trick for third declension neuter nouns. You will simply have to remember their genders as you learn them. As you can imagine, it's becoming increasingly important to memorize the entire Word List entry!

Let's work with an example. Which declension is the word *caput* in? If we look in this week's Word List, we can see that its genitive singular ends in -*īs*. Only third declension nouns have an -*īs* genitive ending, therefore we know *corpus* is in the third declension. But wait, we also know from the Word List that *caput* is neuter—so now we know how to decline it!

The third declension neuter endings are almost exactly the same as the standard third declension endings. Note the three endings where there is a difference—accusative singular, nominative plural, and accusative plural. A helpful trick to remember when declining these neuter nouns is the nominative and accusative endings (both singular and plural) will always match each other. (Again, it's very important that students understand the **x**'s in the chant are only placeholders, not endings.)

In the following chart, you can compare the close similarities between the two. *Caput* has been declined, and the endings, shown in bold, have been applied to its base, *capit-*.

THIRD DECLENSION

	SINGULAR	PLURAL
NOM.	rēx	rēgēs
GEN.	rēgis	rēgum
DAT.	rēgī	rēgibus
ACC.	rēgem	rēgēs
ABL.	rēge	rēgibus

THIRD DECLENSION NEUTER

	SINGULAR	PLURAL
NOM.	caput (**x**)	capit**a**
GEN.	capit**is**	capit**um**
DAT.	capit**ī**	capit**ibus**
ACC.	caput (**x**)	capit**a**
ABL.	capit**e**	capit**ibus**

Run through the ending chant several times, until students feel comfortable saying it. Once they've gotten into the rhythm of chanting the endings, begin applying the endings to whole nouns. Here are more examples:

	SINGULAR	PLURAL
NOM.	corpus	corpora
GEN.	corporis	corporum
DAT.	corporī	corporibus
ACC.	corpus	corpora
ABL.	corpore	corporibus

	SINGULAR	PLURAL
NOM.	crūs	crūra
GEN.	crūris	crūrum
DAT.	crūrī	crūribus
ACC.	crūs	crūra
ABL.	crūre	crūribus

4. Quotation: This week's quotation comes from Cicero (*Pro Murena*). Crows have classically been known as shrewd (and sometimes cruel) creatures, so to "peck the eyes of crows" means to give someone a taste of their own medicine. An alternate meaning is "to fasten shut the eyes of crows," again, taken with the same meaning—cleverly avoiding the notice of the most clever.

Have the students write this week's quotation in the Week 15 "Quotation" section of their student book.

5. Worksheet: Follow the directions given to complete the worksheet.

6. Quiz: Administer Quiz 15 at the end of the week.

WEEK 15

Word List

NOUNS

1. aranea, -ae (f) . . . . .spider
2. bestiola, -ae (f) . . . . .insect
3. caput, capitis (n) . . . . . .head
4. cornix, cornicis (f) . . . . .crow
5. corpus, corporis (n) . . . .body
6. crūs, crūris (n). . . . . . . .leg
7. musca, -ae (f) . . . . .fly
8. pinna, -ae (f) . . . . .feather, wing
9. vulnus, vulneris (n). . . . .wound

ADJECTIVES

10. caeruleus, -a, -um . . . . .blue
11. flavus, -a, -um . . . . . . .yellow, blond

VERBS

12. fīgō, fīgere . . . . .I fasten, attach, make firm
13. mittō, mittere . . . . . . .I send, let go
14. reptō, reptāre . . . . . . .I crawl, creep
15. scalpō, scalpere. . . . . .I carve, scratch

Chant:

Third Declension Neuter Noun Endings

	LATIN			ENGLISH	
	SINGULAR	PLURAL		SINGULAR	PLURAL
NOM.	x	-a		a, the *noun*	the *nouns*
GEN.	-is	-um		of the *noun*, the *noun's*	of the *nouns*, the *nouns'*
DAT.	-ī	-ibus		to, for the *noun*	to, for the *nouns*
ACC.	x	-a		the *noun*	the *nouns*
ABL.	-e	-ibus		by, with, from the *noun*	by, with, from the *nouns*

Quotation:

Cornicum oculōs configere—"To peck the eyes of crows"

Weekly Worksheet 15: Answer Key

A. Complete the chant for this week and answer the questions about it.

	SINGULAR	PLURAL
NOMINATIVE	x	-a
GENITIVE	-is	-um
DATIVE	-ī	-ibus
ACCUSATIVE	x	-a
ABLATIVE	-e	-ibus

1. Which ending tells you a noun's declension? **genitive singular**

2. The genitive ending for the third declension is **-is.**

3. The genitive ending for the third declension neuter is **-is.**

4. The genitive ending for the second declension is **-ī.**

5. The genitive ending for the first declension is **-ae.**

B. Decline *crūs* and *vulnus* in the chart below, then answer the questions.

	SINGULAR	PLURAL		SINGULAR	PLURAL
NOM.	crūs	**crūra**		vulnus	**vulnera**
GEN.	**crūris**	**crūrum**		**vulneris**	**vulnerum**
DAT.	**crūrī**	**crūribus**		**vulnerī**	**vulneribus**
ACC.	**crūs**	**crūra**		**vulnus**	**vulnera**
ABL.	**crūre**	**crūribus**		**vulnere**	**vulneribus**

1. Which declension are *crūs* and *vulnus* in? **third declension**

2. How can you tell? **Both of them have *-is* as their genitive singular ending.**

3. What gender are *crūs* and *vulnus*? **neuter**

C. Decline *cornix* and *rēx* below.

	SINGULAR	PLURAL
NOM.	cornix	**cornicēs**
GEN.	**cornicis**	cornicum
DAT.	**cornicī**	cornicibus
ACC.	**cornicem**	cornicēs
ABL.	**cornice**	cornicibus

	SINGULAR	PLURAL
NOM.	rēx	**rēgēs**
GEN.	**rēgis**	**rēgum**
DAT.	**rēgī**	**rēgibus**
ACC.	**rēgem**	**rēgēs**
ABL.	**rēge**	**rēgibus**

D. Label the picture using the Latin words below.

pinna   cornix   crūs   caput   corpus

caput

pinna

corpus

crūs

This animal is called a **cornix**.

E. Underline the adjective that matches the noun's number and gender, then translate the phrase.

NOUN	ADJECTIVE	TRANSLATION
1. Pinna	**flava** / flavae	**the yellow wing**
2. Vulnera	caeruleae / **caerulea**	**blue wounds**
3. Caput	flavus / **flavum**	**a blond head**
4. Crūs	magna / **magnum**	**big leg**
5. Bestiola	**parva** / parvum	**a little insect**
6. Cornicēs	improbī / **improbae**	**the wicked crows**
7. Insidiae	mīra / **mīrae**	**strange plots**
8. Rēx	**honestus** / honestum	**an honorable king**
9. Servus	**famēlicus** / famēlica	**the hungry servant**
10. Tigridēs	**famēlicī** / famēlica	**hungry tigers**

F. Translate the following sentences into English.

1. Araneae caeruleae reptant. **The blue spiders are crawling.**

2. Balatrō rīdiculus explōrābat. **The funny clown was exploring.**

3. Minūtātim scalpō. **I carve bit by bit.**

4. Circus est magnus et lātus. **The racecourse is large and wide.**

5. Rēgīna flava certātim intrat. **The blond queen enters eagerly.**

6. Semper administrās. **You are always helping.**

7. Simul serēbāmus. **We were planting at the same time.**

8. Hortus minūtātim crescent. **The garden will grow gradually.**

9. Caper magnus oppugnat. **The big billy goat attacks.**

10. Elephantus parvus et cornicēs volant. **The little elephant and the crows are flying.**

G. Translate the following phrases and sentences into English.

1. the spotted insects **bestiolae maculōsae**

2. a little wound **vulnus parvum**

3. The blue fly is not crawling. **Musca caerula nōn reptat.**

4. A blind crow was scratching. **Cornix caeca scalpēbat.**

5. The king and queen will govern. **Rēx et rēgīna regnābunt.**

H. Match the English derivative with its Latin root.

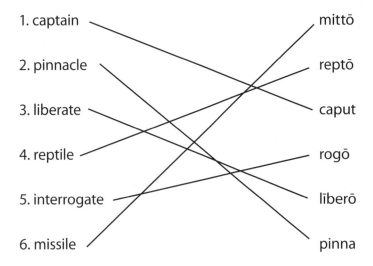

1. captain   mittō

2. pinnacle   reptō

3. liberate   caput

4. reptile   rogō

5. interrogate   līberō

6. missile   pinna

I. Give the stem of each verb, its conjugation, and its family.

	VERB	STEM	CONJUGATION	FAMILY
1.	reptō, reptāre	**reptā-**	1	ā
2.	pāreō, pārēre	**pārē-**	2	ē
3.	confīgō, confīgere	**confīge-**	3	e
4.	gaudeō, gaudēre	**gaudē-**	2	ē
5.	rudō, rudere	**rude-**	3	e

Week 15 Quiz

name:

A. Chant

Complete the chant below, then answer the questions.

	SINGULAR	PLURAL
NOM.	x	
GEN.		
DAT.		
ACC.	x	
ABL.		

1. What is the name of this chant? _____

2. Are these endings for nouns or verbs? _____

3. What are the *x's* in the chant? _____

Decline *caput* and *corpus* and give each word's declension and gender.

DECLENSION _____ GENDER _____   DECLENSION _____ GENDER _____

	SINGULAR	PLURAL
NOM.	caput	
GEN.		
DAT.		
ACC.		
ABL.		

	SINGULAR	PLURAL
NOM.	corpus	
GEN.		
DAT.		
ACC.		
ABL.		

Decline *cornix* and *tigris* and give each word's declension and gender.

DECLENSION _____ GENDER _____

	SINGULAR	PLURAL
NOM.	cornix	
GEN.		
DAT.		
ACC.		
ABL.		

DECLENSION _____ GENDER _____

	SINGULAR	PLURAL
NOM.	tigris	
GEN.		
DAT.		
ACC.		
ABL.		

B. Vocabulary

Give the stem of each verb, its conjugation, and its family.

	VERB	STEM	CONJUGATION	FAMILY
1.	fīgō, fīgere			
2.	obsecrō, obsecrāre			
3.	gaudeō, gaudēre			
4.	mittō, mittere			
5.	intrō, intrāre			

Translate these words into English.

6. musca _____

7. opera _____

8. agricola _____

9. improbus _____

10. crūs _____

11. arō _____

12. līberō _____

13. servus _____

Week 15 Quiz: Answer Key

A. Chant

Complete the chant below, then answer the questions.

	SINGULAR	PLURAL
NOM.	x	-a
GEN.	-is	-um
DAT.	-ī	-ibus
ACC.	x	-a
ABL.	-e	-ibus

1. What is the name of this chant? **third declension neuter**

2. Are these endings for nouns or verbs? **nouns**

3. What are the *x's* in the chant? **They're placeholders.**

Decline *caput* and *corpus* and give each word's declension and gender.

DECLENSION __3__ GENDER __N__

	SINGULAR	PLURAL
NOM.	caput	capita
GEN.	capitis	capitum
DAT.	capitī	capitibus
ACC.	caput	capita
ABL.	capite	capitibus

DECLENSION __3__ GENDER __N__

	SINGULAR	PLURAL
NOM.	corpus	corpora
GEN.	corporis	corporum
DAT.	corporī	corporibus
ACC.	corpus	corpora
ABL.	corpore	corporibus

Decline *cornix* and *tigris* and give each word's declension and gender.

DECLENSION __3__ GENDER __F__

	SINGULAR	PLURAL
NOM.	cornix	**cornicēs**
GEN.	**cornicis**	cornicum
DAT.	**cornicī**	cornicibus
ACC.	**cornicem**	cornicēs
ABL.	**cornice**	cornicibus

DECLENSION __3__ GENDER __M/F__

	SINGULAR	PLURAL
NOM.	tigris	**tigridēs**
GEN.	**tigridis**	**tigridum**
DAT.	**tigridī**	**tigridibus**
ACC.	**tigridem**	**tigridēs**
ABL.	**tigride**	**tigridibus**

B. Vocabulary

Give the stem of each verb, its conjugation, and its family.

	VERB	STEM	CONJUGATION	FAMILY
1.	fīgō, fīgere	**fīge-**	**3**	**e**
2.	obsecrō, obsecrāre	**obsecrā-**	**1**	**ā**
3.	gaudeō, gaudēre	**gaudē-**	**2**	**ē**
4.	mittō, mittere	**mitte-**	**3**	**e**
5.	intrō, intrāre	**intrā-**	**1**	**ā**

Translate these words into English.

6. musca **fly**

7. opera **effort, services**

8. agricola **farmer**

9. improbus **wicked**

10. crūs **leg**

11. arō **I plow**

12. līberō **I set free**

13. servus **servant, slave**

Teaching Notes: Week 16

1. Word List: Introduce the Word List for Week 16. Review this list throughout the week and continue to review vocabulary from previous weeks.

2. Derivatives: Discuss the derivatives for this week's vocabulary:

1. argūmentum, *proof, evidence:* argument
2. discipulus, *apprentice, student:* disciple
3. iūs, *justice, right, law:* conjure, jurisdiction, jurisprudence, justification, perjury
4. lacrima, *tear:* lachrymose
5. magister, *teacher (male):* magistrate, magisterial
6. magistra, *teacher (female)*
7. pax, *peace:* pacify, pacifist, pacific
8. contentus, *satisfied, content:* content, contentious
9. firmus, *strong, firm, steadfast:* firm, infirmary
10. erō, *I will be*
11. fleō, *I weep*
12. moneō, *I warn:* admonish, monitor, premonition
13. repudiō, *I reject, scorn:* repudiate
14. respondeō, *I respond, answer:* respond, responsive
15. sedeō, *I sit:* sedentary, session, obsess, preside, reside
16. timeō, *I fear:* timid, intimidate
17. videō, *I see:* evident, video, vision, visible, vista, visit, visor, visual

Have the students write this week's derivatives in the Week 16 "Derivatives" section of their student book. Look over previous derivatives from Unit 2.

3. Chant: In Week 10, you reviewed the chant for *sum,* "I am." This week, you'll be introducing the future form of *sum,* which is *erō,* meaning "I will be."

Read through the chant starting in the top left corner: *erō, eris, erit, erimus, eritis, erunt.* Chant it a few times, until students catch the rhythm and are comfortable saying it. Then chant through the English translation. Continue to review the chant each day during the week.

As you might expect, the *erō* chant works just like the *sum* chant. *Sum* is an irregular verb, so *erō* is irregular also—it doesn't follow the pattern of any conjugation. And like *sum, erō* is a complete verb, not a verb ending.

Here are some example sentences using *erō* with predicate adjectives:

Erō contenta.	*I will be content.*
Eris pūrus.	*You will be clean.*
Rēgīna nōn erit bona.	*The queen will not be good.*
Erimus famelicī.	*We will be hungry.*
Eritis firmae.	*You all will be steadfast.*
Trochī erunt flavī.	*The hoops will be yellow.*

You know that predicate adjectives follow a linking verb and describe the subject noun. This week, you'll be learning to use nouns in the same way! They are called **predicate nouns.** Like predicate adjectives, predicate nouns tell you something more about the subject noun. *Predicate nouns rename or identify the subject noun and follow a linking verb, like sum.*

Take a look at these sample sentences. The predicate nouns are in bold; notice that they each match the subject noun in number and case.

Avus est **balatrō**.	*The grandfather is a clown.*

Sunt **magistrī.**	*They are teachers.*
Vir nōn est **discipulus.**	*The man is not an apprentice.*
Puella erit **rēgina.**	*The girl will be a queen.*
Servī erunt **amīcī.**	*The slaves will be friends.*
Venēnum erit **argūmentum.**	*The poison will be evidence.*
Cibī erunt **frāga** et **ariēnae.**	*The food will be strawberries and bananas.*

Predicate nouns always take the nominative case, in order to match the case of the subject noun. Usually in sentences with a predicate noun or adjective, the verb will not come at the end of the sentence. Instead it appears in the middle, like an "equals" sign, linking the subject and the predicate noun/adjective.

Follow the directions given to complete the worksheet.

4. Quotation: There is no quotation this week. Look over quotations from previous weeks and test the students' memory of their translations.

5. Worksheet: Follow the directions given to complete the worksheet.

6. Quiz: Since there is a test at the end of the week, this week's quiz is optional. Feel free to use it as practice for the test.

7. Test: The Unit 2 Test should be given at the end of this week.

WEEK 16

Word List

NOUNS

1. argūmentum, -ī (n). . . . . proof, evidence

2. discipulus, -ī (m) . . . . . apprentice, student

3. iūs, iūris (n) . . . . justice, right, law

4. lacrima, -ae (f) . . . . . . tear

5. magister, magistrī (m) . . teacher (male)

6. magistra, -ae (f). . . . . . teacher (female)

7. pax, pācis (f). . . . . peace

ADJECTIVES

8. contentus, -a, -um . . . . satisfied, content

9. firmus, -a, -um . . . . . . strong, firm, steadfast

VERBS

10. erō. . . . . .I will be

11. fleō, flēre . . . . .I weep

12. moneō, monēre . . . . . .I warn

13. repudiō, repudiāre . . . . .I reject, scorn

14. respondeō, respondēre . .I respond, answer

15. sedeō, sedēre . . . . . . .I sit

16. timeō, timēre . . . . . . .I fear

17. videō, vidēre. . . . . . . .I see

Chant:

Erō, *I will be*—Future Active of *Sum*

Irregular Verb

	LATIN			ENGLISH	
	SINGULAR	PLURAL		SINGULAR	PLURAL
1ST	erō	erimus		I will be	we will be
2ND	eris	eritis		you will be	you all will be
3RD	erit	erunt		he/she/it will be	they will be

Quotation:

No new quotation this week.

Weekly Worksheet 16: Answer Key

A. Conjugate *sum* in the present active.

LATIN

ENGLISH

	SINGULAR	PLURAL		SINGULAR	PLURAL
1ST	sum	sumus		I am	we are
2ND	es	estis		you are	you all are
3RD	est	sunt		he/she/it is	they are

1. Is *sum* a regular or irregular verb? **irregular**

2. Is *sum* a verb ending or a complete verb? **a complete verb**

B. Conjugate and translate *sum* in the future active. Try to do it from memory!

LATIN

ENGLISH

	SINGULAR	PLURAL		SINGULAR	PLURAL
1ST	erō	erimus		I will be	we will be
2ND	eris	eritis		you will be	you all will be
3RD	erit	erunt		he/she/it will be	they will be

3. Is *erō* a regular or irregular verb? **irregular**

4. Is *erō* an action verb or a being verb? **a being verb**

C. Fill in the blanks.

1. A **predicate** adjective follows a **linking** verb and describes a subject noun.

2. A predicate **noun** follows a linking verb and identifies or **renames** the subject noun.

3. Which Latin case do you use for this part of speech? **nominative**

4. Which Latin case do you use for the subject? **nominative**

D. These are nouns you learned last year. They are grouped by whether they name a person, place, or thing. Give the English translation for each word. (If you need to use your Latin dictionary, do!)

PERSON	PLACE	THING
1. praefectus **officer**	6. vīcus **village**	11. sagitta **arrow**
2. Iesus **Jesus**	7. forum **marketplace**	12. patientia **patience**
3. lēgātus **lieutenant**	8. patria **native land**	13. praemium **reward**
4. captīvus **captive**	9. campus **athletic field**	14. donum **gift**
5. cīvis **citizen**	10. ecclēsia **church**	15. fossa **ditch**

E. In each English sentence, underline the subject and circle the predicate noun. Then translate the predicate noun into Latin and write it in the blank. (Hint: Remember which case the predicate noun takes!)

1. <u>Fred</u> is my older (brother.) **germānus**

2. <u>Shakespeare</u> is a famous (poet.) **poeta**

3. One day the little <u>nut</u> will be an (elm tree.) **ulmus**

4. <u>Tarantulas</u> are huge, hairy (spiders!) **aranea**

5. <u>This</u> is my favorite (pillow) in the world. **pulvīnus**

F. Translate these short sentences. Be careful about the person and tense of the "being" verb.

1. Sum magistra. **I am a teacher.**

2. Estis discipulī. **You all are students.**

3. Erunt laetī. **They will be happy.**

4. Erimus balatrōnēs! **We will be clowns!**

5. Nōn erō rēx. **I will not be the king.**

6. Erit firmus. **He is steadfast.**

G. Underline the adjective that matches the noun's number and gender, then translate the phrase.

NOUN	ADJECTIVE	TRANSLATION
1. Magister	**firmus** / firmī	**the firm teacher**
2. Pax	pulcher / **pulchra**	**a beautiful peace**
3. Vulnus	caeruleus / **caeruleum**	**the blue wound**
4. Lacrimae	laeta / **laetae**	**joyful tears**
5. Corpus	aptus / aptum	**a fit body**

H. Label each noun's declension (1, 2, or 3) and gender (M, F, or N). Then decline it.

DECLENSION __2__ GENDER __M__

	SINGULAR	PLURAL
NOM.	magister	**magistrī**
GEN.	**magistrī**	**magistrōrum**
DAT.	**magistrō**	**magistrīs**
ACC.	**magistrum**	**magistrōs**
ABL.	**magistrō**	**magistrīs**

DECLENSION __3__ GENDER __N__

	SINGULAR	PLURAL
NOM.	iūs	**iūra**
GEN.	**iūris**	**iūrum**
DAT.	**iūrī**	**iūribus**
ACC.	**iūs**	**iūra**
ABL.	**iūre**	**iūribus**

DECLENSION __3__ GENDER __F__

	SINGULAR	PLURAL
NOM.	pax	**pācēs**
GEN.	**pācis**	**pācum**
DAT.	**pācī**	**pācibus**
ACC.	**pācem**	**pācēs**
ABL.	**pāce**	**pācibus**

DECLENSION __2__ GENDER __N__

	SINGULAR	PLURAL
NOM.	argūmentum	**argūmenta**
GEN.	**argūmentī**	**argūmentōrum**
DAT.	**argūmentō**	**argūmentīs**
ACC.	**argūmentum**	**argūmenta**
ABL.	**argūmentō**	**argūmentīs**

I. Translate these sentences. Circle any *predicate nouns*. You'll notice a couple more words from last year!

1. Rēx bonus respondēbit. **The good king will answer.**

2. Germānus est (discipulus) **The brother is a student.**

3. Iūs nōn est perfectus. **The law is not perfect.**

4. Fābula erit (liber) **The story will be a book.**

5. Puerī erunt (agricolae.) **The boys will be farmers.**

6. Biblia Sacra est (liber) bonus. **The Holy Bible is a good book.**

7. Iesus est (magister) et (rēx) et (Dominus) **Jesus is teacher and king and Lord.**

8. Argūmentum est firmum. **The evidence is strong.**

9. Aranea bona scribet. **The good spider will write.**

10. Cunīculus albus currēbat et properābat. **The white rabbit was running and hurrying.**

11. Lacrimae erunt ūmidae. **Tears will be wet.**

12. Germānae nōn sunt (aviae.) **The sisters are not grandmothers.**

13. Fīlius erit (vir.) **The son will be a man.**

J. Answer the questions, then conjugate and translate *mittō, mittere* in the future active tense.

1. Which conjugation is *mittō* in? **third conjugation**

2. Which family is *mittō* in? **the "e" family**

LATIN

ENGLISH

	SINGULAR	PLURAL		SINGULAR	PLURAL
1ST	mittam	mittēmus		I will send	we will send
2ND	mittēs	mittētis		you will send	you all will send
3RD	mittet	mittent		he/she/it will send	they will send

Week 16 Quiz

name:

A. Chants

Conjugate the following words in the present, future, and imperfect tenses.

Present Active

FIRST CONJUGATION

	SINGULAR	PLURAL
1ST	reptō	
2ND		
3RD		

SECOND CONJUGATION

	SINGULAR	PLURAL
	timeō	

THIRD CONJUGATION

	SINGULAR	PLURAL
	fīgō	

Future Active

FIRST CONJUGATION

	SINGULAR	PLURAL
1ST		
2ND		
3RD		

SECOND CONJUGATION

	SINGULAR	PLURAL

THIRD CONJUGATION

	SINGULAR	PLURAL

Imperfect Active

FIRST CONJUGATION

	SINGULAR	PLURAL
1ST		
2ND		
3RD		

SECOND CONJUGATION

	SINGULAR	PLURAL

THIRD CONJUGATION

	SINGULAR	PLURAL

Conjugate and translate *sum* in the future active tense.

LATIN

	SINGULAR	PLURAL
1ST		
2ND		
3RD		

ENGLISH

	SINGULAR	PLURAL

Label each noun's declension (1, 2, or 3) and gender (M, F, or N). Then decline it.

DECLENSION _____ GENDER _____

	SINGULAR	PLURAL
NOM.	crūs	
GEN.		
DAT.		
ACC.		
ABL.		

DECLENSION _____ GENDER _____

	SINGULAR	PLURAL
NOM.	rēx	
GEN.		
DAT.		
ACC.		
ABL.		

Fill in the blanks.

1. In Latin, the *subject noun* always takes the _____ case.

2. To find the *base* of a Latin noun, you remove its _____ singular ending.

3. A *verb* shows _____ or state of _____.

4. To find the *stem* of a verb, you remove the _____ from the _____ principal part.

5. An adjective answers the questions _____ kind? _____ one? or how _____?

6. A _____ follows a _____ verb and describes a subject noun.

7. A _____ follows a linking verb and identifies or _____ the subject noun.

8. Which Latin case do you use for the part of speech in #7? _____

B. Vocabulary

Give the masculine, feminine, and neuter *nominative plural* of these adjectives in Latin.

	ADJECTIVE	MASCULINE	FEMININE	NEUTER
1.	steadfast			
2.	satisfied			

For each noun, list its genitive singular, gender, declension, and English translation.

	NOUN	GENITIVE	GENDER	DECLENSION	ENGLISH
3.	lacrima				
4.	vulnus				
5.	insidiae				
6.	servus				
7.	tigris				
8.	astrum				

Translate these sentences into English. Circle any predicate nouns or adjectives.

9. Argūmentum firmum repudiābat! _____

10. Discipulus quiētus erit balatrō. _____

11. Caper brūnus semper currit. _____

12. Servus parvus sedet et flet. _____

13. Virī simul erunt magistrī. _____

Week 16 Quiz: Answer Key

A. Chants

Conjugate the following words in the present, future, and imperfect tenses.

Present Active

FIRST CONJUGATION		
	SINGULAR	PLURAL
1ST	reptō	reptāmus
2ND	reptās	reptātis
3RD	reptat	reptant

SECOND CONJUGATION		
	SINGULAR	PLURAL
	timeō	timēmus
	timēs	timētis
	timet	timent

THIRD CONJUGATION		
	SINGULAR	PLURAL
	fīgō	fīgimus
	fīgis	fīgitis
	fīgit	fīgunt

Future Active

FIRST CONJUGATION		
	SINGULAR	PLURAL
1ST	reptābō	reptābimus
2ND	reptābis	reptābitis
3RD	reptābit	reptābunt

SECOND CONJUGATION		
	SINGULAR	PLURAL
	timēbō	timēbimus
	timēbis	timēbitis
	timēbit	timēbunt

THIRD CONJUGATION		
	SINGULAR	PLURAL
	fīgam	fīgēmus
	fīgēs	fīgētis
	fīget	fīgent

Imperfect Active

FIRST CONJUGATION		
	SINGULAR	PLURAL
1ST	reptābam	reptābāmus
2ND	reptābās	reptābātis
3RD	reptābat	reptābant

SECOND CONJUGATION		
	SINGULAR	PLURAL
	timēbam	timēbāmus
	timēbās	timēbātis
	timēbat	timēbant

THIRD CONJUGATION		
	SINGULAR	PLURAL
	fīgēbam	fīgēbāmus
	fīgēbās	fīgēbātis
	fīgēbat	fīgēbant

Conjugate and translate *sum* in the future active tense.

LATIN

	SINGULAR	PLURAL
1ST	erō	erimus
2ND	eris	eritis
3RD	erit	erunt

ENGLISH

	SINGULAR	PLURAL
1ST	I will be	we will be
2ND	you will be	you all will be
3RD	he/she/it will be	they will be

Label each noun's declension (1, 2, or 3) and gender (M, F, or N). Then decline it.

DECLENSION __3__ GENDER __N__

	SINGULAR	PLURAL
NOM.	crūs	crūra
GEN.	crūris	crūrum
DAT.	crūrī	crūribus
ACC.	crūs	crūra
ABL.	crūre	crūribus

DECLENSION __3__ GENDER __M__

	SINGULAR	PLURAL
NOM.	rēx	rēgēs
GEN.	rēgis	rēgum
DAT.	rēgī	rēgibus
ACC.	rēgem	rēgēs
ABL.	rēge	rēgibus

Fill in the blanks.

1. In Latin, the *subject noun* always takes the **nominative** case.

2. To find the *base* of a Latin noun, you remove its **genitive** singular ending.

3. A *verb* shows **action** or state of **being**.

4. To find the *stem* of a verb, you remove the **-re** from the **second** principal part.

5. An adjective answers the questions **what** kind? **which** one? or how **many**?

6. A **predicate adjective** follows a **linking** verb and describes the subject noun.

7. A **predicate noun** follows a linking verb and identifies or **renames** the subject noun.

8. Which Latin case do you use for the part of speech in #7? **nominative**

B. Vocabulary

Give the masculine, feminine, and neuter *nominative plural* of these adjectives in Latin.

	ADJECTIVE	MASCULINE	FEMININE	NEUTER
1.	steadfast	**firmī**	**firmae**	**firma**
2.	satisfied	**contentī**	**contentae**	**contenta**

For each noun, list its genitive singular, gender, declension, and English translation.

	NOUN	GENITIVE	GENDER	DECLENSION	ENGLISH
3.	lacrima	**lacrimae**	**F**	**1**	**tear**
4.	vulnus	**vulneris**	**N**	**3**	**wound**
5.	insidiae	**insidiārum**	**F**	**1**	**ambush, trap**
6.	servus	**servī**	**M**	**2**	**slave, servant**
7.	tigris	**tigridis**	**M/F**	**3**	**tiger**
8.	astrum	**astrī**	**N**	**2**	**star, constellation**

Translate these sentences into English. Circle any predicate nouns or adjectives.

9. Argūmentum firmum repudiābat! **Strong evidence was rejected!**

10. Discipulus quiētus erit (balatrō.) **The quiet apprentice will be a jester.**

11. Caper brūnus semper currit. **The brown billy goat is always running.**

12. Servus parvus sedet et flet. **A little servant sits and weeps.**

13. Virī simul erunt (magistrī.) **The men will be teachers at the same time.**

Unit 2 Test

name:

Chants

A. Fill in the blanks.

1. In Latin, the *subject noun* always takes the _____ case.

2. To find the *base* of a Latin noun, you remove its _____ singular ending.

3. A *verb* shows _____ or state of _____.

4. To find the *stem* of a verb, you remove the _____ from the _____ principal part.

5. An adjective modifies a _____ or _____.

6. An adjective answers the questions _____ kind? _____ one? or how _____?

7. An adverb can modify a _____, an _____, or another _____.

8. An adverb answers the questions _____? _____? _____? or to what extent?

9. A _____ follows a _____ verb and describes a subject noun.

10. A _____ follows a linking verb and identifies or _____ the subject noun.

B. Label each noun's declension (1, 2, or 3) and gender (M, F, or N). Then decline it.

DECLENSION _____ GENDER _____

	SINGULAR	PLURAL
NOM.	caput	
GEN.		
DAT.		
ACC.		
ABL.		

DECLENSION _____ GENDER _____

	SINGULAR	PLURAL
NOM.	pax	
GEN.		
DAT.		
ACC.		
ABL.		

DECLENSION _____ GENDER _____   DECLENSION _____ GENDER _____

	SINGULAR	PLURAL
NOM.	liber	
GEN.		
DAT.		
ACC.		
ABL.		

	SINGULAR	PLURAL
NOM.	verbum	

C. Conjugate the following words in the present, future, and imperfect tenses.

Present Active

FIRST CONJUGATION

	SINGULAR	PLURAL
1ST	rogō	
2ND		
3RD		

SECOND CONJUGATION

	SINGULAR	PLURAL
1ST	fleō	
2ND		
3RD		

THIRD CONJUGATION

	SINGULAR	PLURAL
1ST	dūcō	
2ND		
3RD		

Future Active

FIRST CONJUGATION

	SINGULAR	PLURAL
1ST		
2ND		
3RD		

SECOND CONJUGATION

	SINGULAR	PLURAL
1ST		
2ND		
3RD		

THIRD CONJUGATION

	SINGULAR	PLURAL
1ST		
2ND		
3RD		

Imperfect Active

FIRST CONJUGATION

	SINGULAR	PLURAL
1ST		
2ND		
3RD		

SECOND CONJUGATION

SINGULAR	PLURAL

THIRD CONJUGATION

SINGULAR	PLURAL

D. Conjugate and translate *erō*.

LATIN

	SINGULAR	PLURAL
1ST		
2ND		
3RD		

ENGLISH

SINGULAR	PLURAL

Vocabulary

E. Give the masculine, feminine, and neuter *nominative singular* of these adjectives in Latin.

	ADJECTIVE	MASCULINE	FEMININE	NEUTER
1.	just			
2.	yellow			

F. Translate these sentences into English.

1. Deus est aeternus. _____

2. Vir iūstus lūget. _____

3. Avia et avus hodiē serent. _____

4. Balatrō est laetus servus._____

5. Germānī simul exsultābant. _____

6. Familia hiemābit._____

7. Musca est foeda et caerulea._____

8. Vulnus nōn erit argūmentum._____

9. Rēx improbus minūtātim recuperat._____

10. Nuntius firmus nōn narrābit._____

G. For each noun, give its genitive singular form, gender (M, F, N), base, and declension (1, 2, 3).

	NOUN	GENITIVE	GENDER	BASE	DECLENSION
1.	ariēs				
2.	pax				
3.	aurōra				
4.	flagellum				

H. Match the English derivative with its Latin root.

1. visual   vēlum

2. veil   circus

3. adverb   narrō

4. insomnia   verbum

5. narrator   somnus

6. circle   videō

Unit 2 Test: Answer Key

Chants

A. Fill in the blanks.

1. In Latin, the *subject noun* always takes the **nominative** case.

2. To find the *base* of a Latin noun, you remove its **genitive** singular ending.

3. A *verb* shows **action** or state of **being**.

4. To find the *stem* of a verb, you remove the **-re** from the **second** principal part.

5. An adjective modifies a **noun** or **pronoun**.

6. An adjective answers the questions **what** kind? **which** one? or how **many**?

7. An adverb can modify a **verb**, an **adjective**, or another **adverb**.

8. An adverb answers the questions **how**? **when**? **where**? or to what extent?

9. A **predicate adjective** follows a **linking** verb and describes the subject noun.

10. A **predicate noun** follows a linking verb and identifies or **renames** the subject noun.

B. Label each noun's declension (1, 2, or 3) and gender (M, F, or N). Then decline it.

DECLENSION __3__ GENDER __N__

	SINGULAR	PLURAL
NOM.	caput	**capita**
GEN.	**capitis**	**capitum**
DAT.	**capitī**	**capitibus**
ACC.	**caput**	**capita**
ABL.	**capite**	**capitibus**

DECLENSION __3__ GENDER __F__

	SINGULAR	PLURAL
NOM.	pax	**pācēs**
GEN.	**pācis**	**pācum**
DAT.	**pācī**	**pācibus**
ACC.	**pācem**	**pācēs**
ABL.	**pāce**	**pācibus**

	DECLENSION **2** GENDER **M**	
	SINGULAR	PLURAL
NOM.	liber	librī
GEN.	librī	librōrum
DAT.	librō	librīs
ACC.	librum	librōs
ABL.	librō	librīs

	DECLENSION **2** GENDER **N**	
	SINGULAR	PLURAL
NOM.	verbum	verba
GEN.	verbī	verbōrum
DAT.	verbō	verbīs
ACC.	verbum	verba
ABL.	verbō	verbīs

C. Conjugate the following words in the present, future, and imperfect tenses.

Present Active

FIRST CONJUGATION

	SINGULAR	PLURAL
1ST	rogō	rogāmus
2ND	rogās	rogātis
3RD	rogat	rogant

SECOND CONJUGATION

	SINGULAR	PLURAL
	fleō	flēmus
	flēs	flētis
	flet	flent

THIRD CONJUGATION

	SINGULAR	PLURAL
	dūcō	dūcimus
	dūcis	dūcitis
	dūcit	dūcunt

Future Active

FIRST CONJUGATION

	SINGULAR	PLURAL
1ST	rogābō	rogābimus
2ND	rogābis	rogābitis
3RD	rogābit	rogābunt

SECOND CONJUGATION

	SINGULAR	PLURAL
	flēbō	flēbimus
	flēbis	flēbitis
	flēbit	flēbunt

THIRD CONJUGATION

	SINGULAR	PLURAL
	dūcam	dūcēmus
	dūcēs	dūcētis
	dūcet	dūcent

Imperfect Active

FIRST CONJUGATION		
	SINGULAR	**PLURAL**
1ST	rogābam	rogābāmus
2ND	rogābās	rogābātis
3RD	rogābat	rogābant

SECOND CONJUGATION		
	SINGULAR	**PLURAL**
	flēbam	flēbāmus
	flēbās	flēbātis
	flēbat	flēbant

THIRD CONJUGATION		
	SINGULAR	**PLURAL**
	dūcēbam	dūcēbāmus
	dūcēbās	dūcēbātis
	dūcēbat	dūcēbant

D. Conjugate and translate *erō*.

LATIN			ENGLISH		
	SINGULAR	**PLURAL**		**SINGULAR**	**PLURAL**
1ST	erō	erimus		I will be	we will be
2ND	eris	eritis		you will be	you all will be
3RD	erit	erunt		he/she/it will be	they will be

Vocabulary

E. Give the masculine, feminine, and neuter *nominative singular* of these adjectives in Latin.

	ADJECTIVE	MASCULINE	FEMININE	NEUTER
1.	just	iūstus	iūsta	iūstum
2.	yellow	flavus	flava	flavum

F. Translate these sentences into English.

1. Deus est aeternus. **God is eternal.**

2. Vir iūstus lūget. **The just man is grieving.**

3. Avia et avus hodiē serent. **The grandmother and grandfather will plant today.**

4. Balatrō est laetus servus. **The jester is a happy servant.**

5. Germānī simul exsultābant. **The brothers were dancing at the same time.**

6. Familia hiemābit. **The household will spend the winter.**

7. Musca est foeda et caerulea. **The fly is ugly and blue.**

8. Vulnus nōn erit argūmentum. **The wound will not be proof.**

9. Rēx improbus minūtātim recuperat. **The wicked king recovers bit by bit.**

10. Nuntius firmus nōn narrābit. **The steadfast messenger will not tell.**

G. For each noun, give its genitive singular form, gender (M, F, N), base, and declension (1, 2, 3).

	NOUN	GENITIVE	GENDER	BASE	DECLENSION
1.	ariēs	**arietis**	**M**	**ariet-**	**3**
2.	pax	**pācis**	**F**	**pāc-**	**3**
3.	aurōra	**aurōrae**	**F**	**aurōr-**	**1**
4.	flagellum	**flagellī**	**N**	**flagell-**	**2**

H. Match the English derivative with its Latin root.

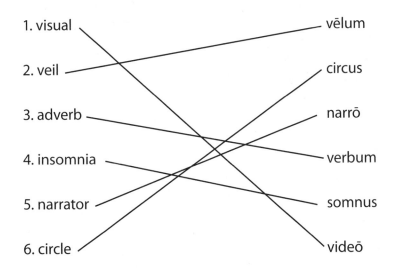

1. visual   vēlum

2. veil   circus

3. adverb   narrō

4. insomnia   verbum

5. narrator   somnus

6. circle   videō

3 UNIT THREE

UNIT 3: GOALS

By the end of Week 24, you should be able to . . .

- Recognize and translate sentences using first, second, and third declension nouns in the accusative case
- Translate and compose Latin questions
- Translate and compose Latin commands
- Recognize and decline masculine and feminine fourth declension nouns

Unit 3 Overview (Weeks 17–24)

During the next four weeks, students will learn about and practice translation using the accusative case. The accusative case is the case used for direct objects—sentence translation will become much more exciting! In Weeks 21 and 22, you'll introduce how to form questions and commands in Latin, and in Weeks 23 and 24, the fourth declension will be introduced and practiced (the fifth declension, which you'll learn next year, is the final Latin declension!).

Teaching Notes: Week 17

1. Word List: Introduce the Word List for Week 17. Students will probably recognize *ferus*—except that last year they learned it as an adjective. This is the same word, but a noun form. (We also do this sometimes in English: I gave him a *blue* tie. They took off into the *blue*.)

Review this list throughout the week and continue to review vocabulary from previous weeks.

2. Derivatives: Discuss derivatives for this week's vocabulary:

1. captīvus, *captive:* captive, captivate
2. disciplīna, *instruction, training:* discipline
3. ferus, *wild animal:* feral, fierce
4. flūmen, *river:* flume
5. habēna, *strap, rein*
6. īnsula, *island:* insulate, insulin, insular, peninsula, isle
7. lēgātus, *lieutenant:* delegate
8. memoria, *memory:* memory, memoir, immemorial
9. patria, *native land:* patriot, expatriate
10. stimulus, *goad, spur:* stimulus, stimulant
11. villa, *farmhouse, country house:* villa, village
12. commemorō, *I remember, mention:* commemorate
13. laxō, *I loosen:* lax, relax, relaxation
14. ornō, *I equip, decorate:* ornate
15. retineō, *I hold back, retain:* retain, retinue
16. servō, *I save:* conserve, conservative, preserve, observatory

Have the students write this week's derivatives in the Week 17 "Derivatives" section of their student book.

3. Chant: There is no new chant this week.

4. Quotation: There is no new quotation this week.

5. Worksheet: *Please note: This introduction to the accusative case assumes both teacher and students are familiar with the basics of English grammar.*

This week, you'll be introducing the accusative case! You've already learned that subject nouns take the nominative case. What takes the accusative case? Direct objects.

A **direct object** *is a noun or pronoun that receives the action of the verb, or the result of that action.* Take a look at these example sentences. The verb has been underlined, and the direct object is italicized.

A dog <u>chases</u> *cars.*
The man <u>ate</u> *a sandwich.*
Waves are <u>hitting</u> *the shore.*

In each sentence, the subject noun is doing something to another noun—the direct object. Below are sample questions and answers you can use to walk students through finding the direct object.

A dog chases cars.

What is the subject? *A dog.*
What is the verb? *Chases.*
What does the dog chase? *Cars.*
Voila! What the dog chases—cars—is the direct object. Let's do another.

The man ate a sandwich.

What is the subject? *The man.*
What is the verb? *Ate.*
What did the man eat? *A sandwich.*
And there you are again. What the man ate—a sandwich—is the direct object.

So, that's English. But what does a direct object look like in Latin? In Latin, **a direct object will always take the accusative case.** (In this book, the accusative case will be used *only* for direct objects.) Here are some sample sentences. Notice that the direct object usually appears before the verb. The accusative endings of the direct objects are bolded.

Agricola habēn**ās** laxat.	*The farmer is loosening the reins.*
Rēx serv**um** mittit.	*The king sends a servant.*
Balatrō tigrid**em** vocābat.	*A clown was calling the tiger.*
Argūment**um** repudiō.	*I scorn the evidence.*

Let's dissect the first sentence. The sentence reads: *Agricola habēnās laxat.*

1. The first step is to **locate the verb:** *laxat*
2. Then ask, **what does the verb mean?** He/she/it is loosening.
Remind students that hidden within each verb is an automatic subject. In this case, it's third person singular—*he, she,* or *it.* If there is a subject noun in the sentence, it must match this verb.
3. **Is there a subject noun that matches** *laxat* (i.e., a noun that is more specific about who he/she/it is)? Yes, *agricola.*
4. **Is there a noun in the accusative case** that tells us whom or what the farmer is loosening? In other words, is there a direct object? Yes, *habēnās.*
5. **Put the pieces together.** The subject noun is *agricola,* "the farmer." The verb is *laxat,* "is loosening." The direct object is *habēnās,* "the reins." All together we get: The farmer is loosening the reins.

It is important for students to understand that in Latin, the noun's ending tells us whether the noun is a subject or a direct object. Subjects are in the nominative case, and direct objects are in the accusative case. Students should be able to explain their translations based on the cases of the words and not guess at a translation based on the definition of the words.

Follow the directions given to complete the worksheet.

6. Quiz: Administer Quiz 17 at the end of the week.

WEEK 17

Word List

NOUNS

1. captīvus, -ī (m) . . . . . . captive
2. disciplīna, -ae (f) . . . . . instruction, training
3. ferus, -ī (m) . . . . wild animal
4. flūmen, flūminis (n) . . . river
5. habēna, -ae (f) . . . . . strap, rein
6. īnsula, -ae (f) . . . . . . island
7. lēgātus, -ī (m) . . . . . . lieutenant
8. memoria, -ae (f) . . . . memory
9. patria, -ae (f) . . . . . . native land
10. stimulus, -ī (m) . . . . . goad, spur
11. villa, -ae (f) . . . . farmhouse, country house

VERBS

12. commemorō, commemorāre . . I remember, mention, call to mind
13. laxō, laxāre . . . . I loosen
14. ornō, ornāre . . . . . . I equip, decorate
15. retineō, retinēre . . . . I hold back, retain
16. servō, servāre . . . . . I save

Chant:

No new chant this week.

Quotation:

No new quotation this week.

Weekly Worksheet 17: Answer Key

A. Write the full names of the cases in order on these lines. Feel free to look below for a hint!

1. **Nominative**

2. **Genitive**

3. **Dative**

4. **Accusative**

5. **Ablative**

B. Label each noun's declension (1, 2, or 3) and gender (M, F, or N). Then decline it.

DECLENSION **1** GENDER **F**

	SINGULAR	PLURAL
NOM.	memoria	**memoriae**
GEN.	**memoriae**	**memoriārum**
DAT.	**memoriae**	**memoriīs**
ACC.	**memoriam**	**memoriās**
ABL.	**memoriā**	**memoriīs**

DECLENSION **2** GENDER **M**

	SINGULAR	PLURAL
NOM.	stimulus	**stimulī**
GEN.	**stimulī**	**stimulōrum**
DAT.	**stimulō**	**stimulīs**
ACC.	**stimulum**	**stimulōs**
ABL.	**stimulō**	**stimulīs**

DECLENSION **3** GENDER **F**

	SINGULAR	PLURAL
NOM.	pax	**pācēs**
GEN.	**pācis**	**pācum**
DAT.	**pācī**	**pācibus**
ACC.	**pācem**	**pācēs**
ABL.	**pāce**	**pācibus**

DECLENSION **3** GENDER **N**

	SINGULAR	PLURAL
NOM.	flūmen	**flūmina**
GEN.	**flūminis**	**flūminum**
DAT.	**flūminī**	**flūminibus**
ACC.	**flūmen**	**flūmina**
ABL.	**flūmine**	**flūminibus**

Now, go back through the nouns you've just declined and circle the accusative case endings for each one.

C. For each noun, list its declension, gender, and its singular and plural accusative forms. The first one is done for you.

	NOUN	DECLENSION	GENDER	SINGULAR ACCUSATIVE	PLURAL ACCUSATIVE
1.	villa	1	F	villam	villās
2.	īnsula	1	F	īnsulam	īnsulās
3.	lēgātus	2	M	lēgātum	lēgātī
4.	pax	3	F	pācem	pācēs
5.	ferus	2	M	ferum	ferī
6.	argūmentum	2	N	argūmentum	argūmenta
7.	corpus	3	N	corpus	corpora
8.	cauda	1	F	caudam	caudās
9.	elephantus	2	M	elephantum	elephantōs
10.	tigris	3	M/F	tigridem	tigridēs
11.	flagellum	2	N	flagellum	flagella

D. Fill in the blanks.

1. The part of speech that *receives the action of the verb* is called the **direct object**.

2. Which Latin case do you use for this part of speech? **accusative**

3. Which Latin case do you use for the subject? **nominative**

4. What is the other meaning of *ferus* you learned last year? **fierce, wild**

5. *Ferus* can be used as either a **noun** or an **adjective**.

6. An adjective must always match the **gender**, number, and **case** of the noun it modifies.

E. For each noun, label whether it is nominative (N) or accusative (A), and whether it's singular (S) or plural (P). The first one is done for you.

1. disciplīnās _____AP_____   5. nauta _____**NS**_____   9. magistrōs _____**AP**_____

2. Deus _____**NS**_____   6. villa _____**NS**_____   10. aquam _____**AS**_____

3. inimīcum _____**AS**_____   7. pācem _____**AS**_____   11. lēgātum _____**AS**_____

4. rēgīnās _____**AP**_____   8. insidiae _____**NP**_____   12. tigridem _____**AS**_____

F. In each English sentence, underline the verb and circle the direct object. Translate the direct object into Latin and write it the blank. (Hint: Remember which case the direct object takes!) The first one is done for you.

1. Once, a lost girl <u>found</u> a (country house) in the woods. _____villam_____

2. Slowly, she **opened** the (door.) **portam**

3. Inside, she **saw** seven (pillows) on seven beds. **pulvinōs**

4. And she **discovered** seven (chairs) at the table. **sellās**

5. "I **will make** (dinner) for these people!" **cēnam**

6. But a cruel queen **had invented** a deadly (plot.) **insidiās**

7. In disguise, the queen **offered** an (apple) to the girl. **mālum**

8. She **had hidden** (poison) in it. **venēnum**

9. The poison **killed** the (girl.) **puellam**

10. But you **know** this (story.) **fābulam**

11. And you **remember** the happy (marriage) at the end! **matrimonium**

G. Translate these Latin sentences.

1. Agricola retinet. **The farmer holds back.**

2. Captīvī servant. **The captives save.**

3. Fēminae ornant. **The women decorate.**

4. Lēgātus laxat. **The lieutenant is loosening.**

5. Populus commemorat. **The people call to mind.**

6. Lēgātus significat. **The lieutenant points out.**

7. Repudiāmus. **We reject.**

H. These sentences include direct objects, which will be in the accusative case. Underline subject nouns and circle direct objects, then translate the sentences into English.

1. **Agricola** (equum) retinet. **The farmer holds back the horse.**

2. **Captīvī** (patriam) servant. **The captives save the native land.**

3. **Fēminae** (villam) ornant. **The women decorate the country house.**

4. **Lēgātus** (habēnās) laxat. **The lieutenant is loosening the reins.**

5. **Populus** (memoriam) commemorat. **The people call to mind the memory.**

6. **Lēgātus** (captivōs) significat. **The lieutenant points out the captives.**

7. (Pācem) repudiāmus. **We reject the peace.**

8. (Lēgātum) nōn timeō. **I do not fear the lieutenant.**

9. **Discipulus** (lacrimās) flēbat. **The apprentice was weeping tears.**

10. **Aranea** (muscam) nōn līberābit. **The spider will not set the fly free.**

I. Translate these English sentences into Latin.

1. I remember the island. **Insulam commemorō.**

2. We see the owls. **Noctuās vidēmus.**

3. The wall holds back the wild animal. **Mūrus ferum retinet.**

4. The elephants obey the clown. **Elephantī balatrōnem pārent.**

Week 17 Quiz

name:

A. *Vocabulary*

Fill in the blanks.

1. The part of speech that _____ the _____ of the verb is called the direct object.

2. Which Latin case do you use for the direct object? _____

3. Which Latin case do you use for the subject? _____

For each noun, list its declension, gender, and its singular and plural accusative forms.

	NOUN	DECLENSION	GENDER	SINGULAR ACCUSATIVE	PLURAL ACCUSATIVE
4.	captīvus				
5.	habēna				
6.	flūmen				
7.	stimulus				
8.	magister				
9.	disciplīna				
10.	caput				
11.	pābulum				

In each English sentence, underline the verb and circle the direct object. Then translate the direct object into Latin and write it the blank.

12. A boy is saluting the lieutenant. _____

13. Our horses feared the spurs. _____

14. A fire destroyed their farmhouse. _____

15. The captain loves the islands. _____

In each sentence underline the verb, circle the direct object, and translate the sentence into English.

16. Servus rēgem respondēbit._____

17. Avus habēnam fīgit._____

18. Arietēs ferum timēbant. _____

19. Argūmentum commemorō. _____

20. Magister bonus verbum declārābit. _____

On the lines below, give the Latin word for each animal.

21. _____   22. _____   23. _____

B. Chants

Conjugate *sum* in the future active tense.

	LATIN			ENGLISH	
	SINGULAR	PLURAL		SINGULAR	PLURAL
1ST					
2ND					
3RD					

Week 17 Quiz: Answer Key

A. Vocabulary

Fill in the blanks.

1. The part of speech that **receives** the **action** of the verb is called the direct object.

2. Which Latin case do you use for the direct object? **accusative**

3. Which Latin case do you use for the subject? **nominative**

For each noun, list its declension, gender, and its singular and plural accusative forms.

	NOUN	DECLENSION	GENDER	SINGULAR ACCUSATIVE	PLURAL ACCUSATIVE
4.	captīvus	**2**	**M**	**captīvum**	**captīvōs**
5.	habēna	**1**	**F**	**habēnam**	**habēnās**
6.	flūmen	**3**	**N**	**flūmen**	**flūmina**
7.	stimulus	**2**	**M**	**stimulum**	**stimulōs**
8.	magister	**2**	**M**	**magistrum**	**magistros**
9.	disciplīna	**1**	**F**	**disciplīnam**	**disciplīnās**
10.	caput	**3**	**N**	**caput**	**capita**
11.	pābulum	**2**	**N**	**pābulum**	**pābula**

In each English sentence, underline the verb and circle the direct object. Then translate the direct object into Latin and write it the blank.

12. A boy is **saluting** the ⟨lieutenant.⟩ **lēgātum**

13. Our horses **feared** the ⟨spurs.⟩ **stimulōs**

14. A fire **destroyed** their (farmhouse.) **villam**

15. The captain **loves** the (islands.) **insulās**

In each sentence underline the verb, circle the direct object, and translate the sentence into English.

16. Servus (rēgem) **respondēbit**. **The slave will answer the king.**

17. Avus (habēnam) **fīgit**. **The grandfather is fastening the strap.**

18. Arietēs (ferum) **timēbant**. **The rams were fearing the wild animal.**

19. (Argūmentum) **commemorō**. **I remember the evidence.**

20. Magister bonus (verbum) **declārābit**. **The good teacher will make the word clear.**

On the lines below, give the Latin word for each animal.

21. **cervus**

22. **noctua**

23. **tigris**

B. Chants

Conjugate *sum* in the future active tense.

	LATIN			ENGLISH	
	SINGULAR	PLURAL		SINGULAR	PLURAL
1ST	erō	erimus		I will be	we will be
2ND	eris	eritis		you will be	you all will be
3RD	erit	erunt		he/she/it will be	they will be

Teaching Notes: Week 18

1. Word List: Introduce the Word List for Week 18. Word #4, *latus*, may seem familiar to students from last year. However, the word they learned last year was *lātus,* an adjective, meaning wide or broad. This week's is a third declension noun and does not have a macron.

Review this list throughout the week and continue to review vocabulary from previous weeks.

2. Derivatives: Discuss derivatives for this week's vocabulary:

1. adulēscēns, *young man:* adolescent
2. bōs, *ox, bull, cow:* bovine
3. labor, *work, labor:* labor, laboratory
4. latus, *flank, side:* lateral, unilateral
5. ōs, *mouth:* oral, orifice
6. pēs, *foot:* pedal, pedestrial, pedestal, pedometer, pedicure, millipede, pedigree, piedmont, pioneer
7. pulvis, *dirt, dust, powder:* pulverize
8. sēmen, *seed:* disseminate, seminal

9. pulvereus, *dusty, full of dust*
10. fessus, *tired, weary*
11. ūnā, *together, in one*
12. dō, *I give:* data, datum, donation, dowry
13. edō, *I eat:* eat, edible
14. iungō, *I join, unite, yoke:* junction, join, conjunction, juncture, injunction
15. quiescō, *I rest, sleep:* acquiesce, requiem, requite, quit, quiet

Have the students write this week's derivatives in the Week 18 "Derivatives" section of their student book.

3. Chant: There is no new chant this week. You may want to review earlier chants and see how comfortable students are repeating them. If you notice they're rusty on a few chants, make time to focus on those.

4. Quotation: This week's quotation is based on Genesis 3:19: "By the sweat of your face you shall eat bread, till you return to the ground, for out of it you were taken; for you are dust, and to dust you shall return." The phrase itself comes from the funeral service in the *Book of Common Prayer* (1549).

Have the students write this week's quotation in the Week 18 "Quotation" section of their student book.

5. Worksheet: Because the neuter accusative looks exactly like the neuter nominative, translation can be a bit more challenging. This week's worksheet focuses on recognizing and translating the neuter accusative. Continue to encourage students to begin translating each sentence by locating and translating the verb.

In Exercise G, you'll come across some adjectives in the accusative, modifying direct objects. As with all adjectives, they will match the noun they modify in *gender, number, and case.* These will be translated exactly as you would an adjective with a subject noun.

You've probably already noticed—when pairing adjectives with third conjugation nouns, students will have to pay particular attention. Adjectives will match in gender, number, and case, but their endings will not match the ending of the noun they modify. For example:

Adulēscēntem pulvereum   *the dusty young man*   accusative singular

Both the noun and the adjective match in gender (masculine), number (singular), and case (accusative), but their endings do not *look* the same.

Let's look at a few examples of sentences where an adjective is modifying the direct object. The accusative endings are in bold.

Agricolae sēmin**a** pulvere**a** crās serent. *The farmers will plant the dusty seeds tomorrow.*
The adjective matches the direct object in gender (neuter), number (plural), and case (accusative).

Coquus fung**ōs** odōrāt**ōs** olefactant. *The cooks are sniffing the fragrant mushrooms.*
The adjective matches the direct object in gender (masculine), number (plural), and case (accusative).

Adulēscēns firm**um** iūs commemorat. *The young man remembers the steadfast justice.*
The adjective matches the direct object in gender (neuter), number (singular), and case (accusative). Notice that *iūs* has no ending bolded because it is a third declension neuter noun—its singular accusative "ending" is **x,** meaning it matches the nominative case form, and there is no standard ending.

Here is one more caution, when working with neuter nouns and adjectives. Take a look at the sentence below.

Adulēscēns fessus iūs commemorat. *The tired young man remembers the law.*
At first glance, *fessus* appears to match *iūs*. However, since *fessus* is masculine, it cannot be paired with *iūs*, which is neuter. To say "the tired law," the phrase would need to be *fessum iūs*. In all translation work, students will need to be led by their understanding of the grammar and not appearances.

Follow the directions given to complete the worksheet.

6. Quiz: Administer Quiz 18 at the end of the week.

WEEK 18

Word List

NOUNS

1. adulēscēns, adulēscentis (m) . young man
2. bōs, bovis (m/f). . . . . ox, bull, cow
3. labor, labōris (m) . . . . work, labor
4. latus, lateris (n). . . . . flank, side
5. ōs, ōris (n) . . . . mouth
6. pēs, pedis (m). . . . . foot
7. pulvis, pulveris (m) . . . . dirt, dust, powder
8. sēmen, sēminis (n). . . . . . . seed

ADJECTIVES

9. pulvereus, -a, -um . . . . dusty, full of dust
10. fessus, -a, -um . . . . . tired, weary

ADVERBS

11. ūnā. . . . . together, in one

VERBS

12. dō, dāre. . . . . I give
13. edō, edere . . . . I eat
14. iungō, iungere . . . . . I join, unite, yoke
15. quiescō, quiescere . . . I rest, sleep

Chant:

No new chant this week.

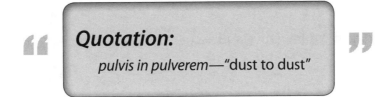

> ## *Quotation:*
> *pulvis in pulverem*—"dust to dust"

Weekly Worksheet 18: Answer Key

A. Translate these review words into English.

1. verbum	**word**	6. aedificium	**building**
2. caelum	**sky, heaven**	7. venēnum	**poison**
3. saxum	**rock**	8. praemium	**reward**
4. vēlum	**sail, curtain**	9. bellum	**war**
5. folium	**leaf**	10. dōnum	**gift**

B. Label each noun's declension (1, 2, or 3) and gender (M, F, or N). Then decline it.

DECLENSION ___2___ GENDER ___N___

	SINGULAR	PLURAL
NOM.	folium	**folia**
GEN.	**foliī**	**foliōrum**
DAT.	**foliō**	**foliīs**
ACC.	**folium**	**folia**
ABL.	**foliō**	**foliīs**

DECLENSION ___3___ GENDER ___N___

	SINGULAR	PLURAL
NOM.	latus	**latera**
GEN.	**lateris**	**laterum**
DAT.	**laterī**	**lateribus**
ACC.	**latus**	**latera**
ABL.	**latere**	**lateribus**

Now, go back and underline the nominative and accusative forms of each noun. Then answer the following questions.

1. Why do you have to be especially careful when translating neuter nouns? **The nominative and accusative forms both look the same, so it's easy to mistake one for the other.**

2. When you translate a sentence, which part of speech should you locate first? **the verb**

C. For each noun, list its declension, gender, and its singular and plural accusative forms.

	NOUN	DECLENSION	GENDER	SINGULAR ACCUSATIVE	PLURAL ACCUSATIVE
1.	vulnus	3	N	vulnus	vulnera
2.	lacrima	1	F	lacrimam	lacrimās
3.	ōs	3	N	ōs	ōra
4.	ferus	2	M	ferum	ferōs
5.	pulvis	3	M	pulverem	pulverēs
6.	iūs	3	N	iūs	iūra
7.	sēmen	3	N	sēmen	sēmina
8.	verbum	2	N	verbum	verba

D. Fill in the blanks.

1. The subject of a sentence takes the **nominative** case.

2. The direct object of a sentence takes the **accusative** case.

3. The direct object receives the action of the **verb**.

E. Translate these sentences. Start by underlining the verb, circling the subject, and drawing a box around the direct object.

1. (Deus) [populum] **commemorābit**. **God will remember the people.**

2. (Populus) [Deum] **commemorābit**. **The people will remember God.**

3. (Bovēs) [agrum] **arant**. **The oxen are plowing the field.**

4. (Adulēscēns) [frāga] et [ariēnās] **edēbat**. **A young man was eating strawberries and bananas.**

5. (Mūrus) magnus [aquam] **retinēbit**. **A large wall will hold back the water.**

6. (Lēgātus) inimīcum **servābit**. **The lieutenant will save a personal enemy.**

7. (Rēgīna) improba pācem **repudiat**. **A wicked queen scorns peace.**

8. Bovēs ūnā **iungēmus**. **We will yoke the oxen together.**

F. Conjugate the following words in the present, future, and imperfect tenses.

Present Active

FIRST CONJUGATION			SECOND CONJUGATION			THIRD CONJUGATION		
	SINGULAR	PLURAL		SINGULAR	PLURAL		SINGULAR	PLURAL
1ST	ornō	ornāmus		fleō	flēmus		edō	edimus
2ND	ornās	ornātis		flēs	flētis		edis	editis
3RD	ornat	ornant		flet	flent		edit	edunt

Future Active

FIRST CONJUGATION			SECOND CONJUGATION			THIRD CONJUGATION		
	SINGULAR	PLURAL		SINGULAR	PLURAL		SINGULAR	PLURAL
1ST	ornābō	ornābimus		flēbō	flēbimus		edam	edēmus
2ND	ornābis	ornābitis		flēbis	flēbitis		edēs	edētis
3RD	ornābit	ornābunt		flēbit	flēbunt		edet	edent

Imperfect Active

FIRST CONJUGATION			SECOND CONJUGATION			THIRD CONJUGATION		
	SINGULAR	PLURAL		SINGULAR	PLURAL		SINGULAR	PLURAL
1ST	ornābam	ornābāmus		flēbam	flēbāmus		edēbam	edēbāmus
2ND	ornābās	ornābātis		flēbās	flēbātis		edēbās	edēbātis
3RD	ornābat	ornābant		flēbat	flēbant		edēbat	edēbant

G. Translate these sentences into English. (Hint: Some adjectives will be in the accusative!)

1. Pedēs saepe sunt pulvereī. **Feet are often dusty.**

2. Insidiās improbās crās nuntiābitis. **You all will announce the wicked plot tomorrow.**

3. Bellum puellam terret. **The war frightens the girl.**

4. Familiae aedificium ornant. **The families are decorating the building.**

5. Lupī famēlicī cervum fessum instant. **Hungry wolves are following the tired stag closely.**

6. Sciūrī nuclueōs ūnā edunt. **The squirrels are eating nuts together.**

7. Saxum fīlius laxat. **The boy is loosening the rock.**

8. Coquī fungōs odōrātōs olefactant. **Cooks are sniffing the fragrant mushrooms.**

9. Elephantī flagella semper pārēbunt. **The elephants will always obey the whips.**

10. Agricola bonus sēmena serit. **A good farmer plants seeds.**

H. Label whether each noun is masculine (M), feminine (F), or neuter (N). Try to do it from memory!

1. balatrō _____**M**_____   5. pax _____**F**_____   9. rēx _____**M**_____

2. servus _____**M**_____   6. caput _____**N**_____   10. cornix _____**F**_____

3. argūmentum _____**N**_____   7. vulnus _____**N**_____   11. labor _____**M**_____

4. flūmen _____**N**_____   8. crūs _____**N**_____   12. latus _____**N**_____

I. Give the masculine, feminine, and neuter *nominative plural* of these adjectives in Latin.

	ADJECTIVE	MASCULINE	FEMININE	NEUTER
1.	strong	**firmī**	**firmae**	**firma**
2.	weary	**fessī**	**fessae**	**fessa**
3.	blond	**flavī**	**flavae**	**flava**

Week 18 Quiz

name:

A. Chants

Label each noun's declension (1, 2, or 3) and gender (M, F, or N). Then decline it.

DECLENSION _____ GENDER _____

	SINGULAR	PLURAL
NOM.	ōs	
GEN.		
DAT.		
ACC.		
ABL.		

DECLENSION _____ GENDER _____

	SINGULAR	PLURAL
NOM.	pābulum	
GEN.		
DAT.		
ACC.		
ABL.		

Now, go back and underline the nominative and accusative forms of each noun. Then answer the following questions.

1. Why do you have to be especially careful when translating neuter nouns? _____

_____

2. When you translate a sentence, which part of speech should you locate first? _____

B. Vocabulary

Translate these sentences into English.

1. Adulēscentēs pinnās ūnā edunt._____

2. Pulverem cumulābās. _____

3. Agricolae sēmina crās serent. _____

4. Adulēscēns fessus iūs commemorat. _____

5. Bovēs pulvereās iungēbamus. _____

6. Captīvus erit rēx. _____

For each adjective/noun phrase, give its gender (M, F, N) whether it is singular (S) or plural (P), then translate it.

	PHRASE	GENDER	NUMBER	TRANSLATION
7.	latus pulvereum			
8.	bovēs fessae			
9.	ōs magnum			
10.	sēmina caerulea			
11.	magister contentus			
12.	pēs pulvereus			
13.	pinnae flavae			
14.	captīvī firmī			

C. Derivatives

Give one English derivative for each Latin word.

1. pēs _____   2. quiescō _____

D. Quotation

Answer the following questions about this week's quotation.

1. What does *pulvis in pulverem* mean? _____

2. What case is *pulvis?* _____

3. What case is *pulverem?* _____

Week 18 Quiz: Answer Key

A. Chants

Label each noun's declension (1, 2, or 3) and gender (M, F, or N). Then decline it.

DECLENSION **3** GENDER **N**

	SINGULAR	PLURAL
NOM.	ōs	ōra
GEN.	ōris	ōrum
DAT.	ōrī	ōribus
ACC.	ōs	ōra
ABL.	ōre	ōribus

DECLENSION **2** GENDER **N**

	SINGULAR	PLURAL
NOM.	pābulum	pābula
GEN.	pābulī	pābulōrum
DAT.	pābulō	pābulīs
ACC.	pābulum	pābula
ABL.	pābulō	pābulīs

Now, go back and underline the nominative and accusative forms of each noun. Then answer the following questions.

1. Why do you have to be especially careful when translating neuter nouns? **The nominative and accusative forms both look the same, so it's easy to mistake one for the other.**

2. When you translate a sentence, which part of speech should you locate first? **the verb**

B. Vocabulary

Translate these sentences into English.

1. Adulēscentēs pinnās ūnā edunt. **The young men were eating wings together.**

2. Pulverem cumulābās. **You were piling up the dirt.**

3. Agricolae sēmina crās serent. **The farmers will plant the seeds tomorrow.**

4. Adulēscēns fessus iūs commemorat. **The weary young man remembers the law.**

5. Bovēs pulvereās iungēbamus. **We were yoking the dusty cows.**

6. Captīvus erit rēx. **The captive will be a king.**

For each adjective/noun phrase, give its gender (M, F, N) whether it is singular (S) or plural (P), then translate it.

	PHRASE	GENDER	NUMBER	TRANSLATION
7.	latus pulvereum	N	S	**dusty flank**
8.	bovēs fessae	F	P	**weary oxen**
9.	ōs magnum	N	S	**large mouth**
10.	sēmina caerulea	N	P	**blue seeds**
11.	magister contentus	M	S	**content teacher**
12.	pēs pulvereus	M	S	**dusty foot**
13.	pinnae flavae	F	P	**yellow feathers**
14.	captīvī firmī	M	P	**steadfast captives**

C. Derivatives

Give one English derivative for each Latin word. **Answers will vary; check them against the derivative list in this week's Teaching Notes. Sample answers are given below.**

1. pēs **pedal, pedestrian**

2. quiescō **quit, quiet**

D. Quotation

Answer the following questions about this week's quotation.

1. What does *pulvis in pulverem* mean? **dust to dust**

2. What case is *pulvis?* **nominative**

3. What case is *pulverem?* **accusative**

Teaching Notes: Week 19

1. Word List: Introduce the Word List for Week 19. Word #3, *mūnicipium,* means "free town." This was a type of town that was subject to Rome but had obtained Roman citizenship. Word #12, *obsideō,* is a Latin word made from two other Latin words—*ob,* which means "in front of," and *sedeō,* which means "I sit."

Review this list throughout the week and continue to review vocabulary from previous weeks.

2. Derivatives: Discuss derivatives for this week's vocabulary:

1. hasta, *spear, lance*
2. luxuria, *luxury, extravagance:* luxury
3. mūnicipium, *free town*
4. oppidum, *town*
5. prōvincia, *province:* province, provincial
6. querēla, *complaint, whining:* quarrel
7. stabulum, *stall, stable:* stable
8. tectum, *roof, ceiling, dwelling*
9. victōria, *victory:* victory, victorious
10. dēmonstrō, *I show:* demonstrate, demo
11. exerceō, *I train, exercise:* exercise
12. obsideō, *I besiege, remain near*
13. pacō, *I pacify, subdue*
14. removeō, *I remove, take away:* remove, removal
15. vulnerō, *I wound:* vulnerable

Have the students write this week's derivatives in the Week 19 "Derivatives" section of their student book.

3. Chant: There is no new chant this week. Continue to practice and review older chants.

4. Quotation: This week's quotation was possibly a battle-cry used by the Romans. Have the students write this week's quotation in the Week 19 "Quotation" section of their student book.

5. Worksheet: This week's worksheet will continue to review the use of direct objects and adjectives. Follow the directions given to complete the worksheet.

6. Quiz: Administer Quiz 19 at the end of the week.

WEEK 19

Word List

NOUNS

1. hasta, -ae (f) . . . . spear, lance
2. luxuria, -ae (f) . . . . . . luxury, extravagance
3. mūnicipium, -ī (n) . . . . free town
4. oppidum, -ī (n) . . . . . town
5. prōvincia, -ae (f) . . . . province
6. querēla, -ae (f) . . . . . complaint, whining
7. stabulum, -ī (n) . . . . . stall, stable
8. tectum, -ī (n) . . . . . . roof, ceiling, dwelling
9. victōria, -ae (f) . . . . . victory

VERBS

10. dēmonstrō, dēmonstrāre . . . . I show
11. exerceō, exercēre . . . . I train, exercise
12. obsideō, obsidēre . . . I remain near, besiege
13. pacō, pacāre . . . . . . I pacify, subdue
14. removeō, removēre . . I remove, take away
15. vulnerō, vulnerāre . . . I wound

Chant:

No new chant this week.

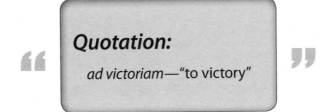

Quotation:

ad victoriam—"to victory"

Weekly Worksheet 19: Answer Key

A. Label each declension and complete the chants. Then circle all of the accusative endings.

1st DECLENSION

	SINGULAR	PLURAL
NOM.	-a	-ae
GEN.	-ae	-ārum
DAT.	-ae	-īs
ACC.	(-am)	(-ās)
ABL.	-ā	-īs

2nd DECLENSION

	SINGULAR	PLURAL
NOM.	-us	-ī
GEN.	-ī	-ōrum
DAT.	-ō	-īs
ACC.	(-um)	(-ōs)
ABL.	-ō	-īs

2ND DECLENSION Neuter

	SINGULAR	PLURAL
NOM.	-um	-a
GEN.	-ī	-ōrum
DAT.	-ō	-īs
ACC.	(-um)	(-a)
ABL.	-ō	-īs

3rd DECLENSION

	SINGULAR	PLURAL
NOM.	x	-ēs
GEN.	-is	-um
DAT.	-ī	-ibus
ACC.	(-em)	(-ēs)
ABL.	-e	-ibus

3RD DECLENSION Neuter

	SINGULAR	PLURAL
NOM.	x	-a
GEN.	-is	-um
DAT.	-ī	-ibus
ACC.	(x)	(-a)
ABL.	-e	-ibus

B. For each noun, list its declension, gender, and its singular and plural accusative forms.

	NOUN	DECLENSION	GENDER	SINGULAR ACCUSATIVE	PLURAL ACCUSATIVE
1.	mūnicipium	2	N	mūnicipium	mūnicipia
2.	pēs	3	M	pedem	pedēs
3.	luxuria	1	F	luxuriam	luxuriās

	NOUN	DECLENSION	GENDER	SINGULAR ACCUSATIVE	PLURAL ACCUSATIVE
4.	labor	3	M	labōrem	labōrēs
5.	querēla	1	F	querēlam	querēlās
6.	oppidum	2	N	oppidum	oppida
7.	magister	2	M	magistrum	magistrōs
8.	ferus	2	M	ferum	ferōs
9.	lacrima	1	F	lacrimam	lacrimās
10.	pax	3	F	pācem	pācēs

C. The following sentences use derivatives. Complete each sentence. Feel free to look back at this week's Word List or use a dictionary if you need help.

1. A knight wearing weak armor is *vulnerable*, meaning he can be **wounded**.

2. The store owner and I had a *quarrel*, because I had a **complaint** about my purchase.

3. The king gave a *demonstration* of his new army, **showing** how ready they were for battle.

D. For each Latin sentence, circle the subject and underline the direct object. Then translate the sentence into English.

1. (Lēgātus) oppidum obsidet. **The lieutenant besieges the town.**

2. (Mūnicipium) victōriam commemorābit. **The free town will remember the victory.**

3. (Lēgātus) equum maculōsum pacat. **The lieutenant is subduing the spotted horse.**

4. (Fīliae) pulchrae cēnam removēbunt. **The beautiful daughters will remove the dinner.**

5. (Victōria) provinciam servābit. **The victory will save the province.**

6. Armentum dēmonstrō. **I am showing the herd.**

7. Portam antīquam removēbit. **He will remove the ancient door.**

8. <u>Deum</u> semper laudat. **He always praises God.**

9. (Fēmina) <u>aquam</u> gelidam lībat. **The woman is sipping cold water.**

10. (Equī) <u>stabulum</u> astant. **The horses are standing by the stable.**

11. (Morbus) <u>colōnōs</u> exanimābit. **The disease will kill the settlers.**

12. (Nimbus) magnus <u>oppidum</u> occultat. **A large cloud is hiding the town.**

13. (Servī) <u>uvās</u> removēbunt. **The slaves will remove the grapes.**

14. (Turba) <u>querēlās</u> clamat. **A crowd is shouting complaints.**

15. <u>Nuntium</u> parāmus. **We are preparing the message.**

16. <u>Provinciam</u> parvam oppugnābunt. **They will attack the little province.**

E. Underline the direct object in these English sentences. Translate the direct object into Latin and write it in the blank. (Hint: Remember which case the direct object takes!)

1. They will repair the <u>roof</u> on the next sunny day. **tectum**

2. The exhausted deer reached the <u>riverbank</u>. **rīpam**

3. Sarah mails one <u>letter</u> every week. **litterās**

4. Fido feared the <u>bull</u>. **taurum**

5. The king chastised the <u>messengers</u>. **nuntiōs**

6. He caught five <u>spiders</u>. **araneās**

F. Here are English sentences and their Latin translations. Each translation contains one word that is incorrect. Cross out that word and write the correct word in the blank.

1. The reins will hold back the horse. *Habēnae ~~equus~~ retinēbunt.* **equum**

2. The sailor is standing near the lieutenant. *Lēgātum nauta ~~astābit~~.* **astat**

3. The slaves are pointing out the islands. *Servī ~~insulam~~ significant.* **insulās**

4. Girls will decorate the buildings. *Puellae ~~tectās~~ ornābunt.* **tecta**

5. The ships are besieging the island. *Navēs insulam ~~obsidet~~.* **obsident**

G. Each of the words below comes from a Latin root! Figure out which of your Latin words is the root, and then give its English meaning.

	ITALIAN	SPANISH	FRENCH	LATIN	ENGLISH
1.	vittoria	victoria	victoire	**victōria**	**victory**
2.	isola	isleno	ile	**īnsula**	**island**
3.	provincia	provincia	province	**prōvincia**	**province**
4.	memoria	memoria	mémoire	**memoria**	**memory**
5.	villa	villa	villa	**villa**	**villa**

H. Fill in the blanks.

1. The **nominative** case is used for the subject of a Latin sentence.

2. The **accusative** case is used for the direct object.

3. To discover which declension a noun is in, you check its **genitive** case.

I. For each English sentence, circle the subject and underline the direct object. Then translate the sentence into Latin.

1. The (wild animal) is standing near the <u>farmhouse</u>. **Ferus villam astat.**

2. A (sailor) is pointing out the <u>land</u>. **Nauta terram significat.**

3. The (quiver) conceals the <u>arrows</u>. **Pharetra saggitās occultat.**

4. The (spears) will wound the <u>wild animal</u>. **Hastae ferum vulnerābunt.**

5. (I) will take away the bad <u>dinner</u>. **Cēnam malam removeō.**

Week 19 Quiz

name:

A. Vocabulary

For each noun, list its declension, gender, and its singular and plural accusative forms.

	NOUN	DECLENSION	GENDER	SINGULAR ACCUSATIVE	PLURAL ACCUSATIVE
1.	oppidum				
2.	luxuria				
3.	tectum				
4.	pulvis				
5.	latus				
6.	lēgātus				
7.	bōs				

For each adjective/noun phrase, give its gender (M, F, N) whether it is singular (S) or plural (P), then translate it.

	PHRASE	GENDER	NUMBER	TRANSLATION
8.	adulēscentēs fessī			
9.	sēminem pulvereum			
10.	victōriae firmae			
11.	mūnicipium honestum			
12.	hastam magnam			
13.	oppida pulverea			

Translate these sentences into English.

14. Lēgātī improbī mūnicipium obsidēbunt. _____

15. Equus stabulum pulvereum commemorat. _____

16. Hastās dēmonstrābimus. _____

17. Adulēscēns tectum fīgit. _____

18. Captīvī luxuriās nōn commemorant. _____

B. Chants

Conjugate and translate *ducō* in the present tense.

LATIN

ENGLISH

	SINGULAR	PLURAL		SINGULAR	PLURAL
1ST					
2ND					
3RD					

Label each declension and complete the chants. Then circle the accusative endings.

_____ DECLENSION

	SINGULAR	PLURAL
NOM.	x	
GEN.		
DAT.		
ACC.		
ABL.		

3RD DECLENSION _____

	SINGULAR	PLURAL
NOM.	x	
GEN.		
DAT.		
ACC.		-a
ABL.		

Week 19 Quiz: Answer Key

A. Vocabulary

For each noun, list its declension, gender, and its singular and plural accusative forms.

	NOUN	DECLENSION	GENDER	SINGULAR ACCUSATIVE	PLURAL ACCUSATIVE
1.	oppidum	2	N	oppidum	oppida
2.	luxuria	1	F	luxuriam	luxuriās
3.	tectum	2	N	tectum	tecta
4.	pulvis	3	M	pulverem	pulverēs
5.	latus	3	N	latus	latera
6.	lēgātus	2	M	lēgātum	lēgātōs
7.	bōs	3	M/F	bovem	bovēs

For each adjective/noun phrase, give its gender (M, F, N) whether it is singular (S) or plural (P), then translate it.

	PHRASE	GENDER	NUMBER	TRANSLATION
8.	adulēscentēs fessī	M	P	tired young men
9.	sēminem pulvereum	N	S	a dusty seed
10.	victōriae firmae	F	P	strong victories
11.	mūnicipium honestum	N	S	honorable free town
12.	hastam magnam	F	S	large spear
13.	oppida pulverea	N	P	dusty towns

Translate these sentences into English.

14. Lēgātī improbī mūnicipium obsidēbunt. **The wicked lieutenants will besiege the free town.**

15. Equus stabulum pulvereum commemorat. **The horse remembers the dusty stable.**

16. Hastās dēmonstrābimus. **We will show the spears.**

17. Adulēscēns tectum fīgit. **The young man will make the roof firm.**

18. Captīvī luxuriās nōn commemorant. **The captives do not remember luxuries.**

B. Chants

Conjugate and translate *ducō* in the present tense.

LATIN

	SINGULAR	PLURAL
1ST	dūcō	dūcimus
2ND	dūcis	dūcitis
3RD	dūcit	dūcunt

ENGLISH

	SINGULAR	PLURAL
1ST	I lead	we lead
2ND	you lead	you all lead
3RD	he/she/it leads	they lead

Label each declension and complete the chants. Then circle the accusative endings.

3rd DECLENSION

	SINGULAR	PLURAL
NOM.	x	-ēs
GEN.	-is	-um
DAT.	-ī	-ibus
ACC.	(-em)	(-ēs)
ABL.	-e	-ibus

3RD DECLENSION **Neuter**

	SINGULAR	PLURAL
NOM.	x	-a
GEN.	-is	-um
DAT.	-ī	-ibus
ACC.	(x)	(-a)
ABL.	-e	-ibus

Teaching Notes: Week 20

1. Word List: Introduce the Word List for Week 20. Review this list throughout the week and continue to review vocabulary from previous weeks.

2. Derivatives: Discuss derivatives for this week's vocabulary:

1. candēla, *candle:* candle
2. carmen, *song, poem*
3. cor, *heart:* cordial, accord, courage
4. flōs, *flower:* flower, florescence, flora
5. lux, *light:* Lucifer, elucidate, lucent, lucid
6. lyra, *lyre:* lyre
7. tempus, *time:* tempo, temporal, temporary, temporize, contemporary
8. vesper, *evening, evening star:* vespers
9. virgō, *maiden:* virgin
10. vox, *voice:* vocal, voice, vowel, equivocal
11. cantō, *I sing, play (music):* chant
12. habeō, *I have, hold:* able, habit, habitable, habitat, inhabit, inhibit, exhibit, prohibit, habeas corpus
13. lūdō, *I play, tease, trick:* allude, illusion, collusion, delude, disillusion, interlude, ludicrous, prelude
14. portō, *I carry:* portage, transportation, portable, important, export, deport, report, rapport, porter (carries luggage)

Have the students write this week's derivatives in the Week 20 "Derivatives" section of their student book.

3. Chant: There is no new chant this week. Continue to practice and review older chants.

4. Quotation: *Sursum corda* is a phrase from one of the oldest Christian communion liturgies, dating back to the third century. The response is *Habēmus ad Dominum,* meaning "We lift them (up) to the Lord."

Have the students write this week's quotation in the Week 20 "Quotation" section of their student book.

5. Worksheet: Follow the directions given to complete the worksheet.

6. Quiz: Administer Quiz 20 at the end of the week.

WEEK 20

Word List

NOUNS

1. candēla, -ae (f) . . . . . . candle
2. carmen, carminis (n). . . song, poem
3. cor, cordis (n) . . . . . . heart
4. flōs, flōris (m) . . . . . . flower
5. lux, lūcis (f) . . . . light
6. lyra, -ae (f) . . . . lyre
7. tempus, temporis (n) . . time
8. vesper, vesperis (m) . . . evening,
                              evening star

9. virgō, virginis (f) . . . . . maiden
10. vox, vōcis (f) . . . . voice

VERBS

11. cantō, cantāre . . . . . . I sing, play (music)
12. habeō, habēre. . . . . . . I have, hold
13. lūdō, lūdere . . . . I play, tease, trick
14. portō, portāre. . . . . . . I carry

Chant:

No new chant this week.

> **Quotation:**
>
> *Sursum corda*—"Lift up your hearts"

Weekly Worksheet 20: Answer Key

A. Conjugate and translate *sum* in the present and future active tenses. Then answer the question.

Present Active

LATIN

	SINGULAR	PLURAL
1ST	sum	sumus
2ND	es	estis
3RD	est	sunt

ENGLISH

SINGULAR	PLURAL
I am	we are
you are	you all are
he/she/it is	they are

Future Active

LATIN

	SINGULAR	PLURAL
1ST	erō	erimus
2ND	eris	eritis
3RD	erit	erunt

ENGLISH

SINGULAR	PLURAL
I will be	we will be
you will be	you all will be
he/she/it will be	they will be

1. Is *sum* a regular or irregular verb? **irregular**

B. Fill in the blank with the English translation of each noun. Underline the Latin nouns that could be used as direct objects. (Hint: Watch your declensions!)

1. stellam **star**

2. dominōs **masters**

3. amīcum **friend**

4. aquilae **eagles**

5. latera **flanks**

6. ripās **riverbanks**

7. carmina **songs**

8. lupus **wolf**

9. latebra **hiding place**

10. vōcēs **voices**

C. Underline the adjective that matches the noun's number, gender, and case. Then translate the phrase.

NOUN	ADJECTIVE	TRANSLATION
1. Candēlae	odōrāta / **odōrātae**	**the sweet-smelling candles**
2. Vox	**fessa** / fessam	**a tired voice**
3. Bovēs	**parvōs** / parva	**small bulls**
4. Iūs	firmus / **firmum**	**the strong law**
5. Flōrēs	**flavī** / flavās	**yellow flowers**
6. Lūcem	**caeruleam** / caeruleās	**a blue light**
7. Carmen	rīdiculam / **rīdiculum**	**the funny song**
8. Stabula	**pulverea** / pulvereae	**dusty stables**

D. Translate these sentences into English.

1. Hastās pulvereās removet. **She (*or* he *or* it) is taking away the dusty spears.**

2. Tempus hodiē nōn habeō. **I don't have time today.**

3. Fīlia serēna auroram spectat. **The calm daughter is watching the dawn.**

4. Equus albus stimulōs pārēbit. **The white horse will obey the spurs.**

5. Ferum parvum servant. **They saved the little wild animal.**

6. Puerī trochōs portant. **The boys are carrying hoops for games.**

7. Ancoram parvam ventus laxābit. **The wind will loosen the small anchor.**

8. Balatrō virōs quiētōs lūdēbat. **A clown was teasing the quiet men.**

9. Poēta lyram crās cantābit. **Tomorrow the poet will play the lyre.**

10. Aranea muscam minūtātim edit. **The spider is eating the fly bit by bit.**

11. Virgō laeta litterās scribet. **The happy maiden will write a letter.**

12. Puer astrum serēnum dēmonstrat. **The boy is pointing out the bright star.**

E. Give the genitive singular form, gender (M, F, N), declension, and the English translation for each Latin noun.

	NOUN	GENITIVE	GENDER	DECLENSION	TRANSLATION
1.	cor	**cordis**	**N**	**3**	**heart**
2.	oppidum	**oppidī**	**N**	**2**	**town**
3.	vesper	**vesperis**	**M**	**3**	**evening, evening star**
4.	latus	**lateris**	**N**	**3**	**flank, side**
5.	lux	**lūcis**	**F**	**3**	**light**
6.	querēla	**querēlae**	**F**	**1**	**complaint, whining**
7.	candēla	**candēlae**	**F**	**1**	**candle**
8.	cibus	**cibī**	**M**	**2**	**food**

F. Translate these English sentences into Latin.

1. The king is summoning the slave. **Rēx servum vocat.**

2. The teacher sees the tears. **Magister (*or* magistra) lacrimās videt.**

3. Students are entering the building. **Discipulī aedificium intrant.**

4. The lieutenant fears an ambush. **Lēgātus insidiās timet.**

5. He will not hesitate. **Nōn dubitābit.**

6. The sailors are decorating the bow of the ship. **Nautae prōram ornant.**

7. The farmers are plowing the land. **Agricolae terram arant.**

8. The woman is imploring the queen. **Fēmina rēgīnam obsecrat.**

G. Conjugate the following words in the present, future, and imperfect tenses.

Present Active

FIRST CONJUGATION		
	SINGULAR	PLURAL
1ST	cantō	**cantāmus**
2ND	**cantās**	**cantātis**
3RD	**cantat**	**cantant**

SECOND CONJUGATION		
	SINGULAR	PLURAL
	habeō	**habēmus**
	habēs	**habētis**
	habet	**habent**

THIRD CONJUGATION		
	SINGULAR	PLURAL
	lūdō	**lūdimus**
	lūdis	**lūditis**
	lūdit	**lūdunt**

Future Active

FIRST CONJUGATION		
	SINGULAR	PLURAL
1ST	**cantābō**	**cantābimus**
2ND	**cantābis**	**cantābitis**
3RD	**cantābit**	**cantābunt**

SECOND CONJUGATION		
	SINGULAR	PLURAL
	habēbō	**habēbimus**
	habēbis	**habēbitis**
	habēbit	**habēbunt**

THIRD CONJUGATION		
	SINGULAR	PLURAL
	lūdam	**lūdēmus**
	lūdēs	**lūdētis**
	lūdet	**lūdent**

Imperfect Active

FIRST CONJUGATION		
	SINGULAR	PLURAL
1ST	**cantābam**	**cantābāmus**
2ND	**cantābās**	**cantābātis**
3RD	**cantābat**	**cantābant**

SECOND CONJUGATION		
	SINGULAR	PLURAL
	habēbam	**habēbāmus**
	habēbās	**habēbātis**
	habēbat	**habēbant**

THIRD CONJUGATION		
	SINGULAR	PLURAL
	lūdēbam	**lūdēbāmus**
	lūdēbās	**lūdēbātis**
	lūdēbat	**lūdēbant**

H. Answer the following questions about this week's quotation.

1. How do you say "Lift up your hearts" in Latin? **sursum corda**

2. Which word means "hearts"? **corda**

3. Which two cases could that word be in? **nominative or accusative (plural)**

Week 20 Quiz

name:

A. Vocabulary

Give the genitive singular form, gender (M, F, N), declension, and the English translation for each Latin noun.

	NOUN	GENITIVE	GENDER	DECLENSION	TRANSLATION
1.	flōs				
2.	vox				
3.	lyra				
4.	virgō				
5.	tempus				
6.	vesper				
7.	carmen				
8.	cor				

Underline the adjective that matches the noun's number, gender, and case. Then translate the phrase.

NOUN	ADJECTIVE	TRANSLATION
9. Cor	contenta / contentum	_____
10. Virgō	quiētōs / quiēta	_____
11. Lūcem	flavam / flavum	_____
12. Prōvinciās	apricam / apricās	_____
13. Carmen	pulcher / pulchrum	_____
14. Tempus	rīdiculus / rīdiculum	_____

Give each verb's second principal part, conjugation (1, 2, 3), and English translation.

	VERB	SECOND PRINCIPAL PART	CONJUGATION	TRANSLATION
15.	portō			
16.	habeō			
17.	cantō			
18.	exerceō			
19.	lūdō			
20.	quiescō			

Translate these English sentences into Latin.

21. A cow was eating the flowers. _____

22. The king loves peace. _____

23. The daughter watches the large waves. _____

B. Chants

Label each declension and complete the chants. Then circle the accusative endings.

_____ DECLENSION

	SINGULAR	PLURAL
NOM.		-ae
GEN.		
DAT.		
ACC.		
ABL.	-ā	

_____ DECLENSION

	SINGULAR	PLURAL
NOM.		-ī
GEN.	-ī	
DAT.		
ACC.		
ABL.		

2ND DECLENSION _____

	SINGULAR	PLURAL
NOM.		-a
GEN.	-ī	
DAT.		
ACC.		
ABL.		

Week 20 Quiz: Answer Key

A. Vocabulary

Give the genitive singular form, gender (M, F, N), declension, and the English translation for each Latin noun.

	NOUN	GENITIVE	GENDER	DECLENSION	TRANSLATION
1.	flōs	**flōris**	**M**	**3**	**flower**
2.	vox	**vōcis**	**F**	**3**	**voice**
3.	lyra	**lyrae**	**F**	**1**	**lyre**
4.	virgō	**virginis**	**F**	**3**	**maiden**
5.	tempus	**temporis**	**N**	**3**	**time**
6.	vesper	**vesperis**	**M**	**3**	**evening, evening star**
7.	carmen	**carminis**	**N**	**3**	**song**
8.	cor	**cordis**	**N**	**3**	**heart**

Underline the adjective that matches the noun's number, gender, and case. Then translate the phrase.

NOUN	ADJECTIVE	TRANSLATION
9. Cor	contenta / **contentum**	**a satisfied heart**
10. Virgō	quiētōs / **quiēta**	**the sleeping maiden**
11. Lūcem	**flavam** / flavum	**the yellow light**
12. Prōvinciās	apricam / **apricās**	**sunny provinces**
13. Carmen	pulcher / **pulchrum**	**a beautiful song**
14. Tempus	rīdiculus / **rīdiculum**	**an amusing time**

Give each verb's second principal part, conjugation (1, 2, 3), and English translation.

	VERB	SECOND PRINCIPAL PART	CONJUGATION	TRANSLATION
15.	portō	**portāre**	1	**I carry**
16.	habeō	**habēre**	2	**I have, hold**
17.	cantō	**cantāre**	1	**I sing, play (music)**
18.	exerceō	**exercēre**	2	**I train, exercise**
19.	lūdō	**lūdere**	3	**I play, tease, trick**
20.	quiescō	**quiescere**	3	**I rest, sleep**

Translate these English sentences into Latin.

21. A cow was eating the flowers. **Bōs flōrēs edēbat.**

22. The king loves peace. **Rēx pācem amat.**

23. The daughter watches the large waves. **Fīliae undās magnās spectat.**

B. Chants

Label each declension and complete the chants. Then circle the accusative endings.

1st DECLENSION

	SINGULAR	PLURAL
NOM.	**-a**	-ae
GEN.	**-ae**	**-ārum**
DAT.	**-ae**	**-īs**
ACC.	(-am)	(-ās)
ABL.	-ā	-īs

2nd DECLENSION

	SINGULAR	PLURAL
NOM.	**-us**	-ī
GEN.	-ī	**-ōrum**
DAT.	-ō	-īs
ACC.	(-um)	(-ōs)
ABL.	-ō	-īs

2ND DECLENSION **Neuter**

	SINGULAR	PLURAL
NOM.	**-um**	-a
GEN.	-ī	**-ōrum**
DAT.	-ō	-īs
ACC.	(-um)	-a
ABL.	-ō	-īs

Teaching Notes: Week 21

1. Word List: Introduce the Word List for Week 21. Review this list throughout the week, continuing to review older vocabulary.

2. Derivatives: Discuss derivatives for this week's vocabulary:

1. asinus, *donkey:* ass, asinine
2. crux, *cross:* crux, crucify, crucial, cross
3. dux, *leader:* duke, duchess, duchy
4. iter, *journey:* itinerary, itinerant
5. moenia, *fortifications, city walls*
6. nōmen, *name:* nomenclature, nominate, noun, misnomer, pronoun, nominal
7. palma, *palm of the hand, palm tree:* palm
8. princeps, *chief:* prince, principal, principle

9. tībia, *flute, pipe:* tibia
10. vestīmentum, *clothing, garment:* vestment
11. flōreō, *I flourish:* flourish
12. imperō, *I order:* imperative, imperious
13. moveō, *I move:* move, remove, mobile, motion, motive, commotion, emotion, promote, remote
14. vehō, *I carry, ride, convey:* invective, vehicle
15. vibrō, *I wave, shake:* vibe, vibrate

Have the students write this week's derivatives in the Week 21 "Derivatives" section of their student book.

3. Chant: There is no new chant this week. Continue to practice and review older chants.

4. Quotation: This week, the quotation is taken from Psalm 92:12. Have the students write this week's quotation in the Week 21 "Quotation" section of their student book.

5. Worksheet: In this lesson, you'll learn how to ask a question in Latin.

Latin questions are very straightforward. To ask a simple "yes" or "no" question, just add -ne to the end of the first word in the sentence. Below is the original sentence, then that sentence turned into a question.

Candēla lūcet.	*The candle is shining.*
Lūcet**ne** candēla?	*Is the candle shining?*

In questions, the verb usually comes first, but it doesn't have to. You could also write *Candēlane lūcet?* and it would mean the same thing.

In Latin, there are no words for "yes" and "no," like there are in English. To answer a "yes" or "no" question, the statement (or part of the statement) has to be repeated. Read the example answers that follow.

Aratne agricola?	*Is the farmer plowing?*
Arat.	*Yes.* (Literally: He is plowing.)
Agricola arat.	*Yes.* (Literally: The farmer is plowing.)
Nōn arat.	*No.* (Literally: He is not plowing.)

Here are a few more sample questions. For fun and practice, you may want to have the students try to answer these!

Rogātisne?	*Are you all asking?*

Habēsne tempus?	*Do you have the time?*
Edēbāsne cēnam?	*Were you eating dinner?*
Removēbisne pulverem?	*Will you remove the dirt?*
Lūdēbatne magistrum?	*Did he/she trick the teacher?*
Explōrābimusne?	*Will we find out?*
Fābulane est rīdicula?	*Is the story funny?*
Quiescōne?	*Did I sleep?*
Estne bonum?	*Is it good?*
Erimusne ūnā?	*Will we be together?*

One more note on questions. The *-ne* ending can be somewhat distracting initially; continue to remind students to check the verb tense.

Follow the directions given to complete the worksheet.

6. Quiz: Administer Quiz 21 at the end of the week.

WEEK 21

Word List

NOUNS

1. asinus, -ī (m) . . . . donkey
2. crux, crucis (f) . . . . . . cross
3. dux, ducis (m) . . . . . . leader
4. iter, itineris (n) . . . . . . journey
5. moenia, -ium (n, pl) . . . fortifications, city walls
6. nōmen, nōminis (n) . . . name
7. palma, -ae (f) . . . . . . palm of the hand, palm tree

8. princeps, principis (n) . . chief
9. tībia, -ae (f) . . . . flute, pipe
10. vestīmentum, -ī (n) . . . clothing, garment

VERBS

11. flōreō, flōrēre . . . . . . I flourish
12. imperō, imperāre . . . . I order
13. moveō, movēre . . . . . I move
14. vehō, vehere . . . . . . I carry, ride, convey
15. vibrō, vibrāre . . . . . . I wave, shake

Chant:

No new chant this week.

Quotation:

iustus ut palma flōrēbit—"the just shall flourish as the palm tree"

Weekly Worksheet 21: Answer Key

A. Answer the following questions about Latin sentences.

1. The subject noun always takes the **nominative** case.

2. In a Latin sentence, the verb is usually at the **end**.

3. To form a question in Latin, **-ne** is added to the first word in the sentence.

4. The first word in a Latin question is usually the **verb**.

B. Translate these verbs into English.

1. cantābimus	**we will sing**	9. veham	**I am riding**
2. liberābit	**he/she/it will set free**	10. accusant	**they are accusing**
3. lūdēmus	**we trick**	11. moneō	**I warn**
4. explōrābunt	**they were exploring**	12. recuperābō	**I will recover**
5. obsecrant	**they are begging**	13. flōrēs	**you are flourishing**
6. manēbit	**he/she/it will remain**	14. augent	**they do increase**
7. mūtābit	**he/she/it will change**	15. dubitant	**they doubt**
8. vibrābitis	**you all will wave**	16. repudiat	**he/she/it is scorning**

C. Compare the Latin sentences and their translations below. Underline the verb in each Latin sentence and circle the -ne ending in each question.

1. Discipulus repudiat. *The student is disputing.*
2. Repudiatne discipulus? *Is the student disputing?*

3. Ventus mūtābit. *The wind will change.*
4. Mūtābitne ventus? *Will the wind change?*

5. Fīlia dubitat. *The daughter is hesitating.*
6. Fīliane dubitat? *Is the daughter hesitating?*

7. Fīliae magistrās <u>administrābant</u>.   *The daughters were helping the teachers.*
8. <u>Administrābantne</u> fīliae magistrās?   *Were the daughters helping the teachers?*

D. Underline the subject noun that matches the verb. Then translate the question into English.

VERB	SUBJECT NOUN	TRANSLATION
1. Cantābitne	**virgō** / virginēs ?	**Will the maiden sing?**
2. Flōrēbuntne	**palmae** / palmās ?	**Will the palm trees flourish?**
3. Rudetne	**asinus** / asinum ?	**Is the donkey braying?**
4. Eduntne	bōs / **bovēs** ?	**Are the oxen eating?**
5. Obsidetne	**dux** / ducis ?	**Is the leader besieging?**
6. Servābitne	**iūs** / iūra ?	**Will the law save?**
7. Lūdentne	**caprī** / caprōs ?	**Are the goats playing?**
8. Imperābitne	principe / **princeps** ?	**Will the chief order?**

E. For each noun, list its declension, gender, and its singular and plural accusative forms.

	NOUN	DECLENSION	GENDER	SINGULAR ACCUSATIVE	PLURAL ACCUSATIVE
1.	nōmen	3	N	**nōmen**	**nōmina**
2.	tībia	1	F	**tībiam**	**tībiās**
3.	crux	3	F	**crucem**	**crucēs**
4.	flōs	3	M	**flōrem**	**flōrēs**
5.	vestīmentum	2	N	**vestīmentum**	**vestīmenta**
6.	lēgātus	2	M	**lēgātum**	**lēgātōs**
7.	iter	3	N	**iter**	**itinera**
8.	lyra	1	F	**lyram**	**lyrās**

F. Give each verb's stem and conjugation. The first one is done for you.

1. vehō   vehe-   3rd   4. quiescō   **quiesce- 3rd**

2. habeō   **habē- 2nd**   5. pacō   **pacā- 1st**

3. vibrō   **vibrā- 1st**   6. iungō   **iunge- 3rd**

G. Label each tense and complete the verb ending chants.

Present TENSE

	SINGULAR	PLURAL
1ST	-ō	**-mus**
2ND	-s	-tis
3RD	-t	-nt

Future TENSE

	SINGULAR	PLURAL
	-bō	**-bimus**
	-bis	**-bitis**
	-bit	**-bunt**

Imperfect TENSE

	SINGULAR	PLURAL
	-bam	**-bāmus**
	-bās	**-bātis**
	-bat	**-bant**

H. Translate the following sentences into English. In each question, underline the verb's *-ne* ending. Some sentences have direct objects—circle the direct objects!

1. Astatne magistra? **Is the teacher standing near?**

2. Administrābitne servus? **Will the slave help?**

3. Explōrābuntne puerī? **Will the boys explore?**

4. Accusatne rēgīna? **Is the queen accusing?**

5. Manēbuntne moenia? **Will the city walls remain?**

6. Spectatne magister? **Is the teacher watching?**

7. Timēbatne (sagittam) germānus? **Was the brother fearing the arrow?**

8. Vehitne (asinum) princeps? **Will the chief ride a donkey?**

9. Familiane (cēnam) imperat? **Is the household ordering a meal?**

10. Occupatne (terram) agricola? **Does the farmer seize the land?**

I. Answer the questions about this week's quotation.

1. How do you say "the just shall flourish as the palm tree" in Latin? **iustus ut palma flōrēbit**

2. Which word means "just"? **iustus**

3. Which word means "shall flourish"? **flōrēbit**

J. This is review from last year! Write these numbers in order on the lines: *trēs, quinque, duo, novem, sex, decem, ūnus, quattuor, septem, octō*. (Hint: Feel free to look the numbers up in your Latin dictionary.)

ūnus, duo, trēs, quattuor, quinque, sex, septem, octō, novem, decem

K. Give the masculine, feminine, and neuter *accusative singular* forms of these adjectives in Latin.

	ADJECTIVE	MASCULINE	FEMININE	NEUTER
1.	weary	**fessum**	**fessam**	**fessum**
2.	strong	**firmum**	**firmam**	**firmum**
3.	dusty	**pulvereum**	**pulveream**	**pulvereum**

L. For each sentence, first underline the verb, then circle the subject. (Hint: The verb may be split up. Watch for "will" and "were"!) Then translate it into Latin.

1. Will the anchor move? **Movēbitne ancora?**

2. Is the effort helping? **Administratne opera?**

3. Is the river cold? **Estne flūmen gelidum?**

4. Were you asking? **Rogābāsne?**

5. Will the flowers flourish? **Flōrēbuntne flōrēs?**

Week 21 Quiz

name: _____

A. Vocabulary

Answer the following questions about Latin sentences.

1. The _____ noun always takes the nominative case.

2. In a Latin sentence, the verb is usually at the _____.

3. The _____ always takes the accusative case.

3. To form a question in Latin, _____ is added to the first word in the sentence.

4. The first word in a Latin question is usually the _____.

For each verb, give its person (1, 2, 3), number (singular: S or plural: P), and tense (present, future, imperfect). Then translate it. The first one is done for you.

	VERB	PERSON	NUMBER	TENSE	TRANSLATION
5.	retinēbam	1	S	imperfect	I was holding back
6.	vibrāmus				
7.	habētis				
8.	flōrēbis				
9.	imperābant				
10.	quiescēs				
11.	vehēbāmus				
12.	lūdam				
13.	movēbō				
14.	cantābit				
15.	obsidet				

Underline the subject noun that matches the verb. Then translate the question into English.

VERB	SUBJECT NOUN	TRANSLATION
15. Habēsne	nōmen / nōminem ?	_____
16. Cantābitne	tībiās / tībiae ?	_____
17. Quiescēbatne	dux / ducēs ?	_____
18. Augentne	querēlae / querēla ?	_____
19. Arābatne	asinum / asinus ?	_____
20. Lūcēbuntne	lux / lūcēs ?	_____
21. Vibrantne	palmā / palmae ?	_____

Translate the following sentences into English.

22. Asinus ducem firmum vehēbat. _____

23. Exercēsne lupōs et ferōs? _____

24. Ventus gelidus vēlum flat. _____

25. Cantābantne ūnā principa lyrās? _____

B. Derivatives

Use your knowledge of Latin to answer the following questions about derivatives.

1. To be *mobile* means you have the ability to move. *Mobile* is a derivative of _____ .

2. An *itinerary* is a travel plan. *Itinerary* is a derivative of the Latin word _____ .

3. A *principal* is the head of a school. *Principal* is a derivative of the Latin word _____ .

4. A car is a type of *vehicle*. *Vehicle* is a derivative of the Latin word _____ .

5. An *imperative* is an order or command. *Imperative* is a derivative of the word _____ .

Week 21 Quiz: Answer Key

A. Vocabulary

Answer the following questions about Latin sentences.

1. The **subject** noun always takes the nominative case.

2. In a Latin sentence, the verb is usually at the **end**.

3. The **direct object** always takes the accusative case.

3. To form a question in Latin, **-ne** is added to the first word in the sentence.

4. The first word in a Latin question is usually the **verb**.

For each verb, give its person (1, 2, 3), number (singular: S or plural: P), and tense (present, future, imperfect). Then translate it. The first one is done for you.

	VERB	PERSON	NUMBER	TENSE	TRANSLATION
5.	retinēbam	1	S	imperfect	I was holding back
6.	vibrāmus	1	P	present	we are waving
7.	habētis	2	P	present	you all hold
8.	flōrēbis	2	S	future	you will flourish
9.	imperābant	3	P	imperfect	they were ordering
10.	quiescēs	2	S	future	you will rest
11.	vehēbāmus	3	P	imperfect	we were conveying
12.	lūdam	1	S	future	I will trick
13.	movēbō	1	S	future	I will move
14.	cantābit	3	S	future	he/she/it will sing
15.	obsidet	3	S	present	he/she/it is besieging

Underline the subject noun that matches the verb. Then translate the question into English.

VERB	SUBJECT NOUN	TRANSLATION
15. Habēsne	**nōmen** / nōminem ?	**Do you have a name?**
16. Cantābitne	tībiās / **tībiae** ?	**Will the flutes play?**
17. Quiescēbatne	**dux** / ducēs ?	**Was the leader resting?**
18. Augentne	**querēlae** / querēla ?	**Are complaints increasing?**
19. Arābatne	asinum / **asinus** ?	**Was a donkey plowing?**
20. Lūcēbuntne	lux / **lūcēs** ?	**Will the lights shine?**
21. Vibrantne	palmā / **palmae** ?	**Are the palm trees shaking?**

Translate the following sentences into English.

22. Asinus ducem firmum vehēbat. **The donkey was carrying the steadfast leader.**

23. Exercēsne lupōs et ferōs? **Do you train wolves and wild animals?**

24. Ventus gelidus vēlum flat. **A cold wind is blowing the sail.**

25. Cantābantne ūnā principa lyrās? **Were the chiefs playing lyres together?**

B. Derivatives

Use your knowledge of Latin to answer the following questions about derivatives.

1. To be *mobile* means you have the ability to move. *Mobile* is a derivative of **moveō**.

2. An *itinerary* is a travel plan. *Itinerary* is a derivative of the Latin word **iter.**

3. A *principal* is the head of a school. *Principal* is a derivative of the Latin word **princeps.**

4. A car is a type of *vehicle. Vehicle* is a derivative of the Latin word **vehō**.

5. An *imperative* is an order or command. *Imperative* is a derivative of the word **imperō**.

Teaching Notes: Week 22

1. Word List: Introduce the Word List for Week 22. Word #9, *mīnōtaurus,* comes from the word *taurus,* which you've learned, combined with the name Minos. Minos was the king of Crete, reigning when the legendary minotaur made its appearance.

Review this list throughout the week. Continue to review vocabulary from previous weeks.

2. Derivatives: Discuss derivatives for this week's vocabulary:

1. architectus, *architect, inventor:* architect, architecture

2. centaurus, *centaur:* centaur

3. cyclops, *cyclops*

4. dracō, *dragon:* dragon, draconic

5. fīlum, *thread, string:* file, filament

6. gigās, *giant:* giant, gigantic, gigabyte

7. grȳps, *griffin:* griffin, gryphaea

8. labyrinthus, *labyrinth, maze:* labyrinth, labyrinthine

9. mīnōtaurus, *minotaur:* minotaur

10. pēgasus, *pegasus:* pegasus

11. satyrus, *satyr, faun:* satyr

12. ruber, *red:* red, rubella, rubric, ruby

13. captō, *I hunt*

14. commūnicō, *I share, inform:* communicate, communique

15. nō, *I swim*

Have the students write this week's derivatives in the Week 22 "Derivatives" section of their student book.

3. Chant: There is no new chant this week. Continue to practice and review the chants you've learned in previous weeks.

4. Quotation: There is no quotation this week. Look over quotations from previous weeks and test the students' memory of their translations.

5. Worksheet: Last week, you learned how to ask a question. This week, you'll learn how to give a command in Latin. The grammatical name for a command is *imperative.*

Latin commands are fairly easy to form. To tell a single person to do something, the imperative is simply the stem; to give a plural command, *–te* is added to the stem.

For example, how do you tell one person to sit? The verb "to sit" is *sedeō.* The stem is *sedē-.* So to tell one person to sit, you would simply say, "*Sedē.*"

To tell a group to sit, add *–te* to the stem: "*Sedēte.*"

Here are some additional examples of singular and plural commands. Notice that the English translation for both singular and plural commands is the same.

stā, stāte	stand
movē, movēte	move
obsidē, obsidēte	remain near
recitā, recitāte	read aloud

Notice that all of the verbs above are from either the first or second conguation. Third conjugation commands work almost exactly, but with just a twist.

A third conjugation command in the singular is formed exactly like in the first or second conjugation: find the verb's stem, and that is the command. For example, how would you tell someone to let go? The verb "to let go" is *mittō*. The stem is *mitte-*. So to tell one person to sit, you would simply say, *"Mitte."*

But, how would you tell a whole group of people to let go? Here's the twist. The "e" of the third conjugation stem changes to an "i", then you add *–te*. So, *mitte* becomes *mitti,* and we add *-te,* giving us *mittite.* (This is somewhat reminiscent of the present tense chant for third conjugation—where you would expect an "e" you get an "i.")

Here are a few more examples of singular and plural commands in the third conjugation.

vehe, vehite	ride
quiesce, quiescite	rest
scrībe, scrībite	write
ede, edite	eat

Once students have the formation of the imperative down, you can start adding direct objects:

Librum recitā.	*Read the book aloud.*
Dracōnem captāte.	*Hunt the dragon.*
Lēgātum commūnicā!	*Inform the lieutenant!*
Flūmen nāte.	*Swim the river.*
Cēnam ede.	*Eat the dinner.*

Follow the directions given to complete the worksheet.

6. Quiz: Administer Quiz 22 at the end of the week.

WEEK 22

Word List

NOUNS

1. architectus, -ī (m). . . . . architect, inventor

2. centaurus, -ī (m) . . . . . centaur

3. cyclops, cyclōpis (m) . . cyclops

4. dracō, dracōnis (m) . . . dragon

5. fīlum, -ī (n). . . . . thread, string

6. gigās, gigantis (m) . . . . giant

7. grȳps, grȳphis (m) . . . . griffin

8. labyrinthus, -ī (m) . . . . labyrinth, maze

9. mīnōtaurus, -ī (m) . . . . minotaur

10. pēgasus, -ī (m). . . . . pegasus

11. satyrus, -ī (m) . . . . . satyr, faun

ADJECTIVES

12. ruber, -bra, -brum . . . red

VERBS

13. captō, captāre. . . . . . I hunt

14. commūnicō, commūnicāre. . I share, inform

15. nō, nāre. . . . . I swim

Chant:

No new chant this week.

Quotation:

No quotation this week.

Weekly Worksheet 22: Answer Key

A. Answer the following questions about commands.

1. When you tell a dog, "Fetch!", you're giving him a **command**.

2. Is a command a noun, a verb, or an adjective? **a verb**

3. Another word for "command" is **imperative**.

4. To give a Latin command, you need to first find the verb's **stem**.

5. To give a singular command, what do you add to the stem? **nothing**

6. To give a plural command using a first or second conjugation verb, what do you add to the

stem? **-te**

7. How do you give a plural command using a third conjugation verb? **Find the verb's stem,**

change the stem "e" to an "i," then add -te.

B. Translate these singular commands into English.

1. Ede.	**Eat.**	3. Commūnicā.	**Inform.**
2. Respondē.	**Answer.**	4. Nā!	**Swim!**

Translate these plural commands into English.

5. Movetē!	**Move!**	7. Quiescite.	**Rest.**
6. Commemorāte.	**Remember.**	8. Cantāte!	**Sing!**

C. Turn each verb into a singular command and a plural command in Latin. Then translate the plural command into English.

	VERB	SINGULAR COMMAND	PLURAL COMMAND	TRANSLATION
1.	vehō	**Vehe.**	**Vehite.**	**Ride.**

	VERB	SINGULAR COMMAND	PLURAL COMMAND	TRANSLATION
2.	captō	**Captā.**	**Captāte.**	**Hunt.**
3.	vibrō	**Vibrā.**	**Vibrāte.**	**Shake.**
4.	dō	**Dā.**	**Dāte.**	**Give.**
5.	moneō	**Monē.**	**Monēte.**	**Warn.**
6.	reptō	**Reptā.**	**Reptāte.**	**Crawl.**
7.	sedeō	**Sedē.**	**Sedēte.**	**Sit.**
8.	mittō	**Mitte.**	**Mittite.**	**Send.**

D. Translate these sentences into English. Some words will be review—feel free to use your dictionary!

1. Architectus rubrum dracōnem captābit. **<u>The inventor will hunt the red dragon.</u>**

2. Septem amīcī manent. **<u>Seven friends remain.</u>**

3. Volatne grȳps fessus? **<u>Is the tired griffin flying?</u>**

4. Puerī quattuor nuntium commemorābunt. **<u>The four boys will remember the message.</u>**

5. Equī decem stant. **<u>Ten horses are standing.</u>**

6. Virgō rubrum fīlum crās dābit. **<u>Tomorrow the maiden will give the red thread.</u>**

7. Candēlam habē. **<u>Hold the candle.</u>**

8. Olefactāsne harēnam et pontum? **<u>Do you smell sand and seawater?</u>**

9. Gigantem improbum vulnerāte! **<u>Wound the wicked giant!</u>**

10. Erratne mīnōtaurus foedus semper? **<u>Is the horrible minotaur always wandering?</u>**

11. Epistulae octō rēgem pacābunt. **<u>The eight letters will pacify the king.</u>**

12. Pābulum est bonum et caper parvus crescit. **<u>The fodder is good and the little billy goat is</u>**

<u>growing.</u>

E. Conjugate the following words in the present, future, and imperfect tenses.

Present Active

FIRST CONJUGATION

	SINGULAR	PLURAL
1ST	captō	captāmus
2ND	captās	captātis
3RD	captat	captant

SECOND CONJUGATION

SINGULAR	PLURAL
flōreō	flōrēmus
flōrēs	flōrētis
flōret	flōrent

THIRD CONJUGATION

SINGULAR	PLURAL
vehō	vehimus
vehis	vehitis
vehit	vehunt

Future Active

FIRST CONJUGATION

	SINGULAR	PLURAL
1ST	captābō	captābimus
2ND	captābis	captābitis
3RD	captābit	captābunt

SECOND CONJUGATION

SINGULAR	PLURAL
flōrēbō	flōrēbimus
flōrēbis	flōrēbitis
flōrēbit	flōrēbunt

THIRD CONJUGATION

SINGULAR	PLURAL
veham	vehēmus
vehēs	vehētis
vehet	vehent

Imperfect Active

FIRST CONJUGATION

	SINGULAR	PLURAL
1ST	captābam	captābāmus
2ND	captābās	captābātis
3RD	captābat	captābant

SECOND CONJUGATION

SINGULAR	PLURAL
flōrēbam	flōrēbāmus
flōrēbās	flōrēbātis
flōrēbat	flōrēbant

THIRD CONJUGATION

SINGULAR	PLURAL
vehēbam	vehēbāmus
vehēbās	vehēbātis
vehēbat	vehēbant

G. Below is a *labyrinthus!* Help the baby *dracō* through it to find his mother.
Below is one of several possible solutions.

Week 22 Quiz

name:

A. *Vocabulary*

Answer the following questions about commands.

1. When you tell a horse, "Giddy-up!", you're giving it a _____.

2. Is a command a verb, a noun, an adverb, or an adjective? _____

3. What is another word for "command"? _____

4. To give a Latin command, you start by find the verb's _____.

5. To give a plural command using a first or second conjugation verb, what do you add to the

stem? _____

6. How do you give a plural command using a third conjugation verb? _____

_____

7. To give a singular command, what do you add to the stem? _____

Change each verb into a singular command and the plural command in Latin. Then translate the plural command into English.

	VERB	SINGULAR COMMAND	PLURAL COMMAND	TRANSLATION
8.	captō			
9.	removeō			
10.	lūdō			
11.	respondeō			
12.	iungō			
13.	commūnicō			

	VERB	SINGULAR COMMAND	PLURAL COMMAND	TRANSLATION
14.	nō			
15.	quiescō			

Translate the following sentences into English. If there are commands, write next to them whether they are singular or plural.

16. Pēgasum mīrum veham. _____

17. Grȳphēs pacāte. _____

18. Dux architectōs fessōs commūnicat. _____

19. Elephantum vehite. _____

20. Vidēsne funga rubra et alba? _____

21. Carmen aliēnum cantā. _____

22. Satyrus foedus virginem captābat. _____

23. Litterās scribe. _____

On the lines below, give the Latin word for each creature.

24. _____   25. _____   26. _____

Week 22 Quiz: Answer Key

A. Vocabulary

Answer the following questions about commands.

1. When you tell a horse, "Giddy-up!", you're giving it a **command**.

2. Is a command a verb, a noun, an adverb, or an adjective? **a verb**

3. What is another word for "command"? **imperative**

4. To give a Latin command, you start by find the verb's **stem**.

5. To give a plural command using a first or second conjugation verb, what do you add to the stem? **-te**

6. How do you give a plural command using a third conjugation verb? **Find the verb's stem, change the stem "e" to an "i," then add -te.**

7. To give a singular command, what do you add to the stem? **nothing**

Change each verb into a singular command and the plural command in Latin. Then translate the plural command into English.

	VERB	SINGULAR COMMAND	PLURAL COMMAND	TRANSLATION
8.	captō	**Captā.**	**Captāte.**	**Hunt.**
9.	removeō	**Removē.**	**Removēte.**	**Remove.**
10.	lūdō	**Lūde.**	**Lūdite.**	**Play.**
11.	respondeō	**Respondē.**	**Respondēte.**	**Respond.**
12.	iungō	**Iunge.**	**Iungite.**	**Join.**
13.	commūnicō	**Commūnicā.**	**Commūnicāte.**	**Inform.**

	VERB	SINGULAR COMMAND	PLURAL COMMAND	TRANSLATION
14.	nō	**Nā.**	**Nāte.**	**Swim.**
15.	quiescō	**Quiesce.**	**Quiescite.**	**Sleep.**

Translate the following sentences into English. If there are commands, write next to them whether they are singular or plural.

15. Pēgasum mīrum veham. **I will ride a wonderful pegasus.**

16. Grȳphēs pacāte. **Subdue the griffins. (plural)**

17. Dux architectōs fessōs commūnicat. **The leader is informing the tired architects.**

18. Elephantum vehite. **Ride the elephant. (plural)**

19. Vidēsne funga rubra et alba? **Do you see the red and white mushrooms?**

20. Carmen aliēnum cantā. **Sing the foreign song. (singular)**

21. Satyrus foedus virginem captābat. **A wicked satyr was hunting the maiden.**

22. Litterās scribe. **Write the letter. (singular)**

On the lines below, give the Latin word for each creature.

24. **pegasus**

25. **grȳps**

26. **satyrus**

Teaching Notes: Week 23

1. Word List: Introduce the Word List for Week 23. This week you'll begin learning fourth declension nouns (see Chants below).

Review this list throughout the week. Continue to review vocabulary from previous weeks.

2. Derivatives: Discuss derivatives for this week's vocabulary:

1. arcus, *arch, bow:* arc, arch
2. frūctus, *fruit, profit:* fructose
3. lacus, *lake, tub, hollow:* lake
4. nix, *snow:* niveous
5. portus, *port, harbor:* port
6. sōl, *sun:* solar, parasol, solstice, solarium
7. tellūs, *earth, ground, land:* tellurian
8. umbra, *shadow, shade:* umbrella, somber
9. vīcus, *village:* vicinity
10. caldus, *warm, hot, fiery:* cauldron
11. novus, *new:* nova, supernova, novel
12. opācus, *dark, shaded:* opaque
13. clam, *secretly:* clandestine
14. exspectō, *I wait, wait for, expect:* expect, expectation
15. foveō, *I cherish, love, esteem*

Have the students write this week's derivatives in the Week 23 "Derivatives" section of their student book.

3. Chant: This week you'll be introducing fourth declension noun endings. This chant works exactly the same way as the other declension chants you've already learned.

Run through the chant several times with the students to familiarize them with it.

Fourth Declension Noun Endings

The first thing to always remember when you learn a new declension is that **a noun's genitive ending will tell you which declension that noun is in**. Fourth declension nouns will *always* have -ūs as their genitive singular ending. Once you see the -ūs genitive ending following a noun, you can be sure you are working with a fourth declension noun.

Fourth declension nouns can be either masculine, feminine, or neuter in gender. This week and next week, you'll only be working with masculine and feminine nouns. (In Week 25, you'll learn the fourth declension neuter chant.)

Let's work with an example. Which declension is the word *arcus* in? At first glance, it looks like a noun from the second declension, doesn't it? (This is another reason why it's crucial to memorize all of the information provided in the Word List.) Looking at this week's Word List, we can see that its genitive singular is -ūs. Since only fourth declension nouns have an -ūs genitive ending, we know *arcus* has to be in the fourth declension.

In the chart below, *arcus* has been declined. The endings, shown in bold, have been applied to the base of *arcus*. Do you still remember how to find a noun's base? Remove the genitive ending from the word, and what remains is the base.

LATIN   ENGLISH

	SINGULAR	PLURAL
NOM.	arc**us**	arc**ūs**
GEN.	arc**ūs**	arc**uum**
DAT.	arc**uī**	arc**ibus**
ACC.	arc**um**	arc**ūs**
ABL.	arc**ū**	arc**ibus**

	SINGULAR	PLURAL
a, the *bow*	the *bows*
of the *bow*, the *bow's*	of the *bows*, the *bows'*
to, for the *bow*	to, for the *bows*
the *bow*	the *bows*
by, with, from the *bow*	by, with, from the *bows*

Make sure students notice how many of the endings are either *-us* or *-ūs,* and help them to pay extra attention when translating.

Once students have gotten into the rhythm of chanting these endings, begin applying the endings to whole nouns. Having visible examples of declined nouns as they are recited often makes the connection easier.

Example:

	SINGULAR	PLURAL
NOM.	frŭctus	frŭctūs
GEN.	frŭctūs	frŭctuum
DAT.	frŭctuī	frŭctibus
ACC.	frŭctum	frŭctūs
ABL.	frŭctū	frŭctibus

	SINGULAR	PLURAL
portus	portūs
portūs	portuum
portuī	portibus
portum	portūs
portū	portibus

4. Quotation: This week's quotation is a phrase from Psalm 51:7, one of King David's prayers: "Purify me with hyssop, and I shall be clean; wash me, and I shall be whiter than snow."

Have the students write this week's quotation in the Week 23 "Quotation" section of their student book.

5. Worksheet: Follow the directions given to complete the worksheet.

6. Quiz: Administer Quiz 23 at the end of the week.

WEEK 23

Word List

NOUNS

1. arcus, -ūs (m) . . . . bow, arch, rainbow
2. frūctus, -ūs (m) . . . . . fruit, profit
3. lacus, -ūs (m) . . . . . . lake, tub, hollow
4. nix, nivis (f) . . . . snow
5. portus, -ūs (m) . . . . . port, harbor
6. sōl, sōlis (m) . . . . sun
7. tellūs, tellūris (f) . . . . . earth, ground, land
8. umbra, -ae (f) . . . . . . shadow, shade
9. vīcus, -ī (m) . . . . village

ADJECTIVES

10. caldus, -a, -um . . . . . warm, hot, fiery
11. novus, -a, -um . . . . . . new
12. opācus, -a, -um . . . . . dark, shaded

ADVERBS

13. clam . . . . secretly

VERBS

14. exspectō, exspectāre . . I wait, wait for, expect
15. foveō, fovēre . . . . I cherish, love, esteem

Chant:

Fourth Declension Noun Endings

	LATIN			ENGLISH	
	SINGULAR	PLURAL		SINGULAR	PLURAL
NOM.	-us	-ūs		a, the *noun*	the *nouns*
GEN.	-ūs	-uum		of the *noun*, the *noun's*	of the *nouns*, the *nouns'*
DAT.	-uī	-ibus		to, for the *noun*	to, for the *nouns*
ACC.	-um	-ūs		the *noun*	the *nouns*
ABL.	-ū	-ibus		by, with, from the *noun*	by, with, from the *nouns*

> ## Quotation:
>
> *albior super nivem*—"whiter than snow"

Weekly Worksheet 23: Answer Key

A. Complete the chant chart for this week and answer the questions about it.

	SINGULAR	PLURAL
NOMINATIVE	-us	-ūs
GENITIVE	-ūs	-uum
DATIVE	-uī	-ibus
ACCUSATIVE	-um	-ūs
ABLATIVE	-ū	-ibus

1. Which case tells you a noun's declension? **genitive**

2. The genitive singular ending for the fourth declension is **-ūs**.

3. The genitive singular ending for the third declension is **-is**.

4. The genitive singular ending for the second declension is **-ī**.

5. The genitive singular ending for the first declension is **-ae**.

B. Decline *arcus* and *frūctus* in the chart below and circle the nominative and accusative cases. Then answer the questions.

	SINGULAR	PLURAL		SINGULAR	PLURAL
NOM.	arcus	arcūs		frūctus	frūctūs
GEN.	arcūs	arcuum		frūctūs	frūctuum
DAT.	arcuī	arcibus		frūctuī	frūctibus
ACC.	arcum	arcūs		frūctum	frūctūs
ABL.	arcū	arcibus		frūctū	frūctibus

1. Which declension are *arcus* and *frūctus* in? **fourth declension**

2. How can you tell? **Both words have -ūs as their genitive singular ending.**

C. For each noun, write in the blank whether it is in the first declension (1), second declension (2), second declension neuter (2N), third declension (3), third declension neuter (3N), or fourth declension (4).

1. cyclops, cyclōpis ____**3**____

6. corpus, corporis ____**3N**____

2. satyrus, -ī ____**2**____

7. asinus, -ī ____**2**____

3. lacus, lacus ____**4**____

8. tībia, -ae ____**1**____

4. umbra, -ae ____**1**____

9. vulnus, vulneris ____**3N**____

5. fīlum, -ī ____**2N**____

10. portus, portus ____**4**____

D. Give the genitive singular form, gender (M, F, N), declension, and the English translation for each noun.

	NOUN	GENITIVE	GENDER	DECLENSION	TRANSLATION
1.	tellūs	**tellūris**	**F**	**3**	**earth, ground**
2.	nix	**nivis**	**F**	**3**	**snow**
3.	centaurus	**centaurī**	**M**	**2**	**centaur**
4.	umbra	**umbrae**	**F**	**1**	**shadow, shade**
5.	frūctus	**frucūs**	**M**	**4**	**fruit, profit**
6.	vīcus	**vīcī**	**M**	**2**	**village**
7.	caput	**capitis**	**N**	**3**	**head**
8.	arcus	**arcūs**	**M**	**4**	**bow, arch**

E. For each sentence, circle any subject nouns and underline any direct objects. Then translate the sentence into English.

1. Agricola tellūrem arābit. **The farmer will plow the ground.**

2. Vīcum (ferus) vītābat. **The wild animal was avoiding the village.**

3. (Nix) nova lūcet. **The new snow shines.**

4. (Centaurī) bonī nuntiōs clam vehēbant. **Good centaurs were conveying the messages secretly.**

5. (Hydrī) ūmidī lacūs fovent. **Wet sea serpents love lakes.**

6. (Dux) caldus nōn est opācus. **The hot leader is not shaded.**

7. Arcum ūnā spectābāmus. **We were looking at the rainbow together.**

8. Portābitisne habēnās et stimulōs? **Will you all carry reins and spurs?**

9. (Vīcus) portūs novōs habet. **The village has new harbors.**

10. Datne (tellūs) frūctūs satis? **Is the ground giving enough fruit?**

11. Cyclōpem exspectāte. **Wait for the cyclops.**

12. Umbrās opācās nōn timēmus. **We do not fear dark shadows.**

F. Draw a line to match each derivative with its Latin root.

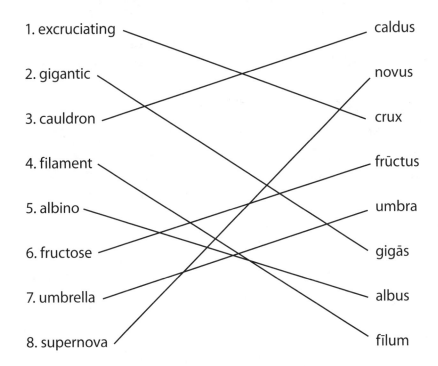

1. excruciating	caldus
2. gigantic	novus
3. cauldron	crux
4. filament	frūctus
5. albino	umbra
6. fructose	gigās
7. umbrella	albus
8. supernova	fīlum

G. Conjugate and translate *foveō* in the imperfect active tense.

Imperfect Active

LATIN

	SINGULAR	PLURAL
1ST	fovēbam	fovēbāmus
2ND	fovēbās	fovēbātis
3RD	fovēbat	fovēbant

ENGLISH

	SINGULAR	PLURAL
1ST	I was cherishing	we were cherishing
2ND	you were cherishing	you all were cherishing
3RD	he/she/it was cherishing	they were cherishing

H. Label each declension and complete the chants. Then circle all of the genitive endings.

1st DECLENSION

	SINGULAR	PLURAL
NOM.	-a	-ae
GEN.	-ae	-ārum
DAT.	-ae	-īs
ACC.	-am	-ās
ABL.	-ā	-īs

2nd DECLENSION

	SINGULAR	PLURAL
NOM.	-us	-ī
GEN.	-ī	-ōrum
DAT.	-ō	-īs
ACC.	-um	-ōs
ABL.	-ō	-īs

2nd DECLENSION **Neuter**

	SINGULAR	PLURAL
NOM.	-um	-a
GEN.	-ī	-ōrum
DAT.	-ō	-īs
ACC.	-um	-a
ABL.	-ō	-īs

3rd DECLENSION

	SINGULAR	PLURAL
NOM.	x	-ēs
GEN.	-is	-um
DAT.	-ī	-ibus
ACC.	-em	-ēs
ABL.	-e	-ibus

3rd DECLENSION **Neuter**

	SINGULAR	PLURAL
NOM.	x	-a
GEN.	-is	-um
DAT.	-ī	-ibus
ACC.	x	-a
ABL.	-e	-ibus

4th DECLENSION

	SINGULAR	PLURAL
NOM.	-us	-ūs
GEN.	-ūs	-uum
DAT.	-uī	-ibus
ACC.	-um	-ūs
ABL.	-ū	-ibus

Week 23 Quiz

name:

A. Chants

Complete the fourth declension chant, then answer the questions about it.

	SINGULAR	PLURAL

1. The genitive singular ending for the fourth declension is _____.

2. The genitive ending for the third declension is _____.

3. The genitive ending for the second declension is _____.

4. The genitive ending for the first declension is _____.

Label each noun's declension (1, 2, 3, or 4) and gender (M, F, or N). Then decline it

.

DECLENSION _____ GENDER _____

	SINGULAR	PLURAL
NOM.	portus	
GEN.		
DAT.		
ACC.		
ABL.		

DECLENSION _____ GENDER _____

	SINGULAR	PLURAL
NOM.	lacus	
GEN.		
DAT.		
ACC.		
ABL.		

DECLENSION _____ GENDER _____   DECLENSION _____ GENDER _____

	SINGULAR	PLURAL
NOM.	nix	
GEN.		
DAT.		
ACC.		
ABL.		

	SINGULAR	PLURAL
NOM.	vīcus	
GEN.		
DAT.		
ACC.		
ABL.		

Now go back and circle the nominative and accusative endings for each word.

B. Vocabulary

Give the masculine, feminine, and neuter *accusative plural* forms of these adjectives in Latin.

	ADJECTIVE	MASCULINE	FEMININE	NEUTER
1.	dark			
2.	new			
3.	fiery			

Translate the following sentences into English.

4. Arcūs sunt rubrī, flavī, et caeruleī. _____

5. Frūctusne est ruber? _____

6. Nauta novus portūs obsidēbit. _____

7. Somnum rēx vītat. _____

8. Fovēsne nivem? _____

9. Dux dracōnem videt et nōn movet. _____

Week 23 Quiz: Answer Key

A. Chants

Complete the fourth declension chant, then answer the questions about it.

	SINGULAR	PLURAL
NOMINATIVE	-us	-ūs
GENITIVE	-ūs	-uum
DATIVE	-uī	-ibus
ACCUSATIVE	-um	-ūs
ABLATIVE	-ū	-ibus

1. The genitive singular ending for the fourth declension is **-ūs**.

2. The genitive ending for the third declension is **-is**.

3. The genitive ending for the second declension is **-ī**.

4. The genitive ending for the first declension is **-ae**.

Label each noun's declension (1, 2, 3, or 4) and gender (M, F, or N). Then decline it

DECLENSION ___4___   GENDER ___M___

	SINGULAR	PLURAL
NOM.	portus	portūs
GEN.	portūs	portuum
DAT.	portuī	portibus
ACC.	portum	portūs
ABL.	portū	portibus

DECLENSION ___4___   GENDER ___M___

	SINGULAR	PLURAL
NOM.	lacus	lacūs
GEN.	lacūs	lacuum
DAT.	lacuī	lacibus
ACC.	lacum	lacūs
ABL.	lacū	lacibus

DECLENSION **3** GENDER **F**

	SINGULAR	PLURAL
NOM.	nix	nivēs
GEN.	nivis	nivum
DAT.	nivī	nivibus
ACC.	nivem	nivēs
ABL.	nive	nivibus

DECLENSION **2** GENDER **M**

	SINGULAR	PLURAL
NOM.	vīcus	vīcī
GEN.	vīcī	vīcōrum
DAT.	vīcō	vīcīs
ACC.	vīcum	vīcōs
ABL.	vīcō	vīcīs

Now go back and circle the nominative and accusative endings for each word.

B. Vocabulary

Give the masculine, feminine, and neuter *accusative plural* forms of these adjectives in Latin.

	ADJECTIVE	MASCULINE	FEMININE	NEUTER
1.	dark	opācōs	opācās	opāca
2.	new	novōs	novās	nova
3.	fiery	caldōs	caldās	calda

Translate the following sentences into English.

4. Arcūs sunt rubrī, flavī, et caeruleī. **Rainbows are red, yellow, and blue.**

5. Frūctusne est ruber? **Is the fruit red?**

6. Nauta novus portūs obsidēbit. **The new sailor will remain near the harbors.**

7. Somnum rēx vītat. **The king avoids sleep.**

8. Fovēsne nivem? **Do you love the snow?**

9. Dux dracōnem videt et nōn movet. **The leader sees the dragon and does not move.**

Teaching Notes: Week 24

1. Word List: Introduce the Word List for Week 24. Review this list throughout the week. Continue to review vocabulary from previous weeks.

2. Derivatives: Discuss derivatives for this week's vocabulary:

1. cantus, *song, singing:* canticle
2. domus, *home, house:* domain, domestic
3. frāter, *brother:* fraternal, fraternity, fraternize, fratricide, friar
4. Iesus, *Jesus:* Jesus
5. manus, *hand:* manual, manacles, manipulate
6. māter, *mother:* maternity, maternal
7. metus, *fear, dread*
8. pater, *father:* paternal

9. soror, *sister:* sorority
10. spīritus, *spirit, breath:* spirit, esprit
11. fīdus, *faithful, trustworthy*
12. repente, *suddenly*
13. appellō, *I name, call by name, call:* appellation
14. commendō, *I commit, entrust:* commend
15. crēdō, I believe: creed, credit, credible, incredible, credence, credential, miscreant, credulous

Have the students write this week's derivatives in the Week 24 "Derivatives" section of their student book. Look over previous derivatives from Unit 3.

3. Chant: There is no new chant this week. Use this week to review the chants from previous weeks, particularly the new fourth declension chant. Check that students can consistently distinguish between first, second, and third conjugation verbs and that they comfortable identifying which declension a noun is in.

4. Quotation: This week's quotation is taken from Luke 23:46, Jesus' final words on the cross: "And Jesus, crying out with a loud voice, said, 'Father, into your hands I commit my spirit.' Having said this, He breathed His last."

Have the students write this week's quotation in the Week 24 "Quotation" section of their student book.

5. Worksheet: Follow the directions given to complete the worksheet.

6. Quiz: Since there is a test at the end of the week, this week's quiz is optional. Feel free to use it as practice for the test.

7. Test: The Unit 3 Test should be given at the end of this week.

WEEK 24

Word List

NOUNS

1. cantus, -ūs (m) . . . . . . song, singing
2. domus, -ūs (f) . . . . . . home, house
3. frāter, frātris (m) . . . . brother
4. Iesus, -ūs (m) . . . . Jesus
5. manus, -ūs (f) . . . . . . hand
6. māter, mātris (f) . . . . mother
7. metus, -ūs (m) . . . . . . fear, dread
8. pater, patris (m) . . . . . father
9. soror, sorōris (f) . . . . . sister
10. spīritus, -ūs (m) . . . . . spirit, breath

ADJECTIVES

11. fīdus, -a, -um . . . . . . faithful, trustworthy

ADVERBS

12. repente . . . . suddenly

VERBS

13. appellō, appellāre . . . I name, call, call by name
14. commendō, commendāre . I commit, entrust
15. crēdō, crēdere . . . . . I believe

Chant:

No new chant this week.

> ### Quotation:
>
> *Pater, in manūs tuās commendō spīritum meum.*
>
> "Father, into Your hands I commit my spirit."

Weekly Worksheet 24: Answer Key

A. Match each genitive singular ending with its declension.

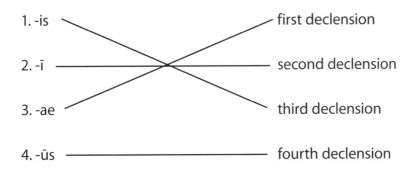

1. -is — third declension

2. -ī — first declension (via crossing lines)

3. -ae — second declension

4. -ūs — fourth declension

B. Label each noun's declension (1, 2, 3, or 4) and gender (M, F, or N). Then decline it.

DECLENSION __4__   GENDER __M__

	SINGULAR	PLURAL
NOM.	cantus	cantūs
GEN.	cantūs	cantuum
DAT.	cantuī	cantibus
ACC.	cantum	cantūs
ABL.	cantū	cantibus

DECLENSION __2__   GENDER __M__

	SINGULAR	PLURAL
NOM.	architectus	architectī
GEN.	architectī	architectōrum
DAT.	architectō	architectīs
ACC.	architectum	architectōs
ABL.	architectō	architectīs

DECLENSION __3__   GENDER __M__

	SINGULAR	PLURAL
NOM.	pater	patrēs
GEN.	patris	patrum
DAT.	patrī	patribus
ACC.	patrem	patrēs
ABL.	patre	patribus

DECLENSION __4__   GENDER __F__

	SINGULAR	PLURAL
NOM.	metus	metūs
GEN.	metūs	metuum
DAT.	metuī	metibus
ACC.	metum	metūs
ABL.	metū	metibus

C. Translate these sentences into English.

   1. Pater et fīlius cervōs captābant. **The father and son were hunting deer.**

   2. Appellābatne māter sorōrem? **Was the mother calling a sister?**

   3. Sōl repente apparēbit. **The sun will suddenly appear.**

   4. Familia frātrem tardum exspectābat. **The family was waiting for the late brother.**

   5. Vehēbāsne pēgasum? **Were you riding a pegasus?**

   6. Grȳphēs ālās magnās et brūnās pinnās habet. **Griffins have large wings and brown feathers.**

   7. Iesus crucem portābat. **Jesus was carrying the cross**.

   8. Māter et pater fābulam nōn crēdunt. **The mother and father do not believe the story.**

   9. Habetne lacus portum parvum? **Does the lake have a little harbor?**

   10. Metūs minūtātim pacābō. **I will pacify fears bit by bit.**

D. Turn each verb into a singular command and the plural command in Latin. Then translate the plural command into English.

	VERB	SINGULAR COMMAND	PLURAL COMMAND	TRANSLATION
1.	crēdō	**Crēde.**	**Crēdite.**	**Believe.**
2.	edō	**Ede.**	**Edite.**	**Eat.**
3.	vibrō	**Vibrā.**	**Vibrāte.**	**Shake.**
4.	appellō	**Appellā.**	**Appellāte.**	**Call.**
5.	foveō	**Fovē.**	**Fovēte.**	**Cherish.**

E. For each sentence, underline the verb and circle the subject. Then translate the sentence into Latin.

   1. The (father) cherishes the land. **Pater tellūrum fovet.**

2. The ⟨brother⟩ was calling the sister. **Frāter sorōrem appellābat.**

3. The horrible ⟨cyclops⟩ will wait for the man. **Cyclops foedus virum exspectābit.**

4. Are ⟨you⟩ loving the song? **Fovēsne cantum?**

5. The ⟨minotaur⟩ has bad breath. **Mīnōtaurus spīritum malum habet.**

F. Each of the nouns below comes from a Latin root in either Word List 23 or 24. Figure out which of your Latin nouns is the root, and then give its English meaning.

	ITALIAN	SPANISH	FRENCH	LATIN	ENGLISH
1.	neve	nieve	neige	**nix**	**snow**
2.	ombra	sombra	ombre	**umbra**	**shadow**
3.	mano	mano	main	**manus**	**hand**

G. Use your knowledge of Latin derivatives to circle the word that completes the definition.

1. *Maternal* love is the love of a _____.

    a) village   ⟨b) mother⟩   c) sister   d) fear

2. *Solar* energy is energy from the _____.

    a) soul   b) moon   c) ground   ⟨d) sun⟩

3. An *appellation* is a title or _____.

    ⟨a) name⟩   b) rainbow   c) fruit   d) mountain

4. A *cauldron* is a pot that contains_____ liquids.

    a) colorful   b) delicious   ⟨c) hot⟩   d) salty

H. Give the genitive forms of these nouns from memory and write whether they are in the first (1), second (2), second neuter (2N), third (3), third neuter (3N), or fourth (4) declension.

1. soror **sorōris (3)**

2. sōl **sōlis (3)**

3. vīcus **vīcī (2)**

4. spīritus **spīritūs (4)**

5. manus **manūs (4)**

6. tellūs **tellūris (3)**

7. pater **patris (3)**

8. māter **mātris (3)**

I. Conjugate and translate *crēdō* in the present and imperfect active tenses.

Present Active

| | LATIN | | ENGLISH | |
	SINGULAR	PLURAL	SINGULAR	PLURAL
1ST	crēdō	**crēdimus**	**I believe**	**we believe**
2ND	**crēdis**	**crēditis**	**you believe**	**you all believe**
3RD	**crēdit**	**crēdunt**	**he/she/it believes**	**they believe**

Imperfect Active

| | LATIN | | ENGLISH | |
	SINGULAR	PLURAL	SINGULAR	PLURAL
1ST	**crēdēbam**	**crēdēbāmus**	**I was believing**	**we were believing**
2ND	**crēdēbās**	**crēdēbātis**	**you were believing**	**you all were believing**
3RD	**crēdēbat**	**crēdēbant**	**he/she/it was believing**	**they were believing**

J. Write this week's quotation from Luke 23:46 in Latin.

Pater, in manūs tuās commendō spīritum meum.

Week 24 Quiz

name:

A. Chants

Label each declension and complete the chants. Then circle all of the genitive endings.

_____ DECLENSION

	SINGULAR	PLURAL
NOM.		
GEN.	-ūs	
DAT.		
ACC.		
ABL.		

_____ DECLENSION _____

	SINGULAR	PLURAL
NOM.		-a
GEN.	-ī	

_____ DECLENSION

	SINGULAR	PLURAL
NOM.		-ēs
GEN.	-is	

_____ DECLENSION

	SINGULAR	PLURAL
NOM.		
GEN.	-ae	
DAT.		
ACC.		
ABL.		

_____ DECLENSION _____

	SINGULAR	PLURAL
NOM.		-a
GEN.	-is	

_____ DECLENSION

	SINGULAR	PLURAL
NOM.		-ī
GEN.	-ī	

B. Vocabulary

Underline the adjective that matches the noun. Then translate the phrase into English.

NOUN	ADJECTIVE	TRANSLATION
1. Lacus	caldus / caldum	_____

2. Frāter   fīdus / fīdum   _____

3. Nivem   novum / novam   _____

4. Domūs   ruber / rubrae   _____

5. Manūs   pulvereōs / pulvereas   _____

6. Tellūs   opācae / opāca   _____

7. Spīritus   contenta / contentus   _____

On the lines below, give the Latin word for each creature.

8. _____   9. _____   10. _____

Translate these sentences into English.

11. Mātrēs et patrēs ūnā edent. _____

12. Sorōrem quiētam appellā. _____

13. Erratne mīnōtaurus labyrinthum foedum? _____

_____

14. Iesus cantum antīquum cantābat. _____

15. Frāter metūs superābit. _____

16. Querēlās repente crēdēmus. _____

17. Movēbatne īnsula mīra? _____

18. Cyclōpem malum nōn commūnicāte. _____

Week 24 Quiz: Answer Key

A. Chants

Label each declension and complete the chants. Then circle all of the genitive endings.

4th DECLENSION

	SINGULAR	PLURAL
NOM.	-us	-ūs
GEN.	-ūs	-uum
DAT.	-uī	-ibus
ACC.	-um	-ūs
ABL.	-ū	-ibus

2nd DECLENSION Neuter

	SINGULAR	PLURAL
NOM.	-um	-a
GEN.	-ī	-ōrum
DAT.	-ō	-īs
ACC.	-um	-a
ABL.	-ō	-īs

3rd DECLENSION

	SINGULAR	PLURAL
NOM.	x	-ēs
GEN.	-is	-um
DAT.	-ī	-ibus
ACC.	-em	-ēs
ABL.	-e	-ibus

1st DECLENSION

	SINGULAR	PLURAL
NOM.	-a	-ae
GEN.	-ae	-ārum
DAT.	-ae	-īs
ACC.	-am	-ās
ABL.	-ā	-īs

3rd DECLENSION Neuter

	SINGULAR	PLURAL
NOM.	x	-a
GEN.	-is	-um
DAT.	-ī	-ibus
ACC.	x	-a
ABL.	-e	-ibus

2nd DECLENSION

	SINGULAR	PLURAL
NOM.	-us	-ī
GEN.	-ī	-ōrum
DAT.	-ō	-īs
ACC.	-um	-ōs
ABL.	-ō	-īs

B. Vocabulary

Underline the adjective that matches the noun. Then translate the phrase into English.

NOUN	ADJECTIVE	TRANSLATION
1. Lacus	**caldus** / caldum	**a hot tub**

2. Frāter   **fīdus** / fīdum   **the faithful brother**

3. Nivem   novum / **novam**   **new snow**

4. Domūs   ruber / **rubrae**   **the red houses**

5. Manūs   **pulvereōs** / pulvereas   **dusty hands**

6. Tellūs   opācae / **opāca**   **a dark land**

7. Spīritus   contenta / **contentus**   **a content spirit**

On the lines below, give the Latin word for each creature.

8. **asinus**   9. **dracō**   10. **grȳps**

Translate these sentences into English.

11. Mātrēs et patrēs ūnā edent. **The mothers and fathers will eat together.**

12. Sorōrem quiētam appellā. **Call the sleeping sister.**

13. Erratne mīnōtaurus labyrinthum foedum? **Does the minotaur wander the horrible labyrinth?**

14. Iesus cantum antīquum cantābat. **Jesus was singing an ancient song.**

15. Frāter metūs superābit. **The brother will conquer the fears.**

16. Querēlās repente crēdēmus. **Suddenly we were believing the complaints.**

17. Movēbatne īnsula mīra? **Was the strange island moving?**

18. Cyclōpem malum nōn commūnicāte. **Do not inform the evil cyclops.**

Unit 3 Test

name: _____

Chants

A. Answer the following questions.

1. The _____ noun always takes the nominative case.

2. In a Latin sentence, the verb is usually at the _____.

3. The _____ always takes the accusative case.

4. To form a question in Latin, _____ is added to the first word in the sentence.

5. The first word in a Latin question is usually the _____.

6. When you tell a dog, "Roll over!", you're giving it a _____.

7. What is another word for "command"? _____

8. To give a Latin command, you start by find the verb's _____.

9. To give a plural command using a first or second conjugation verb, what do you add to the

stem? _____

10. How do you give a plural command using a third conjugation verb? _____

_____

11. To give a singular command, what do you add to the stem? _____

B. In Latin, give these commands to one person.

1. Move. _____   3. Sing! _____

2. Believe. _____   4. Wait. _____

In Latin, give these commands to a group of people.

5. Move. _____   6. Sing! _____

7. Believe. _____   8. Wait._____

C. Label each declension and complete the chants. Then circle all of the genitive endings.

_____ DECLENSION _____

	SINGULAR	PLURAL
NOM.		
GEN.	-ī	
DAT.		
ACC.		-a
ABL.		

_____ DECLENSION _____

	SINGULAR	PLURAL
NOM.		
GEN.	-is	
DAT.		
ACC.	-em	
ABL.		

_____ DECLENSION _____

	SINGULAR	PLURAL
NOM.		
GEN.	-ae	
DAT.		
ACC.		
ABL.		

_____ DECLENSION _____

	SINGULAR	PLURAL
NOM.		
GEN.	-ūs	
DAT.		
ACC.		
ABL.		

_____ DECLENSION _____

	SINGULAR	PLURAL
NOM.		
GEN.	-ī	
DAT.		
ACC.		-ōs
ABL.		

_____ DECLENSION _____

	SINGULAR	PLURAL
NOM.		
GEN.	-is	
DAT.		
ACC.	x	
ABL.		

D. Translate these verbs into English.

1. portābam _____   6. flōrēbās _____

2. vulnerābunt _____   7. nāte _____

3. fovēbitis _____   8. habēmus _____

4. iungit _____   9. laxābant _____

5. crēdam _____   10. retinē _____

E. On the lines below, label what each thing is called in Latin.

1. _____

2. _____

3. _____

4. _____

5. _____

6. _____

F. Finish conjugating and translating this verb.

	LATIN			ENGLISH	
	SINGULAR	PLURAL		SINGULAR	PLURAL
1ST					
2ND	iungēs				
3RD					

G. Translate these sentences into English.

1. Dux mīnōtaurum nōn līberābit. _____

2. Obsidēbuntne stabulum bovēs fessae? _____

3. Gigantēs retinēte! _____

4. Nōn erō improba. _____

5. Edentne clam pēgasī flōrēs rubrōs? _____

6. Lēgātus fīdus hastam removēbit. _____

7. Cantābuntne principēs tibiās et lyrās? _____

8. Dracō spīritum caldum habet. _____

9. Arcus est ruber, flavus, et caeruleus. _____

10. Ferum nōn lūdite. _____

H. Label each noun's declension (1, 2, 3, or 4) and gender (M, F, or N). Then decline it.

DECLENSION _____ GENDER _____

	SINGULAR	PLURAL
NOM.	vīcus	
GEN.		
DAT.		
ACC.		
ABL.		

DECLENSION _____ GENDER _____

	SINGULAR	PLURAL
NOM.	cor	
GEN.		
DAT.		
ACC.		
ABL.		

DECLENSION _____ GENDER _____

	SINGULAR	PLURAL
NOM.	domus	
GEN.		
DAT.		
ACC.		
ABL.		

DECLENSION _____ GENDER _____

	SINGULAR	PLURAL
NOM.	tellūs	
GEN.		
DAT.		
ACC.		
ABL.		

Unit 3 Test: Answer Key

Chants

A. Answer the following questions.

1. The **subject** noun always takes the nominative case.

2. In a Latin sentence, the verb is usually at the **end**.

3. The **direct object** always takes the accusative case.

4. To form a question in Latin, **-ne** is added to the first word in the sentence.

5. The first word in a Latin question is usually the **verb**.

6. When you tell a dog, "Roll over!", you're giving it a **command**.

7. What is another word for "command"? **imperative**

8. To give a Latin command, you start by find the verb's **stem**.

9. To give a plural command using a first or second conjugation verb, what do you add to the

stem? **-te**

10. How do you give a plural command using a third conjugation verb? **First, find the stem, then**

change the stem's "e" to an "i," and add -te.

11. To give a singular command, what do you add to the stem? **nothing**

B. In Latin, give these commands to one person.

1. Move.	**Movē.**	3. Sing!	**Cantā!**
2. Believe.	**Crēde.**	4. Wait.	**Exspectā.**

In Latin, give these commands to a group of people.

5. Move.	**Movēte.**	6. Sing!	**Cantāte!**

7. Believe.   **Crēdite.**   8. Wait.   **Exspectāte.**

C. Label each declension and complete the chants. Then circle all of the genitive endings.

2nd DECLENSION Neuter

	SINGULAR	PLURAL
NOM.	-um	-a
GEN.	-ī	-ōrum
DAT.	-ō	-īs
ACC.	-um	-a
ABL.	-ō	-īs

3rd DECLENSION

	SINGULAR	PLURAL
NOM.	x	-ēs
GEN.	-is	-um
DAT.	-ī	-ibus
ACC.	-em	-ēs
ABL.	-e	-ibus

1st DECLENSION

	SINGULAR	PLURAL
NOM.	-a	-ae
GEN.	-ae	-ārum
DAT.	-ae	-īs
ACC.	-am	-ās
ABL.	-ā	-īs

4th DECLENSION

	SINGULAR	PLURAL
NOM.	-us	-ūs
GEN.	-ūs	-uum
DAT.	-uī	-ibus
ACC.	-um	-ūs
ABL.	-ū	-ibus

2nd DECLENSION

	SINGULAR	PLURAL
NOM.	-us	-ī
GEN.	-ī	-ōrum
DAT.	-ō	-īs
ACC.	-um	-ōs
ABL.	-ō	-īs

3rd DECLENSION Neuter

	SINGULAR	PLURAL
NOM.	x	-a
GEN.	-is	-um
DAT.	-ī	-ibus
ACC.	x	-a
ABL.	-e	-ibus

D. Translate these verbs into English.

1. portābam   **I was carrying**

2. vulnerābunt   **they will wound**

3. fovēbitis   **you all will cherish**

4. iungit   **he/she/it is joining**

5. crēdam   **I will believe**

6. flōrēbās   **you were flourishing**

7. nāte   **swim**

8. habēmus   **we hold**

9. laxābant   **they were loosening**

10. retinē   **hold back**

E. On the lines below, label what each thing is called in Latin.

1. **bōs**

2. **sōl**

3. **satyrus**

4. **flōs**

5. **centaurus**

6. **asinus**

F. Finish conjugating and translating this verb.

	LATIN			ENGLISH	
	SINGULAR	PLURAL		SINGULAR	PLURAL
1ST	iungam	iungēmus		I will join	we will join
2ND	iungēs	iungētis		you will join	you all will join
3RD	iunget	iungent		he/she/it will join	they will join

G. Translate these sentences into English.

1. Dux mīnōtaurum nōn līberābit. **The leader will not set the minotaur free.**

2. Obsidēbuntne stabulum bovēs fessae? **Will the tired cows remain near the stable?**

3. Gigantēs retinēte! **Hold back the giants!**

4. Nōn erō improba. **I will not be wicked.**

5. Edentne clam pēgasī flōrēs rubrōs? **Do pegasuses secretly eat red flowers?**

6. Lēgātus fīdus hastam removēbit. **The faithful lieutenant will remove the lance.**

7. Cantābuntne principēs tibiās et lyrās? **Will the chiefs play flutes and lyres?**

8. Dracō spīritum caldum habet. **The dragon has fiery breath.**

9. Arcus est ruber, flavus, et caeruleus. **The rainbow is red, yellow, and blue.**

10. Ferum nōn lūdite. **Do not tease the wild animal.**

H. Label each noun's declension (1, 2, 3, or 4) and gender (M, F, or N). Then decline it.

DECLENSION __2__ GENDER __M__

	SINGULAR	PLURAL
NOM.	vīcus	vīcī
GEN.	vīcī	vīcōrum
DAT.	vīcō	vīcīs
ACC.	vīcum	vīcōs
ABL.	vīcō	vīcīs

DECLENSION __3__ GENDER __N__

	SINGULAR	PLURAL
NOM.	cor	corda
GEN.	cordis	cordum
DAT.	cordī	cordibus
ACC.	cor	corda
ABL.	corde	cordibus

DECLENSION __4__ GENDER __F__

	SINGULAR	PLURAL
NOM.	domus	domūs
GEN.	domūs	domuum
DAT.	domuī	domibus
ACC.	domum	domūs
ABL.	domū	domibus

DECLENSION __3__ GENDER __F__

	SINGULAR	PLURAL
NOM.	tellūs	tellūrēs
GEN.	tellūris	tellūrum
DAT.	tellūrī	tellūribus
ACC.	tellūrem	tellūrēs
ABL.	tellūre	tellūribus

4 UNIT FOUR

UNIT 4: GOALS

By the end of Week 32, students should be able to . . .

- Recognize and decline any fourth declension noun
- Conjugate *possum* in the present tense
- Recognize and translate infinitives
- Conjugate *sum* in the present, future, and imperfect tenses

Unit 4 Overview (Weeks 25–32)

Congratulations! This is the final Unit of the *Latin Primer 2*. In this Unit, you'll introduce and practice the neuter endings for the fourth declension (Weeks 25 and 26). In Week 27, students will learn how to translate sentences using the infinitive (or second principal part) of a verb. Weeks 28 and 29 will be review, then in Week 30, you'll learn the imperfect chant for *sum—eram*. The last two weeks will be dedicated to general review in preparation for the final Unit test.

Teaching Notes: Week 25

1. Word List: Introduce the Word List for Week 25. Many of these are fourth declension neuter nouns, which you'll be learning about this week. Notice that you're learning two nouns with similar meanings—*grex* and *pecū*. (There isn't much difference between the two, just like there isn't much difference in English between *herd* and *flock!*) Review this list throughout the week. Continue to review vocabulary from previous weeks.

2. Derivatives: Discuss derivatives for this week's vocabulary:

1. cornū, *horn:* cornucopia, unicorn, corner
2. culter, *knife:* cutlery, cutlass
4. gelū, *chill, frost*
5. genū, *knee:* genuflect
6. grex, *flock, herd:* gregarious, segregate, congregation
7. leō, *lion:* lion, leonine, lionize
8. pastor, *shepherd:* pastor, pastoral
9. pecū, *herd, flock:* peculiar

10. tempestās, *weather, storm:* tempest
11. verū, *javelin, spit (for roasting meat)*
12. tūtus, *safe, secure:* tutor, tutorial
13. cūrō, *I care for:* curator
14. terreō, *I frighten, terrify:* deter, terrible, terrific, terrify
15. tondeō, *I clip, give a haircut, shear:* tonsure
16. vigilō, *I guard, watch over:* vigilant

Have the students write this week's derivatives in the Week 25 "Derivatives" section of their student book.

3. Chant: This week, you'll be learning the noun ending chant for the fourth declension *neuter*. There are only six fourth declension neuter nouns in the Latin language, yet somehow they managed to get their very own chant! You'll be learning five of the six this week. The sixth one is *specus,* cave. (Oddly, *specus* is also masculine and feminine as well.)

The fourth declension neuter is a variation on the fourth declension endings that you learned in Week 23. The only difference is this week's chant is for nouns of the fourth declension that are *neuter.*

Fourth Declension Neuter Noun Endings

Since there are only six neuter nouns in the fourth declension, you may find it easiest to simply memorize them. However, there's also a trick to discovering if a noun in the fourth declension is neuter, in case you forget one!

Do you remember how you learned last year to identify second declension neuter nouns? **Look at the nominative and genitive singular endings together.** You can use this same trick to find out if a fourth declension noun is neuter!

Every fourth declension noun has -ūs as its genitive singular ending. But only fourth declension *neuter* nouns also have -ū as their nominative singular ending.

For example, what family is the word *cornū* in? If we look in this Week's Word list, we see that *cornū's* genitive singular ending is *-ūs,* so we know *cornū* is in the fourth declension. But *cornū* also ends in *-ū* in the nominative singular. Only fourth declension neuter nouns follow the *-ū, -ūs* progression, so we know *cornū* has to be a fourth declension neuter noun.

In the chart below, *cornū* has been declined. The endings, shown in bold, have been applied to the base of *cornū.* (To find a noun's base, remove the genitive ending from the word.)

LATIN

	SINGULAR	PLURAL
NOM.	corn**ū**	corn**ua**
GEN.	corn**ūs**	corn**uum**
DAT.	corn**ū**	corn**ibus**
ACC.	corn**ū**	corn**ua**
ABL.	corn**ū**	corn**ibus**

ENGLISH

	SINGULAR	PLURAL
NOM.	a, the *horn*	the *horns*
GEN.	of the *horn,* the *horn's*	of the *horns,* the *horns'*
DAT.	to, for the *horn*	to, for the *horns*
ACC.	the *horn*	the *horns*
ABL.	by, with, from the *horn*	by, with, from the *horns*

Notice that, like all neuter nouns, the nominative and accusative forms match each other in the singular and plural. Once students have gotten into the rhythm of chanting these endings, begin applying the endings to whole nouns.

Example:

	SINGULAR	PLURAL
NOM.	gelū	gelua
GEN.	gelūs	geluum
DAT.	gelū	gelibus
ACC.	gelū	gelua
ABL.	gelū	gelibus

	SINGULAR	PLURAL
NOM.	verū	verua
GEN.	verūs	veruum
DAT.	verū	veribus
ACC.	verū	verua
ABL.	verū	veribus

4. Quotation: This week's quotation is a sentence from Horace's *Satires.* Horace was a famous Roman lyric poet. In its original context, this quotation refers to the fact that everyone attacks using their greatest strength. Another way of looking at it—no one expects a wolf to attack with his tail, or a bull with his teeth!

Have the students write this week's quotation in the Week 25 "Quotation" section of their student book..

5. Worksheet: Follow the directions given to complete the worksheet.

6. Quiz: Administer Quiz 25 at the end of the week.

WEEK 25

Word List

NOUNS

1. cornū, -ūs (n) . . . . horn
2. culter, -trī (m) . . . . knife
4. gelū, -ūs (n) . . . . chill, frost
5. genū, -ūs (n). . . . . knee
6. grex, gregis (m). . . . . . . flock, herd
7. leō, leōnis (m) . . . . lion
8. pastor, pastōris (m) . . . . . shepherd
9. tempestās, tempestātis (f) . weather, storm
10. pecū, -ūs (n) . . . . cattle, flock
11. verū, -ūs (n). . . . . javelin, spit (for roasting meat)

ADJECTIVES

12. tūtus, -a, -um . . . . . . safe, secure

VERBS

13. cūrō, cūrāre . . . . I care for
14. terreō, terrēre . . . . . I frighten, terrify
15. tondeō, tondēre . . . . I clip, give a haircut, shear
16. vigilō, vigilāre . . . . . . I guard, watch over

Chant:

Fourth Declension Neuter Noun Endings

	LATIN			ENGLISH	
	SINGULAR	PLURAL		SINGULAR	PLURAL
NOM.	-ū	-ua		a, the *noun*	the *nouns*
GEN.	-ūs	-uum		of the *noun*, the *noun's*	of the *nouns*, the *nouns'*
DAT.	-ū	-ibus		to, for the *noun*	to, for the *nouns*
ACC.	-ū	-ua		the *noun*	the *nouns*
ABL.	-ū	-ibus		by, with, from the *noun*	by, with, from the *nouns*

(Continued on the next page)

Quotation:

Dente lupus, cornū taurus petit.

"The wolf attacks with his fang, the bull with its horn."

Weekly Worksheet 25: Answer Key

A. Write the chant for this week and answer the questions about it.

	SINGULAR	PLURAL
NOM.	-ū	-ua
GEN.	-ūs	-uum
DAT.	-ū	-ibus
ACC.	-ū	-ua
ABL.	-ū	-ibus

1. Which case tells you a noun's declension? **genitive**

2. The genitive singular ending for the fourth declension is **-ūs.**

3. How can you tell if a noun is in the fourth declension neuter? **All fourth declension neuter**

nouns have -ūs as their genitive singular ending and -ū as their nominative singular ending.

B. Decline *cornū* and *genū* in the chart below and circle the accusative endings. Then answer the questions.

	SINGULAR	PLURAL		SINGULAR	PLURAL
NOM.	cornū	cornua		genū	genua
GEN.	cornūs	cornuum		genūs	genuum
DAT.	cornū	cornibus		genū	genibus
ACC.	cornū̃	cornua		genū̃	genua
ABL.	cornū	cornibus		genū	genibus

1. Which declension are *cornū* and *genū* in? **fourth declension**

2. What is their gender? **neuter**

C. Give the genitive singular form, gender (M, F, N), declension, and the English translation for each noun.

	NOUN	GENITIVE	GENDER	DECLENSION	TRANSLATION
1.	grex	gregis	M	3	flock, herd
2.	culter	cultrī	M	2	knife
3.	cantus	cantī	M	2	song, singing
4.	pecū	pecūs	N	4	cattle, flock
5.	arcus	arcūs	M	4	bow, arch, rainbow
6.	asinus	asinī	M	2	donkey
7.	palma	palmae	F	1	palm tree
8.	gelū	gelūs	N	4	chill, frost
9.	fīlum	fīlī	N	2	thread, string
10.	iter	itineris	N	3	journey

D. Underline the adjective that matches the noun's number, gender, and case. Then translate the phrase.

NOUN	ADJECTIVE	TRANSLATION
1. Pastor	**fīdus** / fīdum	**the faithful shepherd**
2. Domūs	caldus / **caldās**	**the warm homes**
3. Gelū	mīrus / **mīrum**	**a wonderful frost**
4. Tellūs	opācus / **opāca**	**the dark land**
5. Arcus	**pulcher** / pulchrōs	**a beautiful rainbow**
6. Matrimonia	beātum / **beāta**	**the happy marriages**
7. Cornua	**alba** / albae	**white horns**

E. Complete the chants. Then circle all of the accusative endings.

	FIRST DECLENSION	
	SINGULAR	**PLURAL**
NOM.	-a	**-ae**
GEN.	**-ae**	**-ārum**
DAT.	**-ae**	**-īs**
ACC.	(-am)	(-ās)
ABL.	**-ā**	**-īs**

	SECOND DECLENSION	
	SINGULAR	**PLURAL**
NOM.	-us	**-ī**
GEN.	**-ī**	**-ōrum**
DAT.	**-ō**	**-īs**
ACC.	(-um)	(-ōs)
ABL.	**-ō**	**-īs**

	THIRD DECLENSION	
	SINGULAR	**PLURAL**
NOM.	x	**-ēs**
GEN.	**-is**	**-um**
DAT.	**-ī**	**-ibus**
ACC.	(-em)	(-ēs)
ABL.	**-e**	**-ibus**

F. Decline each of the nouns below.

	SINGULAR	PLURAL
NOM.	nōmen	**nōmina**
GEN.	**nōminis**	**nōminum**
DAT.	**nōminī**	**nōminibus**
ACC.	**nōmen**	**nōmina**
ABL.	**nōmine**	**nōminibus**

	SINGULAR	PLURAL
NOM.	portus	**portūs**
GEN.	**portūs**	**portuum**
DAT.	**portuī**	**portibus**
ACC.	**portum**	**portūs**
ABL.	**portū**	**portibus**

	SINGULAR	PLURAL
NOM.	leō	**leōnēs**
GEN.	**leōnis**	**leōnum**
DAT.	**leōnī**	**leōnibus**
ACC.	**leōnem**	**leōnēs**
ABL.	**leōne**	**leōnibus**

	SINGULAR	PLURAL
NOM.	fīlum	**fīla**
GEN.	**fīlī**	**fīlōrum**
DAT.	**fīlō**	**fīlīs**
ACC.	**fīlum**	**fīla**
ABL.	**fīlō**	**fīlīs**

G. Translate these sentences into English.

1. Pastor gregem fovet. **The shepherd loves the flock.**

2. Tempestātem exspectābat. **She was expecting a storm.**

3. Gregem tempestās terrēbit. **The storm will frighten the flock.**

4. Pastor gregem vigilat et cūrat. **The shepherd watches over and takes care of the flock.**

5. Grex est tūtus et nōn errābit. **The flock is safe and will not wander.**

6. Coquus verū vigilābat. **The cook was watching over the spit.**

7. Soror frātrēs tondēbit. **The sister will give the brothers haircuts.**

8. Habetne leō cornua? **Does a lion have horns?**

9. Genua sunt magna et ridicula. **Knees are big and funny.**

10. Gelū gelidum ventum vehit. **A cold chill rides the wind.**

H. Answer true (T) or false (F) for each statement about Latin sentences. The first one is done for you.

    T   1. The subject always takes the nominative case.

    T   2. A command is a verb.

    T   3. Direct objects take the accusative case.

    F   4. Subject nouns must match a verb's gender.

    T   5. To form a question, you can add -*ne* to the end of a verb.

    F   6. A noun's genitive singular form tells you which conjugation it's in.

    T   7. The accusative singular ending for the third declension is -*em*.

    T   8. To find the base of a noun, you drop the genitive singular ending.

    F   9. The stem of a verb is also a plural command.

    F   10. *Terreō* is an "ā" family verb.

Week 25 Quiz

name:

A. Chants

Write the chant for this week and answer the questions about it.

	SINGULAR	PLURAL
NOM.		
GEN.		
DAT.		
ACC.		
ABL.		

1. The genitive singular ending for the fourth declension is _____.

2. How can you tell if a noun is in the fourth declension neuter? _____

_____

Label each noun's declension (1, 2, 3, or 4) and gender (M, F, or N). Then decline it.

DECLENSION _____ GENDER _____   DECLENSION _____ GENDER _____

	SINGULAR	PLURAL
NOM.	gelū	
GEN.		
DAT.		
ACC.		
ABL.		

	SINGULAR	PLURAL
NOM.	grex	
GEN.		
DAT.		
ACC.		
ABL.		

B. Vocabulary

Translate these sentences into English.

1. Alba rēgīna nivēs et gelū cumulat. _____

2. Bonus satyrus albam rēgīnam nōn fovet. _____

3. Satyrus puellam cūrābat et vigilābat. _____

4. Mīrus leō clam exspectat. _____

5. Rēgīna et leō pugnābunt. _____

6. Improba rēgīna leōnem fīdum exanimat. _____

7. Leō repente vīvit! _____

8. Rēgīnane erō tūta? _____

C. Quotation

Answer the following questions about this week's quotation.

1. Write in Latin, "The wolf attacks with his fang, the bull with its horn." _____

_____

2. Which word means "horn"? _____

3. What is its gender and number? _____

3. Which word means "wolf"? _____

4. What is its case and number? _____

D. Derivatives

Give one derivative for each of the following Latin words.

1. grex _____   2. cornū _____

Week 25 Quiz: Answer Key

A. Chants

Write the chant for this week and answer the questions about it.

	SINGULAR	PLURAL
NOM.	-ū	-ua
GEN.	-ūs	-uum
DAT.	-ū	-ibus
ACC.	-ū	-ua
ABL.	-ū	-ibus

1. The genitive singular ending for the fourth declension is **_-ūs._**

2. How can you tell if a noun is in the fourth declension neuter? **All fourth declension neuter**

nouns have _-ūs_ as their genitive singular ending and _-ū_ as their nominative singular ending.

Label each noun's declension (1, 2, 3, or 4) and gender (M, F, or N). Then decline it.

DECLENSION **4** GENDER **N**

	SINGULAR	PLURAL
NOM.	gelū	gelua
GEN.	gelūs	geluum
DAT.	gelū	gelibus
ACC.	gelū	gelua
ABL.	gelū	gelibus

DECLENSION **3** GENDER **M**

	SINGULAR	PLURAL
NOM.	grex	gregēs
GEN.	gregis	gregum
DAT.	gregī	gregibus
ACC.	gregem	gregēs
ABL.	grege	gregibus

B. Vocabulary

Translate these sentences into English.

1. Alba rēgīna nivēs et gelū cumulat. **The white queen piles up snow and frost.**

2. Bonus satyrus albam rēgīnam nōn fovet. **The good faun does not cherish the white queen.**

3. Satyrus puellam cūrābat et vigilābat. **The faun was caring for and guarding the girl.**

4. Mīrus leō clam exspectat. **A wonderful lion is secretly waiting.**

5. Rēgīna et leō pugnābunt. **The lion and the queen will fight.**

6. Improba rēgīna leōnem fīdum exanimat. **The wicked queen kills the faithful lion.**

7. Leō repente vīvit! **The lion suddenly lives!**

8. Rēgīnane erō tūta? **Will the queen be safe?**

C. Quotation

Answer the following questions about this week's quotation.

1. Write in Latin, "The wolf attacks with his fang, the bull with its horn." **Dente lupus, cornū taurus**

petit.

2. Which word means "horn"? **cornū**

3. What is its gender and number? **neuter, singular**

3. Which word means "wolf"? **lupus**

4. What is its case and number? **nominative, singular**

D. Derivatives

Give one derivative for each of the following Latin words. **Answers will vary and will need to be checked individually.**

1. grex **gregarious, segregate, congregation**   2. cornū **unicorn, cornucopia, corner**

Teaching Notes: Week 26

1. Word List: Introduce the Word List for Week 26. Notice that Words #12 and #13 have similar meanings—*flagrō* is used when an object itself is on fire (e.g., the wood is burning); *incendō* is used when someone is setting an object on fire (e.g., we are setting the wood on fire).

Review this list throughout the week. Continue to review vocabulary from previous weeks.

2. Derivatives: Discuss derivatives for this week's vocabulary:

1. arbor, *tree:* arbor, arboreal, aboretum
2. fulmen, *lightning, thunderbolt:* fulminate
3. imber, *rain*
4. lignum, *wood, timber*
5. lutum, *mud:* lutarious
6. nūbēs, *cloud, gloom*
7. rādix, *root:* radish, radical, eradicate
8. rāmus, *branch, twig:* ramification

9. tonitrus, *thunder*
10. mox, *soon*
11. cadō, *I fall, sink, drop:* cadence, cascade, casualty, decadent, incidental, occident
12. flagrō, *I blaze, flame, burn:* flagrant, conflagration
13. incendō, *I kindle, set on fire:* incendiary
14. tangō, *I touch, strike:* tactful, tangible, tactile, tangent, contiguous, contingent
15. vastō, *I devastate, lay waste:* devastate

Have the students write this week's derivatives in the Week 26 "Derivatives" section of their student book.

3. Chant: There is no new chant this week. Continue to practice and review last week's fourth declension neuter chant, as well as the chants you've learned in previous weeks.

4. Quotation: This week's quotation comes from Matthew 12:33, " Either make the tree good and its fruit good, or make the tree bad and its fruit bad; for the tree is known by its fruit."

Have the students write this week's quotation in the Week 26 "Quotation" section of their student book.

5. Worksheet: Follow the directions given to complete the worksheet.

6. Quiz: Administer Quiz 26 at the end of the week.

WEEK 26

Word List

NOUNS

1. arbor, arboris (f) . . . . . tree
2. fulmen, fulmenis (n) . . . lightning, thunderbolt
3. imber, imbris (m) . . . . . rain
4. lignum, -ī (n) . . . . wood, timber
5. lutum, -ī (n) . . . . mud
6. nūbēs, nūbis (f) . . . . . cloud, gloom
7. rādix, rādīcis (f) . . . . . root
8. rāmus, -ī (m) . . . . branch, twig
9. tonitrus, -ūs (m) . . . . . thunder

ADVERBS

10. mox . . . . soon

VERBS

11. cadō, cadere . . . . I fall, sink, drop
12. flagrō, flagrāre . . . . . I blaze, flame, burn
13. incendō, incendere . . . I kindle, set on fire
14. tangō, tangere . . . . . . I touch, strike
15. vastō, vastāre . . . . . . I devastate, lay waste

Chant:

No new chant this week.

> **Quotation:**
>
> *Frūctū cognoscitur arbor*—"The tree is known by its fruit"

Weekly Worksheet 26: Answer Key

A. For each noun, write its declension and gender on the line above, then decline it.

DECLENSION __4__ GENDER __N__

	SINGULAR	PLURAL
NOM.	pecū	pecua
GEN.	pecūs	pecuum
DAT.	pecū	pecibus
ACC.	pecū	pecua
ABL.	pecū	pecibus

DECLENSION __4__ GENDER __M__

	SINGULAR	PLURAL
NOM.	tonitrus	tonitrūs
GEN.	tonitrūs	tonitruum
DAT.	tonitruī	tonitribus
ACC.	tonitrum	tonitrūs
ABL.	tonitrū	tonitribus

DECLENSION __3__ GENDER __N__

	SINGULAR	PLURAL
NOM.	fulmen	fulmena
GEN.	fulmenis	fulmenum
DAT.	fulmenī	fulmenibus
ACC.	fulmen	fulmena
ABL.	fulmene	fulmenibus

DECLENSION __4__ GENDER __N__

	SINGULAR	PLURAL
NOM.	genū	genua
GEN.	genūs	genuum
DAT.	genū	genibus
ACC.	genū	genua
ABL.	genū	genibus

B. Give the gender, case, and number of these nouns. Gender: masculine (M), feminine (F), or neuter (N). Case: nominative (NOM) or accusative (ACC). Number: singular (SG) or plural (PL). The first one is done for you.

1. tellūrem __F ACC SG__
2. rādix __F NOM SG__
3. rāmum __M ACC SG__
4. portus __M NOM SG__
5. umbrās __F ACC PL__
6. tempestātem __F ACC SG__
7. leō __M NOM SG__
8. cornū __N NOM SG__ or __N ACC SG__

C. Underline the adjective that matches the noun's number, gender, and case. Then translate the phrase.

NOUN	ADJECTIVE	TRANSLATION
1. Rādix	rubrum / **rubra**	**a red radish**
2. Nūbēs	**opācās** / opācus	**the dark clouds**
3. Ligna	ūmidum / **ūmida**	**wet wood**
4. Rāmī	nova / **novī**	**the new branches**
5. Tonitrus	**foedus** / foeda	**horrible thunder**
6. Manus	pulvereus / **pulverea**	**a dusty hand**
7. Verūa	antīquae / **antīqua**	**the ancient javelins**
8. Arborem	firmum / **firmam**	**a strong tree**

D. Conjugate each verb in the given tense.

Tondeō—Present Tense

LATIN

	SINGULAR	PLURAL
1ST	tondēō	tondēmus
2ND	tondēs	tondētis
3RD	tondet	tondent

ENGLISH

	SINGULAR	PLURAL
1ST	I clip	we clip
2ND	you clip	you all clip
3RD	he/she/it clips	they clip

Cadō—Future Tense

LATIN

	SINGULAR	PLURAL
1ST	cadam	cadēmus
2ND	cadēs	cadētis
3RD	cadet	cadent

ENGLISH

	SINGULAR	PLURAL
1ST	I will drop	we will drop
2ND	you will drop	you will all drop
3RD	he/she/it will drop	they will drop

Vastō—Imperfect Tense

	LATIN			ENGLISH	
	SINGULAR	**PLURAL**		**SINGULAR**	**PLURAL**
1ST	**vastābam**	**vastābāmus**		I was devastating	we were devastating
2ND	**vastābās**	**vastābātis**		you were devastating	you were all devastating
3RD	**vastābat**	**vastābant**		he/she/it was devastating	they were devastating

E. Translate these sentences into English.

1. Fulmen arborem antīquam incendit. **A thunderbolt set the ancient tree on fire.**

2. Tempestās gelida flōrēs vastat. **The cold weather is devastating the flowers.**

3. Cadentne imbrēs mox? **Will the rains fall soon?**

4. Cyclops gregem tondēbat. **The cyclops was shearing the flock.**

5. Arbor rādicēs firmās crescēbat. **The tree was growing firm roots.**

6. Leōnem videt et vītat. **He sees and avoids the lion.**

7. Ligna flagrant et nivēs cadunt. **The wood is burning and snow is falling.**

8. Pater mātrem fovet. **The father cherishes the mother.**

9. Timēbātisne tonitrum? **Do you all fear thunder?**

10. Nivēs frātrēs removēbant. **The brothers were removing the snow.**

F. Pick a subject, verb, and direct object and write your own sentence, using the words from Weeks 25 and 26. Write it in English first, and then translate it into Latin. **Answers will vary and will need to be checked individually. Sample answers are provided below.**

Elephantus lutum habet. The elephant is holding mud.

Leōnēs pecū terrēbant. The lions were terrifying the flock.

G. Label the *corpus* of the *leō* using the Latin terms below!

crūs   nasus   caput   cauda   oculus   latus   coma
pēs   ōs

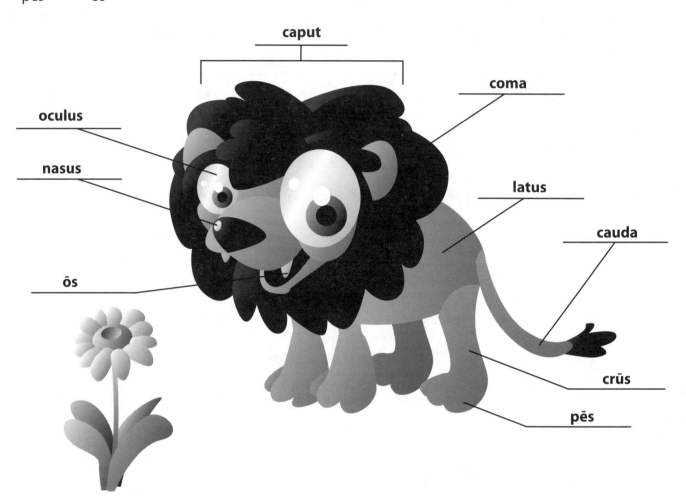

caput

coma

oculus

nasus

latus

cauda

ōs

crūs

pēs

H. Use your knowledge of Latin to match the English derivatives on the left with their definitions on the right! Write the letter of the correct definition in the blank.

D	1. radish	a) a violent windstorm
E	2. florist	b) a waterfall
C	3. vigilant	c) watchful
A	4. tempest	d) a root vegetable
B	5. cascade	e) a person who grows or sells flowers

Week 26 Quiz

name:

A. Chants

Complete the noun ending chants. Then circle all of the nominative and accusative endings.

2ND DECLENSION NEUTER

	SINGULAR	PLURAL
NOM.		
GEN.		
DAT.		
ACC.		
ABL.		

3RD DECLENSION NEUTER

	SINGULAR	PLURAL
NOM.		
GEN.		
DAT.		
ACC.		
ABL.		

4TH DECLENSION NEUTER

	SINGULAR	PLURAL
NOM.		
GEN.		
DAT.		
ACC.		
ABL.		

Conjugate *incendō* in the future tense.

LATIN

	SINGULAR	PLURAL
1ST		
2ND		
3RD		

ENGLISH

	SINGULAR	PLURAL
1ST		
2ND		
3RD		

B. Quotation

Answer the following questions about this week's quotation.

1. Write in Latin, "A tree is known by its fruit." _____

2. Which word means "tree"? _____

3. What is its case and number? _____

4. Which word means "fruit"? _____

5. What is its case and number? _____

C. Vocabulary

Underline the adjective that matches the noun's number, gender, and case. Then translate the phrase.

NOUN	ADJECTIVE	TRANSLATION
1. Pastōrēs	fīdum / fīdōs	_____
2. Tempestās	opācās / opāca	_____
3. Cornua	nova / novum	_____
4. Verū	caldum / calda	_____
5. Rādīcēs	tūtae / tūtōs	_____

Give the genitive singular form, gender (M, F, N), declension, and the English translation for each noun.

	NOUN	GENITIVE	GENDER	DECLENSION	TRANSLATION
1.	fulmen				
2.	tonitrus				
3.	cornū				

Translate the following sentences into English.

1. Porcī laetī lutum fovēbant. _____

2. Agricola gregēs mox tondēbit. _____

3. Fulmen domum parvam nōn tanget. _____

4. Caditne foliī? _____

5. Cultrum nōn tange! _____

Week 26 Quiz: Answer Key

A. Chants

Complete the noun ending chants. Then circle all of the nominative and accusative endings.

2ND DECLENSION NEUTER

	SINGULAR	PLURAL
NOM.	(-um)	(-a)
GEN.	-ī	-ōrum
DAT.	-ō	-īs
ACC.	(-um)	(-a)
ABL.	-ō	-īs

3RD DECLENSION NEUTER

	SINGULAR	PLURAL
NOM.	(x)	(-a)
GEN.	-is	-um
DAT.	-ī	-ibus
ACC.	(x)	(-a)
ABL.	-e	-ibus

4TH DECLENSION NEUTER

	SINGULAR	PLURAL
NOM.	(-ū)	(-ua)
GEN.	-ūs	-uum
DAT.	-ū	-ibus
ACC.	(-ū)	(-ua)
ABL.	-ū	-ibus

Conjugate *incendō* in the future tense.

	LATIN SINGULAR	LATIN PLURAL		ENGLISH SINGULAR	ENGLISH PLURAL
1ST	incendam	incendēmus		I will kindle	we will kindle
2ND	incendēs	incendētis		you will kindle	you all will kindle
3RD	incendet	incendent		he/she/it will kindle	they will kindle

B. Quotation

Answer the following questions about this week's quotation.

1. Write in Latin, "A tree is known by its fruit." **Fructū cognoscitur arbor.**

2. Which word means "tree"? **arbor**

3. What is its case and number? **nominative singular**

4. Which word means "fruit"? **fructū**

5. What is its case and number? **ablative singular**

C. Vocabulary

Underline the adjective that matches the noun's number, gender, and case. Then translate the phrase.

NOUN	ADJECTIVE	TRANSLATION
1. Pastōrēs	fīdum / **fīdōs**	**the faithful shepherds**
2. Tempestās	opācās / **opāca**	**the dark storm**
3. Cornua	**nova** / novum	**new horns**
4. Verū	**caldum** / calda	**the hot spit**
5. Rādīcēs	**tūtae** / tūtōs	**secure roots**

Give the genitive singular form, gender (M, F, N), declension, and the English translation for each noun.

	NOUN	GENITIVE	GENDER	DECLENSION	TRANSLATION
1.	fulmen	**fulmenis**	**N**	**3**	**lightning**
2.	tonitrus	**tonitrūs**	**M**	**4**	**thunder**
3.	cornū	**cornūs**	**N**	**4**	**horn**

Translate the following sentences into English.

1. Porcī laetī lutum fovēbant. **The happy pigs were loving the mud.**

2. Agricola gregēs mox tondēbit. **The farmer will soon shear the flocks.**

3. Fulmen domum parvam nōn tanget. **The lightning will not strike the little house.**

4. Caditne foliī? **Are the leaves falling?**

5. Cultrum nōn tange! **Do not touch the knife!**

Teaching Notes: Week 27

1. Word List: Introduce the Word List for Week 27. Review this list throughout the week. Continue to review vocabulary from previous weeks.

2. Derivatives: Discuss derivatives for this week's vocabulary:

1. carcer, *prison:* incarcerate
2. latrō, *robber*
3. lēx, *law:* legal, legislature, illegal, legislative, legitimate, privilege
4. mīles, *soldier:* military, militia
5. mūnus, *duty, office:* common, immune, commonwealth
6. pecūnia, *money:* pecuniary
7. sepulcrum, *tomb, grave:* sepulcher
8. avārus, *greedy:* avarice
9. ēgregius, *outstanding:* egregious
10. caveō, *I guard against, beware:* caution, cautious, precautionary
11. dēbeō, *I owe, ought:* debt, debtor, debit, due, endeavor, indebted, overdue
12. iaceō, *I lie down*
13. mereō, *I deserve, earn, am worthy of:* merit, demerit, meritorious
14. possum, *I am able:* potent, omnipotent, posse, possible, impossible
15. quaerō, *I search for, seek:* acquisition, conquistador, inquest, inquisition, query, require

Have the students write this week's derivatives in the Week 27 "Derivatives" section of their student book.

3. Chants: Introduce this week's chant, *possum. Possum* means "I am able." Students will most likely remember learning it last year.

Like the *sum* chant, its forms are irregular—not following any conjugation. (However, you can see that they are the forms of *sum* with "pot-" or "pos-" added at the beginning.)

Run through the chant several times, until students are comfortable again with saying it. *Possum* will be used quite a bit in this week's exercises.

4. Quotation: It's probably obvious that this week's quotation isn't classical (though somehow, you can imagine some of the ancient satirists using it)! This one is just for fun.

Have the students write this week's quotation in the Week 27 "Quotation" section of their student book.

5. Worksheet: This week, you'll be learning about a verb form called the *infinitive.* We use infinitives in English all the time! Some examples of English infinitives would be: *to walk, to run, to guard, to write, to search, to love, to climb, to think, to eat.*

In Latin, the infinitive and the second principal part of a verb are the same thing. (This means you've been memorizing infinitives all year, and you didn't even realize it!) Every Latin verb has a second principal part, which means every Latin verb has an infinitive.

The infinitive is simply translated "to —." For example, *captāre* means "to capture." *Nāre* means "to swim." Let's look at examples from this week's Word List.

caveō	*I guard against*	dēbeō	*I owe, ought*
cavēre	*to guard against*	dēbēre	*to owe, ought*

iaceō	I lie down	possum	I am able
iacēre	to lie down	posse	to be able
mereō	I deserve, earn	quaerō	I search for, seek
merēre	to deserve, earn	quaerere	to search for, seek

Pretty straightforward, right? Practice a few more from last week's Word List, until students are comfortable finding and translating the infinitives.

Next, we're going to look at how to use an infinitive in a Latin sentence. An infinitive can be used in several ways. In this book, you'll be using it as a direct object (I decided *to run*) and as a complementary infinitive, which completes the meaning of another verb (We are able *to go*).

One of the wonderful things about infinitives is that they never change or conjugate. Take a look at these sample sentences below (the infinitives are bolded). Do you see how the infinitive is simply added to the sentence?

Dēbēs **labōrāre.**	*You ought to work.*
Possum **tondēre.**	*I am able to give a haircut.*
Nōn potest **commendāre.**	*He is not able to commit.*
Potestisne **nāre?**	*Are you all able to swim?*
Latrōnem dēbēmus **quaerere.**	*We ought to search for the robber.*
Mīles meret **regnāre.**	*The soldier does not deserve to rule.*
Quiescō **somniāre.**	*I sleep to dream.*

While each of the sentences above could be translated without an infinitive, adding infintives makes them much more fun and interesting! Remember, even when translating with infinitives, always locate the main verb first.

Follow the directions given to complete the worksheet.

6. Quiz: Administer Quiz 27 at the end of the week.

WEEK 27

Word List

NOUNS

1. carcer, carceris (m) . . . . prison
2. latrō, latrōnis (m) . . . . . robber
3. lēx, lēgis (f) . . . . law
4. mīles, mīlitis (m) . . . . . soldier
5. mūnus, mūneris (n) . . . duty, office
6. pecūnia, -ae (f) . . . . . money
7. sepulcrum, -ī (n) . . . . tomb, grave

ADJECTIVES

8. avārus, -a, -um . . . . . . greedy
9. ēgregius, -a, -um . . . . . outstanding

VERBS

10. caveō, cavēre . . . . . . I guard against, beware
11. dēbeō, dēbēre . . . . . . I owe, ought
12. iaceō, iacēre . . . . . . I lie down
13. mereō, merēre . . . . . I deserve, earn, am worthy of
14. possum, posse . . . . . I am able
15. quaerō, quaerere . . . . I search for, seek

Chant:

Possum, *I am able*—Present Active
Irregular Verb

LATIN

	SINGULAR	PLURAL
1ST	possum	possumus
2ND	potes	potestis
3RD	potest	possunt

ENGLISH

	SINGULAR	PLURAL
1ST	I am able	we are able
2ND	you are able	you all are able
3RD	he/she/it is able	they are able

 Quotation:
Tē audīre nōn possum —"I can't hear you"

Weekly Worksheet 27: Answer Key

A. Answer the following questions.

1. In this week's Word List, *caveō* has two Latin forms. The first form, *caveō*, is called the **first principal part**.

2. Does every verb have a first form? **yes**

3. Write the second form of *caveō* given in the Word List: **cavēre**

4. The second form of a verb is called the **second principal part**.

5. The second principal part is also called the **infinitive**.

6. Does every verb have a second principal part? **yes**

7. Give the second principal part of *quaerō*: **quaerere**

B. Translate the following infinitives into English. The first one is done for you.

1. iacēre _____ to lie down _____

2. merēre _____ **to deserve, earn** _____

3. dēbēre _____ **to owe, ought** _____

4. cadere _____ **to fall, sink, drop** _____

5. habēre _____ **to have, hold** _____

6. tondēre _____ **to clip, shear** _____

7. appellāre _____ **to name, call** _____

8. tangere _____ **to touch, strike** _____

9. retinēre _____ **to hold back, retain** _____

10. posse _____ **to be able** _____

C. Translate these infinitives into Latin.

1. to beware _____ **cavēre** _____

2. to lay waste _____ **vastāre** _____

3. to care for _____ **cūrāre** _____

4. to watch over _____ **vigilāre** _____

5. to believe _____ **crēdere** _____

6. to entrust _____ **commendāre** _____

7. to trick _____ **lūdere** _____

8. to taste _____ **gustāre** _____

D. Each of these short sentences uses an infinitive. First, find the main verb, then underline the infinitive, and translate the sentence. The first one is done for you.

1. Potes <u>iacēre</u>. _____ You are able to lie down. _____

2. Mereō <u>edere</u>. _____ **I deserve to eat.** _____

3. Dēbēmus <u>amāre</u>. _____ **We ought to love.** _____

4. Possum <u>tondēre</u>. _____ **I am able to give a haircut.** _____

5. Dēbēs <u>cavēre</u>. _____ **You ought to beware.** _____

6. Potestis <u>cantāre</u> et <u>exsultāre</u>. _____ **You all are able to sing and dance.** _____

E. Write this week's chant in the box and translate it. Then answer the questions about it.

LATIN

	SINGULAR	PLURAL
1ST	possum	**possumus**
2ND	**potes**	**potestis**
3RD	**potest**	**possunt**

ENGLISH

	SINGULAR	PLURAL
1ST	**I am able**	**we are able**
2ND	**you are able**	**you all are able**
3RD	**he/she/it is able**	**they are able**

1. Does *possum* conjugate regularly or irregularly? **irregularly**

2. Is this a chant of a complete verb or of verb endings? **a complete verb**

F. Conjugate *dēbeō* in the present tense and translate it.

LATIN

	SINGULAR	PLURAL
1ST	dēbeō	**dēbēmus**
2ND	**dēbēs**	**dēbētis**
3RD	**dēbet**	**dēbent**

ENGLISH

	SINGULAR	PLURAL
1ST	**I ought**	**we ought**
2ND	**you ought**	**you all ought**
3RD	**he/she/it ought**	**they ought**

G. Give the stem of each verb, then write whether it is in the "ā" family (ā), "ē" family (ē), "e" family (e), or is irregular (IRR). Do not give a stem for irregular verbs.

1. flagrō, flagrāre _____**flagrā-**____**ā**____

2. mereō, merēre _____**merē-**____**ē**____

3. quaerō, quaerere _____**quaere-**__**e**___

4. possum, posse _____**IRR**_____

5. caveō, cavēre _____**cavē-**____**ē**____

6. incendō, incendere __**incende-**___**e**___

7. nō, nāre _____**nā-**_____**ā**___

8. iaceō, iacēre _____**iacē-**_____**ē**___

9. tangō, tangere _____**tange-**____**e**___

10. vastō, vastāre _____**vastā-**____**ā**___

H. For each noun, write its declension and gender on the line above, then decline it.

DECLENSION __**3**__ GENDER __**M**__

	SINGULAR	PLURAL
NOM.	mīles	**mīlitēs**
GEN.	**mīlitis**	**mīlitum**
DAT.	**mīlitī**	**mīlitibus**
ACC.	**mīlitem**	**mīlitēs**
ABL.	**mīlite**	**mīlitibus**

DECLENSION __**2**__ GENDER __**N**__

	SINGULAR	PLURAL
NOM.	sepulcrum	**sepulcra**
GEN.	**sepulcrī**	**sepulcrōrum**
DAT.	**sepulcrō**	**sepulcrīs**
ACC.	**sepulcrum**	**sepulcra**
ABL.	**sepulcrō**	**sepulcrīs**

DECLENSION __**4**__ GENDER __**N**__

	SINGULAR	PLURAL
NOM.	verū	**verua**
GEN.	**verūs**	**veruum**
DAT.	**verū**	**veribus**
ACC.	**verū**	**verua**
ABL.	**verū**	**veribus**

DECLENSION __**3**__ GENDER __**N**__

	SINGULAR	PLURAL
NOM.	mūnus	**mūnera**
GEN.	**mūneris**	**mūnerum**
DAT.	**mūnerī**	**mūneribus**
ACC.	**mūnus**	**mūnera**
ABL.	**mūnere**	**mūneribus**

I. Translate these sentences into English. Underline any infinitives.

1. Latrōnēs dēbent <u>labōrāre</u>. **The robbers ought to work.**

2. Legātus mīlitem egregium commemorat. **The lieutenant remembers the outstanding soldier.**

3. Merētne <u>regnāre</u>? **Does she deserve to rule?**

4. Latrō carcerem intrābit. **A robber will enter the prison.**

5. Pastor ferum pācābat. **The shepherd was pacifying the wild animal.**

6. Non possum <u>volāre</u>. **I am not able to fly.**

7. Mīles legem dēbet <u>commemorāre</u>. **A soldier ought to remember the law.**

8. Sepulcra mīra quaerēmus. **We will search for the strange graves.**

9. Rēx grȳphem avārum cavet. **The king guards against the greedy griffin.**

10. Agricolae agrōs properābunt <u>arāre</u>. **The farmers will hasten to plow the fields.**

J. Use your knowledge of Latin derivatives to circle the word that completes the definition.

1. A *sepulcher* is a _____.

   a) skyscraper   b) ghost   (c) tomb)   d) village

2. *Avarice* is a _____ desire for money and wealth.

   a) natural   (b) greedy)   c) funny   d) kind

3. If someone is *incarcerated,* he is put in _____ .

   a) oil   (b) prison)   c) space   d) a grave

4. An *insomniac* is a person who often cannot _____ .

   (a) sleep)   b) sing   c) lie down   d) eat

Week 27 Quiz

name:

A. Vocabulary

Translate each verb, then write whether it is in the first (1), second (2), or third conjugation (3).

1. dāre _____

6. rogāre _____

2. iacēre _____

7. incendere _____

3. cūrāre _____

8. cavēre _____

4. dēbēre _____

9. commūnicāre _____

5. exspectāre _____

10. quaerere _____

Fill in the blanks.

11. The infinitive of a Latin verb is also called the _____ .

12. Does every Latin verb have an infinitive? _____

13. Give the infinitive of *dēbeō:* _____

14. Give the infinitive of *possum:* _____

In each sentence, underline the main verb and circle subject nouns. Then translate the sentences into English.

15. Dux militēs dēbet curāre. _____

16. Latrō avārus pecūniam nōn meret. _____

17. Elephantum nōn exspectābāmus vehere! _____

18. Mīles sepulchrum intrābit. _____

19. Nōn dēbēmus peccāre. _____

20. Ligna ūmida possum incendere. _____

B. Derivatives

Use your knowledge of Latin to match the English derivatives on the left with their definitions on the right! Write the letter of the correct definition in the blank.

_____ 1. cautious   a) able to do anything

_____ 2. debtor   b) on guard, careful

_____ 3. omnipotent   c) against the law

_____ 4. illegal   d) someone who owes money

C. Chants

Conjugate and translate *possum*.

LATIN   ENGLISH

	SINGULAR	PLURAL		SINGULAR	PLURAL
1ST					
2ND					
3RD					

For each noun, write its declension and gender on the line above, then decline it.

DECLENSION _____ GENDER _____   DECLENSION _____ GENDER _____

	SINGULAR	PLURAL		SINGULAR	PLURAL
NOM.	pecū			metus	
GEN.					
DAT.					
ACC.					
ABL.					

Week 27 Quiz: Answer Key

A. Vocabulary

Translate each verb, then write whether it is in the first (1), second (2), or third conjugation (3).

1. dāre _____**to give**_____ **(1)**

2. iacēre _____**to lay down**___ **(2)**

3. cūrāre _____**to care for**____ **(1)**

4. dēbēre _____**to owe**_____ **(2)**

5. exspectāre ___**to wait for**____ **(1)**

6. rogāre _____**to ask**_____ **(1)**

7. incendere _____**to kindle**_____ **(3)**

8. cavēre _____**to beware**_____ **(2)**

9. commūnicāre __**to inform**_____ **(1)**

10. quaerere _____**to seek**_____ **(3)**

Fill in the blanks.

11. The infinitive of a Latin verb is also called the **second principal part**.

12. Does every Latin verb have an infinitive? **yes**

13. Give the infinitive of *dēbeō:* **dēbēre**

14. Give the infinitive of *possum:* **posse**

In each sentence, underline the main verb and circle subject nouns. Then translate the sentences into English.

15. (Dux) militēs dēbet curāre. **A leader ought to care for the soldiers.**

16. (Latrō) avārus pecūniam nōn meret. **The greedy robber does not earn money.**

17. Elephantum nōn exspectābāmus vehere! **We were not expecting to ride an elephant!**

18. (Mīles) sepulchrum intrābit. **The soldier will enter the tomb.**

19. Nōn dēbēmus peccāre. **We ought not to sin.**

20. Ligna ūmida possum incendere. **I am able to kindle the wet wood.**

B. Derivatives

Use your knowledge of Latin to match the English derivatives on the left with their definitions on the right! Write the letter of the correct definition in the blank.

___**B**___ 1. cautious   a) able to do anything

___**D**___ 2. debtor   b) on guard, careful

___**A**___ 3. omnipotent   c) against the law

___**C**___ 4. illegal   d) someone who owes money

C. Chants

Conjugate and translate *possum*.

LATIN

	SINGULAR	PLURAL
1ST	possum	possumus
2ND	potes	potestis
3RD	potest	possunt

ENGLISH

	SINGULAR	PLURAL
1ST	I am able	we are able
2ND	you are able	you all are able
3RD	he/she/it is able	they are able

For each noun, write its declension and gender on the line above, then decline it.

DECLENSION __4__ GENDER __N__

	SINGULAR	PLURAL
NOM.	pecū	pecua
GEN.	pecūs	pecuum
DAT.	pecū	pecibus
ACC.	pecū	pecua
ABL.	pecū	pecibus

DECLENSION __4__ GENDER __M__

	SINGULAR	PLURAL
NOM.	metus	metūs
GEN.	metūs	metuum
DAT.	metuī	metibus
ACC.	metum	metūs
ABL.	metū	metibus

Teaching Notes: Week 28

1. Word List: Introduce the Word List for Week 28. The "p" in Word #8, *psittācus,* is silent, as in "psalm." Review this list throughout the week. Continue to review vocabulary from previous weeks.

2. Derivatives: Discuss derivatives for this week's vocabulary:

1. camēlus, *camel:* camel
2. carō, *flesh, meat:* carnivore, carnage, carnal, carrion, incarnate, carnival
3. cȳgnus, *swan:* cygnet
4. herba, *herb, grass:* herb, herbarium, herbivore, herbaceous, herbicide
5. hippopotāmus, *hippopotamus:* hippopotamus
6. hyaena, *hyena:* hyena
7. pardus, *panther, leopard:* leopard
8. psittācus, *parrot*
9. rhīnocerōs, *rhinoceros:* rhinoceros
10. serpēns, *serpent, snake:* serpent, serpentine
11. sīmia, *ape, monkey:* simian
12. ursa *or* ursus, *bear:* ursine
13. numquam, *never*
14. domō, *I tame, subdue*
15. mordeō, *I bite, sting:* morsel, remorse

Have the students write this week's derivatives in the Week 28 "Derivatives" section of their student book.

3. Chant: There is no new chant this week. Continue to practice and review the chants you've learned in previous weeks.

4. Quotation: This week's quotation is a common saying in English and finds its roots in Jesus' command in Matthew 10:16, "Behold, I send you out as sheep in the midst of wolves. Therefore be wise as serpents and harmless as doves." The phrase "wise as a serpent" may also call to mind Genesis 3:1a, "Now the serpent was more cunning than any beast of the field which the Lord God had made."

Have the students write this week's quotation in the Week 28 "Quotation" section of their student book.

5. Worksheet: Follow the directions given to complete the worksheet.

6. Quiz: Administer Quiz 28 at the end of the week.

WEEK 28

Word List

NOUNS

1. camēlus, -ī (m) . . . . camel
2. carō, carnis (f). . . . . meat, flesh
3. cȳgnus, -ī (m) . . . . swan
4. herba, -ae (f) . . . . herb, grass
5. hippopotāmus, -ī (m) . . . . . hippopotamus
6. hyaena, -ae (f). . . . . hyena
7. pardus, -ī (m) . . . . panther, leopard
8. psittācus, -ī (m) . . . . parrot
9. rhīnocerōs, rhīnocerōtis (m) . rhinoceros

10. serpēns, serpentis (m/f) . . .serpent, snake
11. sīmia, -ae (f) . . . . ape, monkey
12. ursa, -ae (f) *or* ursus, -ī (m) . bear

ADVERBS

13. numquam . . . . never

VERBS

14. domō, domāre . . . . I tame, subdue
15. mordeō, mordēre . . . . . . I bite, sting

Chant:

No new chant this week.

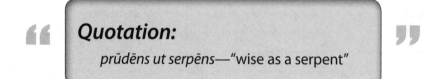

Quotation:

prūdēns ut serpēns—"wise as a serpent"

Weekly Worksheet 28: Answer Key

A. For each noun, write its declension and gender on the line above, then decline it.

DECLENSION **2**   GENDER **M**

	SINGULAR	PLURAL
NOM.	pardus	**pardī**
GEN.	**pardī**	**pardōrum**
DAT.	**pardō**	**pardīs**
ACC.	**pardum**	**pardōs**
ABL.	**pardō**	**pardīs**

DECLENSION **3**   GENDER **F**

	SINGULAR	PLURAL
NOM.	carō	**carnēs**
GEN.	**carnis**	**carnum**
DAT.	**carnī**	**carnibus**
ACC.	**carnem**	**carnēs**
ABL.	**carne**	**carnibus**

DECLENSION **4**   GENDER **M**

	SINGULAR	PLURAL
NOM.	spīritus	**spīritūs**
GEN.	**spīritūs**	**spīrituum**
DAT.	**spīrituī**	**spīritibus**
ACC.	**spīritum**	**spīritūs**
ABL.	**spīritū**	**spīritibus**

DECLENSION **1**   GENDER **F**

	SINGULAR	PLURAL
NOM.	**sīmia**	**sīmiae**
GEN.	**sīmiae**	**sīmiārum**
DAT.	**sīmiae**	**sīmiīs**
ACC.	**sīmiam**	**sīmiās**
ABL.	**sīmiā**	**sīmiīs**

B. Translate the following infinitives into English.

1. mordēre   **to bite, sting**

2. peccāre   **to sin**

3. domāre   **to tame, subdue**

4. gaudēre   **to rejoice**

5. commendāre   **to commit, entrust**

6. hiemāre   **to spend the winter**

7. repudiāre   **to reject, scorn**

8. cūrāre   **to care for**

C. Translate these infinitives into Latin.

1. to owe **dēbēre**

2. to seek **quaerere**

3. to devastate **vastāre**

4. to fall **cadere**

5. to lie down **iacēre**

6. to be able **posse**

D. Conjugate *mordeō* in the present, future, and imperfect tenses.

Present Tense

LATIN

	SINGULAR	PLURAL
1ST	mordeō	**mordēmus**
2ND	**mordēs**	**mordētis**
3RD	**mordet**	**mordent**

ENGLISH

	SINGULAR	PLURAL
1ST	**I bite**	**we bite**
2ND	**you bite**	**you all bite**
3RD	**he/she/it bites**	**they bite**

Future Tense

LATIN

	SINGULAR	PLURAL
1ST	**mordēbō**	**mordēbimus**
2ND	**mordēbis**	**mordēbitis**
3RD	**mordēbit**	**mordēbunt**

ENGLISH

	SINGULAR	PLURAL
1ST	**I was biting**	**we were biting**
2ND	**you were biting**	**you all were biting**
3RD	**he/she/it was biting**	**they were biting**

Imperfect Tense

LATIN

	SINGULAR	PLURAL
1ST	**mordēbam**	**mordēbāmus**
2ND	**mordēbās**	**mordēbātis**
3RD	**mordēbat**	**mordēbant**

ENGLISH

	SINGULAR	PLURAL
1ST	**I will bite**	**we will bite**
2ND	**you will bite**	**you all will bite**
3RD	**he/she/it will bite**	**they will bite**

E. Translate these sentences into Latin.

1. The woman was taming a blue parrot. **Femina caeruleum psittācum domābat.**

2. Do you see the yellow dragon? **Vidēsne flavum dracōnem?**

3. The swans are not able to bite. **Cȳgnī nōn possunt mordēre.**

4. Always beware! (plural) **Semper cavēte!**

F. On the lines below, give the Latin word for each zoo animal!

1. **caper**   2. **sīmia**   3. **cȳgnus**   4. **rhīnocerōs**

5. **tigris**   6. **psittācus**   7. **hippopotāmus**   8. **elephantus**

G. Translate these sentences into English.

1. Cȳgnī et psittācī possunt volāre. **Swans and parrots are able to fly.**

2. Mīlites sepulchrum vigilābant. **The soldiers were guarding the tomb.**

3. Numquam mordē! **Never bite!**

4. Frāter camēlum vehēbat. **The brother was riding a camel.**

5. Homō caecus lūcem nōn potest vidēre. **The blind man is not able to see the light.**

6. Intratne lūx carcerem? **Does light enter the prison?**

7. Hyaenae improbae rident. **The wicked hyenas are laughing.**

8. Rēx avārus pecūniam amat. **The greedy king loves money.**

9. Rhīnocerōtem mox domābō! **Soon I will tame the rhinoceros.**

10. Potesne nāre? **Are you able to swim?**

H. Underline the adjective that matches the noun's number, gender, and case. Then translate the phrase.

NOUN	ADJECTIVE	TRANSLATION
1. Herba	ēgregiās / **ēgregia**	**an outstanding herb**
2. Sepulcra	album / **alba**	**white tombs**
3. Pardōs	maculōsa / **maculōsōs**	**the spotted leopards**
4. Serpēns	**pulcher** / pulchram	**a beautiful serpent**
5. Carō	dēliciōsus / **dēliciōsa**	**the delicious meat**
6. Sīmiae	**rīdiculae** / rīdicula	**funny monkeys**
7. Mīlitēs	fessus / **fessī**	**the tired soldiers**
8. Dracō	caldō / **caldus**	**a fiery dragon**

I. Fill in the blank by writing the noun in the correct case.

1. "flesh" in the genitive singular **carnis**

2. "trees" in the accusative plural **arborēs**

3. "snakes" in the nominative plural **serpentēs**

4. "swan" in the accusative singular **cȳgnum**

Week 28 Quiz

name:

A. Vocabulary

On the lines below, give the Latin word for each animal!

1._____   2._____   3._____   4._____

Give the masculine, feminine, and neuter *nominative plural* forms of these adjectives in Latin.

	ADJECTIVE	MASCULINE	FEMININE	NEUTER
5.	outstanding			
6.	greedy			
7.	safe			

Translate the following infinitives into English.

8. incendere _____ 11. fovēre _____

9. crēdere _____ 12. captāre _____

10. terrēre _____ 13. imperāre _____

Translate these infinitives into Latin.

14. to beware _____ 16. to sting _____

15. to tame _____ 17. to strike _____

Give the genitive singular form, gender (M, F, N), declension, and the English translation for each noun.

	NOUN	GENITIVE	GENDER	DECLENSION	TRANSLATION
18.	psittācus				
19.	serpēns				
20.	carō				
21.	sīmia				
22.	tonitrus				

Translate these sentences into English.

23. Hyaenae et pardī carnem edunt. _____

24. Ursōs numquam cibāte! _____

25. Amantne edere herbam hippopotāmī? _____

26. Serpēns dominum nōn mordēbat. _____

27. Psittācum salsum dēbemus appellāre. _____

B. Chants

Conjugate *sum* in the present tense.

LATIN

	SINGULAR	PLURAL
1ST		
2ND		
3RD		

ENGLISH

	SINGULAR	PLURAL
1ST		
2ND		
3RD		

Week 28 Quiz: Answer Key

A. Vocabulary

On the lines below, give the Latin word for each animal!

1. **ursa** *or* **ursus**   2. **hyaena**   3. **camēlus**   4. **pardus**

Give the masculine, feminine, and neuter *nominative plural* forms of these adjectives in Latin.

	ADJECTIVE	MASCULINE	FEMININE	NEUTER
5.	outstanding	**ēgregiī**	**ēgregiae**	**ēgregia**
6.	greedy	**avārī**	**avārae**	**avāra**
7.	safe	**tūtī**	**tūtae**	**tūta**

Translate the following infinitives into English.

8. incendere   **to set on fire**

9. crēdere   **to believe**

10. terrēre   **to frighten, terrify**

11. fovēre   **to cherish, love**

12. captāre   **to hunt**

13. imperāre   **to order**

Translate these infinitives into Latin.

14. to beware   **cavēre**

15. to tame   **domāre**

16. to sting   **mordēre**

17. to strike   **tangere**

Give the genitive singular form, gender (M, F, N), declension, and the English translation for each noun.

	NOUN	GENITIVE	GENDER	DECLENSION	TRANSLATION
18.	psittācus	**psittācī**	**M**	**2**	**parrot**
19.	serpēns	**serpentis**	**M/F**	**3**	**serpent, snake**
20.	carō	**carnis**	**F**	**3**	**flesh, meat**
21.	sīmia	**sīmiae**	**F**	**1**	**ape, monkey**
22.	tonitrus	**tonitrūs**	**M**	**4**	**thunder**

Translate these sentences into English.

23. Hyaenae et pardī carnem edunt. **Hyenas and leopards eat meat.**

24. Ursōs numquam cibāte! **Never feed the bears!**

25. Amantne edere herbam hippopotāmī? **Do hippopotamuses love to eat grass?**

26. Serpēns dominum nōn mordēbat. **The snake was not biting the master.**

27. Psittācum salsum dēbemus appellāre. **We ought to name the witty parrot.**

B. Chants

Conjugate *sum* in the present tense.

LATIN ENGLISH

	SINGULAR	PLURAL		SINGULAR	PLURAL
1ST	**sum**	**sumus**		**I am**	**we are**
2ND	**es**	**estis**		**you are**	**you all are**
3RD	**est**	**sunt**		**he/she/it is**	**they are**

Teaching Notes: Week 29

1. Word List: Introduce the Word List for Week 29. Review this list throughout the week. Continue to review vocabulary from previous weeks.

2. Derivatives: Discuss derivatives for this week's vocabulary:

1. aestās, *summer*
2. Carthāgō, *Carthage*
3. Eurōpa, *Europe:* Europe
4. fīnitimus, *neighbor*
5. Gallia, *Gaul*
6. hiems, *winter, bad weather:* hiemal
7. homō, *man, human being:* homo sapiens
8. Ītalia, *Italy:* Italy
9. Rōma, *Rome*
10. terminus, *end, boundary, limit:* terminal, term
11. celsus, *tall, high, lofty*
12. undique, *on/from all sides, from every direction*
13. vexō, *I vex, harass:* vex, vexation
14. vītō, *I avoid:* inevitable

Have the students write this week's derivatives in the Week 29 "Derivatives" section of their student book.

3. Chant: There is no new chant this week. Continue to practice and review the chants you've learned in previous weeks.

4. Quotation: This week, your quotation is a statement made by Pontius Pilate, the governor of the Roman province of Judea, during the trial of Jesus. After having Jesus scourged, Pilate brought Him out to the mobs who wanted to crucify Him, saying, "Behold the man!" (Jn. 19:1–5).

Have the students write this week's quotation in the Week 29 "Quotation" section of their student book.

5. Worksheet: In Exercise F, students will be asked to label a map. Though the ancient country divisions did not exactly correspond to our own, students may label the map according to modern boundaries (e.g., *Gallia* corresponds with modern day France).

Follow the directions given to complete the worksheet.

6. Quiz: Administer Quiz 29 at the end of the week.

WEEK 29

Word List

NOUNS

1. aestās, aestātis (f) . . . . summer
2. Carthāgō, Carthāginis (f) . . .Carthage
3. Eurōpa, -ae (f). . . . . . Europe
4. fīnitimus, -ī (m) . . . . . neighbor
5. Gallia, -ae (f). . . . . . . Gaul
6. hiems, hiemis (f) . . . . . winter, bad weather
7. homō, hominis (m). . . . man, human being
8. Ītalia, -ae (f) . . . . Italy
9. Rōma, -ae (f). . . . . . . Rome
10. terminus, -ī (m) . . . . . end, boundary, limit

ADJECTIVES

11. celsus, -a, -um . . . . . . .tall, high, lofty

ADVERBS

12. undique . . . . on/from all sides,
from every direction

VERBS

13. vexō, vexāre . . . . I annoy, harass
14. vītō, vītāre . . . . I avoid

Chant:

No new chant this week.

> ### Quotation:
>
> *Ecce homō!*—"Behold the man!"

Weekly Worksheet 29: Answer Key

A. Fill in the blanks.

1. The **accusative** case is used for direct objects.

2. A *direct object* receives the action of the **verb**.

3. A *verb* expresses **action** or a state of **being**.

4. The part of speech that *renames or identifies the subject* is called the **predicate noun**.

5. Which Latin case do you use for this part of speech? **nominative**

6. Which Latin case do you use for the subject? **nominative**

B. List each noun's gender, declension, and its nominative plural form. The first one is done for you.

	NOUN	GENDER	DECLENSION	NOMINATIVE PLURAL
1.	terminus	M	2	terminī
2.	hiems	F	3	hiemēs
3.	fīnitimus	M	2	fīnitimī
4.	ursa	F	1	ursae
5.	aestās	F	3	aestātēs
6.	carō	F	3	carnēs
7.	homō	M	3	hominēs
8.	sepulcrum	N	2	sepulcra
9.	mūnus	N	3	mūnera
10.	Gallia	F	1	Galliae

C. Circle all the *being verbs* below.

move   (are)   frighten   show   (is)   avoid

(am)   increase   teach   (will be)   sniff   (was)

D. Conjugate and translate *sum* in the present and future tenses.

Present Tense

LATIN

ENGLISH

	SINGULAR	PLURAL		SINGULAR	PLURAL
1ST	sum	sumus		I am	we are
2ND	es	estis		you are	you all are
3RD	est	sunt		he/she/it is	they are

Future Tense

LATIN

ENGLISH

	SINGULAR	PLURAL		SINGULAR	PLURAL
1ST	erō	erimus		I will be	we will be
2ND	eris	eritis		you will be	you all will be
3RD	erit	erunt		he/she/it will be	they will be

E. In each English sentence, underline subject nouns and circle predicate nouns. If there is a predicate noun, translate it into Latin and write it in the blank. (Hint: Remember which case the predicate noun takes!) The first one is done for you.

1. A <u>wolf</u> is a (wild animal.) _____ferus_____

2. <u>Little Red Riding Hood</u> was a (girl.) **puella**

3. <u>It</u> will not always be (summer.) **aestās**

4. <u>One</u> of the four seasons is (winter.) **hiems**

5. <u>Princess Aurora</u> will be the (queen.) **rēgīna**

6. The wicked <u>witch</u> was her (enemy). **inimīcus**

7. <u>Turkey</u>, <u>bacon</u>, and <u>ham</u> are all (meats.) **carnēs**

8. My favorite <u>city</u> in all the world is (Rome) **Rōma**

9. <u>Coco</u> is the (name) of our parrot. **nōmen**

F. For each sentence, first find the verb. Once you've found it, underline the subject and circle the predicate noun. Then translate the sentence into English.

1. <u>Fīlius</u> est (agricola.) **The son is a farmer.**

2. <u>Frātrēs</u> sunt (latrōnēs.) **The brothers are robbers.**

3. <u>Pastor</u> nōn est (nauta.) **The shepherd is not a sailor.**

4. <u>Hominēs</u> sunt (fīnitimī.) **The men are neighbors.**

5. Nōn sumus (gigantēs.) **We are not giants.**

G. Label the parts of each sentence: S for subject, V for verb, DO for direct object, and PN for predicate noun. Then translate the sentence into English.

    S   DO   V

1. Muscae equum undique vexant. **The flies are harrassing the horse on all sides.**

   S V PN

2. Fīlia est rēgīna. **The daughter is a queen.**

      V   DO

3. Portābisne pulvīnōs rubrōs? **Will you carry the red pillows?**

     S   V PN

4. Hominēs sunt legātī. **The men are lieutenants.**

    S   V   PN

5. Colōnī celsī sunt agricolae. **The tall settlers are farmers.**

     S   DO   V

6. Taurus ferus campum vastābit. **The fierce bull will devastate the plain.**

   S   DO V

7. Pecū umbram videt. **The cattle see the shade.**

    V   PN

8. Sumus discipulī rīdiculī. **We are funny students.**

        V   PN
9. Esne coquus? **Are you the cook?**

        S   V   PN
10. Fluvius erit terminus. **The river will be the boundary.**

F. Use a map, an encyclopedia, or the internet to find the following places and label them below.

    Carthāgō   Gallia   Ītalia   Rōma

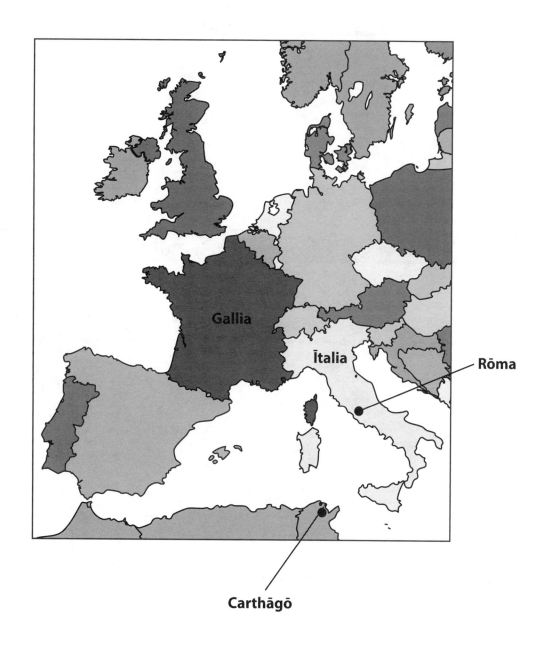

Week 29 Quiz

name:

A. Chants

Conjugate and translate *sum* in the present and future tenses.

Present Tense

LATIN

	SINGULAR	PLURAL
1ST		
2ND		
3RD		

ENGLISH

	SINGULAR	PLURAL
1ST		
2ND		
3RD		

Future Tense

LATIN

	SINGULAR	PLURAL
1ST		
2ND		
3RD		

ENGLISH

	SINGULAR	PLURAL
1ST		
2ND		
3RD		

B. Vocabulary

Fill in the blanks.

1. A *verb* shows _____ or state of _____ .

2. The part of speech that *renames or identifies the subject* is called the _____ .

3. Which Latin case do you use for this part of speech? _____

4. Which Latin case do you use for the subject? _____

5. The second principal part of a verb is also known as the _____ .

Translate these sentences into English.

6. Carthāgō est oppidum magnum. _____

7. Muscae rhīnocerōtem fessum vexābant. _____

8. Hiems numquam est calda. _____

9. Adulēscēns Rōmam dēbet vītāre. _____

10. Potesne habēre serpentem? _____

Give the genitive singular form, gender (M, F, N), declension, and the English translation for each noun.

	NOUN	GENITIVE	GENDER	DECLENSION	TRANSLATION
11.	Carthāgō				
12.	aestās				
13.	Gallia				
14.	terminus				
15.	sīmia				

C. Derivatives

Use your knowledge of Latin to match the English derivatives on the left with their definitions on the right! Write the letter of the correct definition in the blank.

_____ 1. inevitable   a) shaped or winding like a snake

_____ 2. serpentine   b) having to do with winter

_____ 3. incarcerate   c) a creature which eats only plants

_____ 4. hiemal   d) unavoidable

_____ 5. herbivore   e) to put in prison

Week 29 Quiz: Answer Key

A. Chants

Conjugate and translate *sum* in the present and future tenses.

Present Tense

LATIN

	SINGULAR	PLURAL
1ST	sum	sumus
2ND	es	estis
3RD	est	sunt

ENGLISH

	SINGULAR	PLURAL
1ST	I am	we are
2ND	you are	you all are
3RD	he/she/it is	they are

Future Tense

LATIN

	SINGULAR	PLURAL
1ST	erō	erimus
2ND	eris	eritis
3RD	erit	erunt

ENGLISH

	SINGULAR	PLURAL
1ST	I will be	we will be
2ND	you will be	you all will be
3RD	he/she/it will be	they will be

B. Vocabulary

Fill in the blanks.

1. A *verb* shows **action** or state of **being**.

2. The part of speech that *renames or identifies the subject* is called the **predicate noun**.

3. Which Latin case do you use for this part of speech? **nominative**

4. Which Latin case do you use for the subject? **nominative**

5. The second principal part of a verb is also known as the **infinitive**.

Translate these sentences into English.

6. Carthāgō est oppidum magnum. **Carthage is a large town.**

7. Muscae rhīnocerōtem fessum vexābant. **The flies were annoying the tired rhinoceros.**

8. Hiems numquam est calda. **Winter is never hot.**

9. Adulēscēns Rōmam dēbet vītāre. **The young man ought to avoid Rome.**

10. Potesne habēre serpentem? **Are you able to hold a snake?**

Give the genitive singular form, gender (M, F, N), declension, and the English translation for each noun.

	NOUN	GENITIVE	GENDER	DECLENSION	TRANSLATION
11.	Carthāgō	**Carthāginis**	**F**	**3**	**Carthage**
12.	aestās	**aestātis**	**F**	**3**	**summer**
13.	Gallia	**Galliae**	**F**	**1**	**Gaul**
14.	terminus	**terminī**	**M**	**2**	**end, boundary**
15.	sīmia	**sīmiae**	**F**	**1**	**ape, monkey**

C. Derivatives

Use your knowledge of Latin to match the English derivatives on the left with their definitions on the right! Write the letter of the correct definition in the blank.

D   1. inevitable   a) shaped or winding like a snake

A   2. serpentine   b) having to do with winter

E   3. incarcerate   c) a creature which eats only plants

B   4. hiemal   d) unavoidable

C   5. herbivore   e) to put in prison

Teaching Notes: Week 30

1. Word List: Introduce the Word List for Week 30. Review this list throughout the week. Continue to review vocabulary from previous weeks.

2. Derivatives: Discuss derivatives for this week's vocabulary:

1. būtūrum, *butter:* butter
2. crūstulum, *cookie, small cake*
3. farīna, *flour:* farina
4. lāc, *milk:* lactate, lactic
5. ōvum, *egg:* ovary, ovule, ovulation
6. patella, *plate, dish:* patella
7. pōculum, *cup*
8. sacchārum, *sugar:* saccharine, saccharide

9. sīve, *or*
10. bibō, *I drink:* imbibe
11. consecō, *I chop, cut up*
12. coquō, *I cook, bake:* cook
13. emō, *I buy, purchase:* exempt, peremptory, preemptive
14. eram, *I was*
15. frangō, *I break:* fraction, fractious, fragile, infraction, infringe, refract, refractory

Have the students write this week's derivatives in the Week 30 "Derivatives" section of their student book.

3. Chant: In Week 16, you learned the future chant for *sum*—*erō*. This week, you'll be introducing the imperfect form of *sum,* which is *eram,* meaning "I was."

Read through the chant starting in the top left corner: *eram, erās, erat, erāmus, erātis, erant.* Chant it a few times until students catch the rhythm and are comfortable saying it. Then chant through the English translation. Continue to review the chant each day during the week.

As you've probably already guessed, the *eram* chant works just like its parent chant, *sum. Sum* is an irregular verb, so *eram* is irregular also—not following the pattern of any conjugation. And like *sum, eram* is a complete verb, not a verb ending.

Here are some example sentences using predicate nouns and adjectives:

Eram latrō.	*I was a robber.*
Erās ēgregia!	*You were outstanding!*
Lāc numquam erat caldum.	*The milk was never warm.*
Erāmus architectī.	*We were inventors.*
Erātis novae.	*You all were new.*
Crūstula erant dēliciōsus.	*The cookies were delicious.*

4. Quotation: This week, your quotation is a handy question—one which may have frequently been asked of Roman mothers.

Have the students write this week's quotation in the Week 30 "Quotation" section of their student book.

5. Worksheet: Follow the directions to complete the worksheet.

6. Quiz: Administer Quiz 30 at the end of the week.

WEEK 30

Word List

NOUNS

1. būtūrum, -ī (n) . . . . . . butter
2. crūstulum, -ī (n) . . . . . cookie, small cake
3. farīna, -ae (f) . . . . flour
4. lāc, lactis (n) . . . . milk
5. ōvum, -ī (n) . . . . egg
6. patella, -ae (f) . . . . . . plate, dish
7. pōculum, -ī (n) . . . . . cup
8. sacchārum, -ī (n) . . . . sugar

CONJUNCTIONS

9. sīve . . . . or

VERBS

10. bibō, bibere . . . . I drink
11. consecō, consecāre . . . I chop, cut up
12. coquō, coquere . . . . . I cook, bake
13. emō, emere . . . . I buy, purchase
14. eram . . . . I was
15. frangō, frangere . . . . I break

Chant:

Eram, *I was*—Imperfect Active of *Sum*
Irregular Verb

LATIN

	SINGULAR	PLURAL
1ST	eram	erāmus
2ND	erās	erātis
3RD	erat	erant

ENGLISH

	SINGULAR	PLURAL
1ST	I was	we were
2ND	you were	you all were
3RD	he/she/it was	they were

Quotation:

Mihine crūstula coquēs?—"Will you bake cookies for me?"

Weekly Worksheet 30: Answer Key

A. Conjugate *sum* in the imperfect tense and translate it. Then answer the questions about it.

LATIN

ENGLISH

	SINGULAR	PLURAL
1ST	eram	**erāmus**
2ND	**erās**	**erātis**
3RD	**erat**	**erant**

	SINGULAR	PLURAL
	I was	**we were**
	you were	**you all were**
	he/she/it was	**they were**

1. Is *eram* a regular or irregular verb? **irregular verb**

2. Is *eram* an action verb or a being verb? **being verb**

B. For each noun, write its declension and gender on the line above. Then decline each noun by adding the endings to the base that is given. Each noun's nominative and genitive singular forms are provided.

DECLENSION __2__ GENDER __N__

	SINGULAR	PLURAL
NOM.	būtūrum	būtūr**a**
GEN.	būtūr**ī**	būtūr**ōrum**
DAT.	būtūr**ō**	būtūr**īs**
ACC.	būtūr**um**	būtūr**a**
ABL.	būtūr**ō**	būtūr**īs**

DECLENSION __3__ GENDER __N__

	SINGULAR	PLURAL
NOM.	lāc	lact**a**
GEN.	lactis	lact**um**
DAT.	lact**ī**	lact**ibus**
ACC.	lāc	lact**a**
ABL.	lact**e**	lact**ibus**

C. In each English sentence, underline the subject and circle the predicate noun. Then translate the predicate noun into Latin and write it in the blank. (Hint: Remember which case the predicate noun takes!)

1. The first <u>ingredient</u> is (butter.) **būtūrum**

2. Her <u>surprise</u> was a small (cake.) **crūstulum**

3. That <u>bird</u> is a(swan.) **cȳgnus**

4. <u>Italy</u> is a neighbor to(Gaul.) **Gallia**

5. A <u>birch</u> is a(tree.) **arbor**

D. Fill in the blanks.

1. The **accusative** case is used for direct objects.

2. A *direct object* receives the action of the **verb**.

3. A *verb* expresses **action** or **state of being**.

4. The part of speech that *renames or identifies the subject* is called the **predicate noun**.

5. Which Latin case do you use for this part of speech? **nominative**

E. Label the parts of each sentence: S for subject, V for main verb, DO for direct object, and PN for predicate noun. Then translate the sentence into English.

    S DO   V

1. Coquus ōva quattuor frangit. **The cook broke four eggs.**

    S V PN

2. Frāter est fīnitimus. **The brother is a neighbor.**

    DO   S/V

3. Crūstula dēliciōsa amō coquere! **I love to bake delicious little cakes!**

    S V PN

4. Ursī sunt ferī. **Bears are wild animals.**

    S   DO   V

5. Dux Eurōpam nōn potest vastāre. **The general is not able to devastate Europe.**

    DO   S   V

6. Carthāginem copiae undique vexābant. **Troops were harassing Carthage on all sides.**

    S/V   DO   DO   DO

7. Emēsne farīnam, lacte, sīve sacchārum? **Will you buy flour, milk, or sugar?**

    S   DO   V

8. Mīles ligna consecābat. **The soldier was chopping the wood.**

F. Each of the nouns below comes from a Latin root in either Word List 29 or 30. Figure out which of your Latin nouns is the root, and then give its English meaning.

	ITALIAN	SPANISH	FRENCH	LATIN	ENGLISH
1.	uomo	hombre	homme	**homō**	**man, human being**
2.	latte	leche	lait	**lāc**	**milk**
3.	farina	harina	farine	**farīna**	**flour**

G. Conjugate and translate *bibō* in the present, future, and imperfect tenses.

Present Tense

LATIN

	SINGULAR	PLURAL
1ST	**bibō**	**bibimus**
2ND	**bibis**	**bibitis**
3RD	**bibit**	**bibunt**

ENGLISH

	SINGULAR	PLURAL
1ST	**I drink**	**we drink**
2ND	**you drink**	**you all drink**
3RD	**he/she/it drinks**	**they drink**

Future Tense

LATIN

	SINGULAR	PLURAL
1ST	**bibam**	**bibēmus**
2ND	**bibēs**	**bibētis**
3RD	**bibet**	**bibent**

ENGLISH

	SINGULAR	PLURAL
1ST	**I will drink**	**we will drink**
2ND	**you will drink**	**you all will drink**
3RD	**he/she/it will drink**	**they will drink**

Imperfect Tense

	LATIN			ENGLISH	
	SINGULAR	PLURAL		SINGULAR	PLURAL
1ST	bibēbam	bibēbāmus		I was drinking	we were drinking
2ND	bibēbās	bibēbātis		you were drinking	you all were drinking
3RD	bibēbat	bibēbant		he/she/it was drinking	they were drinking

H. Below are *direct object* nouns. Underline the adjective that matches each noun's number, gender, and case. Then translate the phrase.

NOUN	ADJECTIVE	TRANSLATION
1. Farīnam	albās / **albam**	**white flour**
2. Būtūrum	flavus / **flavum**	**yellow butter**
3. Carthāginem	antīquus / **antīquum**	**ancient Carthage**
4. Rāmum	celsus / **celsum**	**the high branch**
5. Patellās	pulchrīs / **pulchrās**	**beautiful plates**
6. Cornū	**maculōsum** / maculōsōs	**a spotted horn**
7. Cantūs	laetum / **laetōs**	**joyful songs**
8. Gregēs	tūtum / **tūtōs**	**secure flocks**
9. Camēlōs	**avārōs** / avārās	**greedy camels**
10. Aestātem	**ēgregiam** / ēgregium	**an outstanding summer**

I. Answer the following questions about your Latin quotations.

1. Translate *Mihine crūstula coquēs?* into English. **Will you bake cookies for me?**

2. Which Latin word is the verb? **coques**

3. Is the verb in the "ā" family, the "ē" family, or the "e" family? **"e" family**

4. What Latin ending tells you that this is a question? **-ne**

Week 30 Quiz

name:

A. Chants

Conjugate and translate *eram.* Then answer the questions about it.

LATIN

	SINGULAR	PLURAL
1ST	eram	
2ND		
3RD		

ENGLISH

	SINGULAR	PLURAL

1. *Eram* is the _____ tense of _____ .

2. Is *eram* an action verb or a being verb? _____

Conjugate and translate *possum* in the present tense.

LATIN

	SINGULAR	PLURAL
1ST		
2ND		
3RD		

ENGLISH

	SINGULAR	PLURAL

B. Quotations

Answer the following questions about this week's quotation.

1. Translate *Mihine crūstula coquēs?* into English. _____

2. Is the verb present, future, or imperfect tense? _____

3. Is the verb in the 1st, 2nd, or 3rd person? _____

4. Which Latin word is the direct object? _____

5. What is the gender and number of the direct object? _____

C. Vocabulary

Translate the following sentences into English.

1. Rhīnocerōs est ferus. _____

2. Nōn frange pōcula sīve patellās! _____

3. Puellane erit rēgina? _____

4. Gigantēs rubram carnem coquēbant. _____

5. Farinam et ōva dēbēmus emere. _____

6. Adulēscentēs erunt fīnitimī. _____

7. Serpentēs lactem nōn possunt bibere. _____

8. Estne cēna calda sīve gelida? _____

9. Consecābisne mala et pira? _____

Decline *celsus* in the neuter and *avārus* in the feminine.

	SINGULAR	PLURAL		SINGULAR	PLURAL
NOM.					
GEN.					
DAT.					
ACC.					
ABL.					

Week 30 Quiz: Answer Key

A. Chants

Conjugate and translate *eram*. Then answer the questions about it.

LATIN

	SINGULAR	PLURAL
1ST	eram	erāmus
2ND	erās	erātis
3RD	erat	erant

ENGLISH

	SINGULAR	PLURAL
1ST	I was	we were
2ND	you were	you all were
3RD	he/she/it was	they were

1. *Eram* is the **imperfect** tense of **_sum_**.

2. Is *eram* an action verb or a being verb? **being verb**

Conjugate and translate *possum* in the present tense.

LATIN

	SINGULAR	PLURAL
1ST	possum	possumus
2ND	potes	potestis
3RD	potest	possunt

ENGLISH

	SINGULAR	PLURAL
1ST	I am able	we are able
2ND	you are able	you all are able
3RD	he/she/it is able	they are able

B. Quotations

Answer the following questions about this week's quotation.

1. Translate *Mihine crūstula coquēs?* into English. **Will you bake cookies for me?**

2. Is the verb present, future, or imperfect tense? **future tense**

3. Is the verb in the 1st, 2nd, or 3rd person? **2nd person**

4. Which Latin word is the direct object? *crūstula*

5. What is the gender and number of the direct object? **neuter plural**

C. Vocabulary

Translate the following sentences into English.

1. Rhīnocerōs est ferus. **The rhinoceros is a wild animal.**

2. Nōn frange pōcula sīve patellās! **Do not break the cups or plates!**

3. Puellane erit rēgina? **Will the girl be a queen?**

4. Gigantēs rubram carnem coquēbant. **The giants were cooking red meat.**

5. Farinam et ōva dēbēmus emere. **We ought to buy flour and eggs.**

6. Adulēscentēs erunt fīnitimī. **The young men will be neighbors.**

7. Serpentēs lactem nōn possunt bibere. **Snakes are not able to drink milk.**

8. Estne cēna calda sīve gelida? **Is the dinner hot or cold?**

9. Consecābisne mala et pira? **Will you cut up the apples and pears?**

Decline *celsus* in the neuter and *avārus* in the feminine.

	SINGULAR	PLURAL
NOM.	celsum	celsa
GEN.	celsī	celsōrum
DAT.	celsō	celsīs
ACC.	celsum	celsa
ABL.	celsō	celsīs

	SINGULAR	PLURAL
NOM.	avāra	avārae
GEN.	avārae	avārārum
DAT.	avārae	avārīs
ACC.	avāram	avārās
ABL.	avārā	avārīs

Teaching Notes: Week 31

1. Word List: Introduce the Word List for Week 31. Review this list throughout the week. Continue to review vocabulary from previous weeks.

2. Derivatives: Discuss derivatives for this week's vocabulary:

1. Brittania, *Britain:* Britain
2. eques, *horseman, knight:* equestrian
3. exercitus, *army:* exercise
4. Germānia, *Germany:* Germany
5. Hispānia, *Spain:* Hispanic
6. regnum, *kingdom*
7. tuba, *trumpet:* tuba
8. vadum, *ford, shallows:* wade
9. extrēmus, *last, farthest, outermost:* extreme, extremity
10. longinquus, *far away, distant*
11. quondam, *once, formerly*
12. equitō, *I ride (horseback)*
13. habitō, *I live in, dwell, inhabit:* habitat, inhabit, cohabitation

Have the students write this week's derivatives in the Week 31 "Derivatives" section of their student book.

3. Chant: There is no new chant this week. Take this opportunity to begin reviewing for the final exam. Students should be able to decline any first, second, third, or fourth declension noun, and should be able to conjugate any first, second, or third conjugation verb.

4. Quotation: This week's quotation is another one by the Roman lyric poet, Horace, taken from his *Odes* (3.12). Bellerophon was the legendary Roman hero who tamed and rode Pegasus, the divine winged horse. To be a better horseman than he was would be quite an accomplishment.

Have the students write this week's quotation in the Week 31 "Quotation" section of their student book.

5. Worksheet: The next two weeks' worksheets will focus on reviewing in preparation for the final exam.

In Exercise G, students will be asked to label a map. Though the ancient country divisions did not exactly correspond to our own, students may label the map according to modern boundaries (e.g., *Gallia* corresponds with modern day France).

Follow the directions to complete the worksheet.

6. Quiz: Administer Quiz 31 at the end of the week.

WEEK 31

Word List

NOUNS

1. Brittania, -ae (f) . . . . . Britain
2. eques, equitis (m) . . . . horseman, knight
3. exercitus, -ūs (m) . . . . . army
4. Germānia, -ae (f) . . . . . Germany
5. Hispānia, -ae (f) . . . . . Spain
6. regnum, -ī (n) . . . . . . kingdom
7. tuba, -ae (f) . . . . trumpet
8. vadum, -ī (n) . . . . ford, shallows

ADJECTIVES

9. extrēmus, -a, -um . . . . last, farthest, outermost
10. longinquus, -a, -um . . far away, distant

ADVERBS

11. quondam . . . . once, formerly

VERBS

12. equitō, equitāre . . . . . I ride (horseback)
13. habitō, habitāre . . . . . I live in, dwell, inhabit

Chant:

No new chant this week.

Quotation:

eques ipso melior Bellerophonte

"A better horseman than Bellerophon himself"

Weekly Worksheet 31: Answer Key

A. Answer the following questions about this week's Word List.

1. What are the two second declension nouns in this week's Word List? **regnum, vadum**

2. What is their gender? **neuter**

3. *Exercitus* and *lacus* look like second declension nouns. What tells you that they are not? **They both have -*us* as their genitive singular ending, which means they are in the fourth declension.**

B. Write each Latin word in the given form.

1. *latrō* in accusative singular **latrōnem**

2. *exercitus* in accusative singular **exercitum**

3. *mūrus* in accusative singular **mūrum**

4. *tuba* in accusative singular **tubam**

5. *puella* in accusative plural **puellās**

6. *regnum* in nominative plural **regna**

7. *vīcus* in nominative plural **vīcī**

8. *tellūs* in nominative plural **tellūrēs**

C. Conjugate and translate *eram*. Then answer the questions about it.

| | LATIN | | | ENGLISH | |
	SINGULAR	PLURAL		SINGULAR	PLURAL
1ST	eram	**erāmus**		**I was**	**we were**
2ND	**erās**	**erātis**		**you were**	**you all were**
3RD	**erat**	**erant**		**he/she/it was**	**they were**

D. Give the masculine, feminine, and neuter *accusative plural* forms of these adjectives in Latin.

	ADJECTIVE	MASCULINE	FEMININE	NEUTER
1.	last	**extrēmōs**	**extrēmās**	**extrēma**
2.	distant	**longinqōs**	**longinqās**	**longinqa**
3.	sunny	**apricōs**	**apricās**	**aprica**

E. Label each noun's declension (1, 2, or 3) and gender (M, F, or N). Then decline it.

DECLENSION **3** GENDER **M**

	SINGULAR	PLURAL
NOM.	**eques**	**equitēs**
GEN.	equitis	**equitum**
DAT.	**equitī**	**equitibus**
ACC.	**equitem**	**equitēs**
ABL.	equite	**equitibus**

DECLENSION **4** GENDER **M**

	SINGULAR	PLURAL
NOM.	**exercitus**	**exercitūs**
GEN.	exercitūs	**exercituum**
DAT.	**exercituī**	**exercitibus**
ACC.	**exercitum**	**exercitūs**
ABL.	**exercitū**	**exercitibus**

F. Translate these sentences into English.

1. Exercitūs Brittaniam vexābant undique. **The armies were harassing Britain on all sides.**

2. Brittania est īnsula. **Britain is an island.**

3. Estne Brittania īnsula parva? **Is Britain a small island?**

4. Agricola mūrum removēbit. **The farmer will remove the wall.**

5. Mīles salsus est poēta. **The witty soldier is a poet.**

6. Bovem quondam equitabam! **Once I was riding a cow horseback!**

7. Rēgīna Hispāniam longinquam habitāt. **The queen lives in distant Spain.**

8. Equus fīdus stabulum astābat. **The faithful horse was standing near the stable.**

9. Latrō quondam erat eques mīrus. **The robber was once a wonderful knight.**

10. Carthāgō erat regnum antīquum. **Carthage was an ancient kingdom.**

G. Use a map, an encyclopedia, or the internet to find the following places and label them below.

Brittania   Carthāgō   Gallia   Germānia   Hispānia   Ītalia   Rōma

H. Translate these commands into English.

1. Amīcum astā. **Stand by the friend.**

2. Pecūniam nōn amāte. **Do not love money.**

3. Arā terram. **Plow the land.**

4. Vītā hominēs improbōs. **Avoid wicked men.**

5. Occultā librum statim! **Hide the book immediately!**

I. Underline the predicate nouns in these sentences, then translate the sentence into Latin.

1. The letter was a <u>complaint</u>. **Epistula erat querēla.**

2. Britain and Spain are <u>kingdoms</u>. **Brittania et Hispānia sunt regna.**

3. The men will be outstanding <u>knights</u>. **Hominēs erunt ēgregiī equitēs.**

4. The girl will be a <u>teacher</u>. **Puella erit magistra.**

5. The fruits were <u>strawberries</u> and <u>bananas</u>. **Frūctūs erant frāga et ariēnae.**

J. Find and circle the hidden vocabulary words!

| vadum | eram | sive | psittacus | regnum | bibo |
| tuba | extremus | emo | Germania | undique | quondam |

Week 31 Quiz

name:

A. Vocabulary

Give the masculine, feminine, and neuter *accusative singular* forms of these adjectives in Latin.

	ADJECTIVE	MASCULINE	FEMININE	NEUTER
1.	lofty			
2.	outermost			

Provide the infintive, conjugation, and English translation of each verb.

	VERB	INFINITIVE	CONJUGATION	TRANSLATION
3.	iaceō			
4.	equitō			
5.	mordeō			
6.	emō			
7.	habitō			

Give the Latin translation for each word.

8. trumpet _____

9. Spain _____

10. formerly _____

11. flour _____

12. duty _____

13. parrot _____

In each sentence, underline the main verb and circle the subject. Then translate the sentence into English.

14. Quondam exercitus eram ēgregius. _____

15. Hydrum magnum dēbēs pugnāre. _____

16. Rēgīna lactem et saccarum habēbit. _____

17. Germāniane est longinquum regnum? _____

18. Pontum nōn amātis bibere. _____

B. Chants

Conjugate and translate *sum* in the future and imperfect tenses.

Future Tense

LATIN			ENGLISH		
	SINGULAR	PLURAL		SINGULAR	PLURAL
1ST					
2ND					
3RD					

Imperfect Tense

LATIN			ENGLISH		
	SINGULAR	PLURAL		SINGULAR	PLURAL
1ST					
2ND					
3RD					

C. Quotations

1. Write in Latin, "A better horseman than Bellerophon himself": _____

_____

2. What kind of "horse" did Bellerophon ride? _____

Week 31 Quiz: Answer Key

A. Vocabulary

Give the masculine, feminine, and neuter *accusative singular* forms of these adjectives in Latin.

	ADJECTIVE	MASCULINE	FEMININE	NEUTER
1.	lofty	**celsum**	**celsam**	**celsum**
2.	outermost	**extrēmum**	**extrēmam**	**extrēmum**

Provide the infintive, conjugation, and English translation of each verb.

	VERB	INFINITIVE	CONJUGATION	TRANSLATION
3.	iaceō	**iacēre**	**2**	**I lie down**
4.	equitō	**equitāre**	**1**	**I ride (horseback)**
5.	mordeō	**mordēre**	**2**	**I bite, sting**
6.	emō	**emere**	**3**	**I buy, purchase**
7.	habitō	**habitāre**	**1**	**I live in, dwell, inhabit**

Give the Latin translation for each word.

8. trumpet   **tuba**

9. Spain   **Hispānia**

10. formerly   **quondam**

11. flour   **farīna**

12. duty   **mūnus**

13. parrot   **psittācus**

In each sentence, underline the main verb and circle the subject. Then translate the sentence into English.

14. Quondam (exercitus) eram ēgregius. **Once, the army was outstanding.**

15. Hydrum magnum <u>dēbēs</u> pugnāre. **You ought to fight the large sea serpent.**

16. (Rēgīna) lactem et saccarum <u>habēbit</u>. **The queen will have milk and sugar.**

17. (Germāniane) est longinquum regnum? **Is Germany a distant kingdom?**

18. Pontum nōn <u>amātis</u> bibere. **You all do not love to drink seawater.**

B. Chants

Conjugate and translate *sum* in the future and imperfect tenses.

Future Tense

LATIN

ENGLISH

	SINGULAR	PLURAL		SINGULAR	PLURAL
1ST	erō	erimus		I will be	we will be
2ND	eris	eritis		you will be	you all will be
3RD	erit	erunt		he/she/it will be	they will be

Imperfect Tense

LATIN

ENGLISH

	SINGULAR	PLURAL		SINGULAR	PLURAL
1ST	eram	erāmus		I was	we were
2ND	erās	erātis		you were	you all were
3RD	erat	erant		he/she/it was	they were

C. Quotations

1. Write in Latin, "A better horseman than Bellerophon himself": **eques ipso melior Bellerophonte**

2. What kind of "horse" did Bellerophon ride? **Pegasus**

Teaching Notes: Week 32

1. Word List: Introduce the Word List for Week 32. This week's list is short to allow the maximum time to review prior Word Lists, in preparation for the Unit 4 Test.

2. Derivatives: Discuss derivatives for this week's vocabulary:

1. dīrigō, *I direct:* dirigible
2. pōnō, *I put, place:* deposit, expose, impostor, opponent, opposite
3. praedīcō, *I proclaim:* predicate, predict, predicament
4. vincō, *I conquer:* evict, invincible, vincible, vanquish, victor, convince

   Have the students write this week's derivatives in the Week 32 "Derivatives" section of their student book. Look over previous derivatives from Unit 4.

3. Chant: There is no new chant this week. Use this time to review the chants you've learned throughout the year. Students should be able to chant all of them and be comfortable with their use.

4. Quotation: There is no quotation this week. Look over quotations from this Unit and test the students' memory of the translations. (The final test will only cover quotations from Unit 4.)

5. Worksheet: Follow the directions given to complete the worksheet.

6. Quiz: Since there is a test at the end of the week, this week's quiz is optional. Feel free to use it as practice for the final test.

7. Test: The Unit 4 Test should be given at the end of this week. Congratulations on completing *Latin Primer 2!*

WEEK 32

Word List

VERBS

1. dīrigō, dīrigere . . . . . . I direct
2. pōnō, pōnere . . . . I put, place
3. praedīcō, pradīcere . . . I proclaim
4. vincō, vincere . . . . . . I conquer

Chant:

No new chant this week.

Quotation:

No new quotation this week.

Weekly Worksheet 32: Answer Key

A. Conjugate the following words in the present, future, and imperfect tenses.

Present Active

FIRST CONJUGATION

	SINGULAR	PLURAL
1ST	domō	domāmus
2ND	domās	domātis
3RD	domat	domant

SECOND CONJUGATION

	SINGULAR	PLURAL
1ST	caveō	cavēmus
2ND	cavēs	cavētis
3RD	cavet	cavent

THIRD CONJUGATION

	SINGULAR	PLURAL
1ST	pōnō	pōnimus
2ND	pōnis	pōnitis
3RD	pōnit	pōnunt

Future Active

FIRST CONJUGATION

	SINGULAR	PLURAL
1ST	domābō	domābimus
2ND	domābis	domābitis
3RD	domābit	domābunt

SECOND CONJUGATION

	SINGULAR	PLURAL
1ST	cavēbō	cavēbimus
2ND	cavēbis	cavēbitis
3RD	cavēbit	cavēbunt

THIRD CONJUGATION

	SINGULAR	PLURAL
1ST	pōnam	pōnēmus
2ND	pōnēs	pōnētis
3RD	pōnet	pōnent

Imperfect Active

FIRST CONJUGATION

	SINGULAR	PLURAL
1ST	domābam	domābāmus
2ND	domābās	domābātis
3RD	domābat	domābant

SECOND CONJUGATION

	SINGULAR	PLURAL
1ST	cavēbam	cavēbāmus
2ND	cavēbās	cavēbātis
3RD	cavēbat	cavēbant

THIRD CONJUGATION

	SINGULAR	PLURAL
1ST	pōnēbam	pōnēbāmus
2ND	pōnēbās	pōnēbātis
3RD	pōnēbat	pōnēbant

B. Give the function (subject, direct object, predicate noun), case, number, and Latin form of each underlined noun. The first one is done for you.

1. The dove's <u>wing</u> is broken. _____ subject, nominative, singular, āla

2. The <u>sailor</u> does not see the wave. _____ **subject, nominative, singular, nauta**_____

3. The <u>clouds</u> hide the sun. _____ **subject, nominative, plural, nūbēs**_____

4. The farmer is a <u>settler</u>. _____ **predicate noun, nominative, singular, colōnus**_____

5. A <u>rabbit</u> is approaching the hiding place. __ **subject, nominative, singular, cunīculus**_____

6. Those neighbors are <u>brothers</u>. _____ **predicate noun, nominative, plural, germānī**_____

7. The horse carries the <u>master</u>. _____ **direct object, accusative, singular, dominum**_____

8. The horse is avoiding the <u>spurs</u>. _____ **direct object, accusative, plural, stimulōs**_____

9. Suddenly the archer sees a <u>deer</u>. _____ **direct object, accusative, singular, cervum**_____

10. The boy is a <u>poet</u>. _____ **predicate noun, nominative, singular, poeta**_____

11. The woman will save the <u>sons</u>. _____ **direct object, accusative, plural, fīliōs**_____

C. Draw a line to match each derivative with its Latin root.

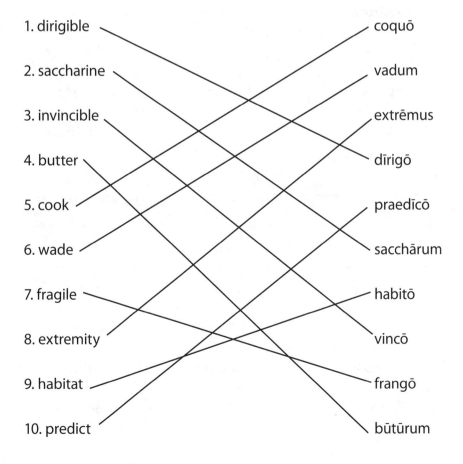

1. dirigible	coquō
2. saccharine	vadum
3. invincible	extrēmus
4. butter	dīrigō
5. cook	praedīcō
6. wade	sacchārum
7. fragile	habitō
8. extremity	vincō
9. habitat	frangō
10. predict	būtūrum

D. For each noun, give its declension and gender, then decline it.

DECLENSION ___4___ GENDER ___M___

	SINGULAR	PLURAL
NOM.	exercitus	exercitūs
GEN.	exercitūs	exercituum
DAT.	exercituī	exercitibus
ACC.	exercitum	exercitūs
ABL.	exercitū	exercitibus

DECLENSION ___2___ GENDER ___N___

	SINGULAR	PLURAL
NOM.	pōculum	pōcula
GEN.	pōculī	pōculōrum
DAT.	pōculō	pōculīs
ACC.	pōculum	pōcula
ABL.	pōculō	pōculīs

DECLENSION ___1___ GENDER ___F___

	SINGULAR	PLURAL
NOM.	tuba	tubae
GEN.	tubae	tubārum
DAT.	tubae	tubīs
ACC.	tubam	tubās
ABL.	tubā	tubīs

DECLENSION ___3___ GENDER ___N___

	SINGULAR	PLURAL
NOM.	lāc	lācta
GEN.	lāctis	lāctum
DAT.	lāctī	lāctibus
ACC.	lāc	lācta
ABL.	lācte	lāctibus

DECLENSION ___2___ GENDER ___M___

	SINGULAR	PLURAL
NOM.	cȳgnus	cȳgnī
GEN.	cȳgnī	cȳgnōrum
DAT.	cȳgnō	cȳgnīs
ACC.	cȳgnum	cȳgnōs
ABL.	cȳgnō	cȳgnīs

DECLENSION ___4___ GENDER ___F___

	SINGULAR	PLURAL
NOM.	domus	domūs
GEN.	domūs	domuum
DAT.	domuī	domibus
ACC.	domum	domūs
ABL.	domū	domibus

DECLENSION	3	GENDER	F

	SINGULAR	PLURAL
NOM.	aestās	**aestātēs**
GEN.	**aestātis**	**aestātum**
DAT.	**aestātī**	**aestātibus**
ACC.	**aestātem**	**aestātēs**
ABL.	**aestāte**	**aestātibus**

DECLENSION	4	GENDER	N

	SINGULAR	PLURAL
NOM.	verū	**verua**
GEN.	**verūs**	**veruum**
DAT.	**verū**	**veribus**
ACC.	**verū**	**verua**
ABL.	**verū**	**veribus**

E. Fill in the blanks.

1. The **accusative** case is used for direct objects.

2. A *direct object* receives the action of the **verb**.

3. A *verb* expresses **action** or **state of being**.

4. The part of speech that *renames or identifies the subject* is called the **predicate noun**.

5. Which Latin case do you use for this part of speech? **nominative**

6. Which Latin case do you use for the subject? **nominative**

F. Underline the adjective that matches the noun's number, gender, and case. Then translate the phrase.

NOUN	ADJECTIVE	TRANSLATION
1. Cunīculus	**albus** / albōs	**the white rabbit**
2. Rēgīna	ruber / **rubra**	**the red queen**
3. Regna	extrēmum / **extrēma**	**farthest kingdoms**
4. Lacūs	opācus / **opācī**	**the dark lakes**
5. Gigās	**salsus** / salsās	**the witty giant**
6. Hominem	**bonum** / bonōrum	**a good man**

7. Arbor   celsus / **celsa**   **a tall tree**

8. Equitēs   honestum / **honestī**   **the honorable knights**

G. Give the stem of each verb and which conjugation it's in. The first one is done for you.

	VERB	STEM	CONJUGATION
1.	vigilō, vigilāre	vigilā-	1
2.	mordeō, mordēre	**mordē-**	**2**
3.	equitō, equitāre	**equitā-**	1
4.	praedīcō, pradīcere	**pradīce-**	**3**
5.	vītō, vītāre	**vītā-**	1
6.	tangō, tangere	**tange-**	3
7.	caveō, cavēre	**cavē-**	2
8.	vincō, vincere	**vince-**	3

H. Translate these sentences into English.

1. Gallia erat provincia antīqua. **Gaul was an ancient province.**

2. Parva puella fungum edēbat. **The little girl was eating a mushroom.**

3. Dux vadum significat. **The leader is pointing out the ford.**

4. Lacus nunc est serēnus. **The lake is calm now.**

5. Lacus nōn erat serēnus herī. **The lake was not calm yesterday.**

6. Pontus erat longinquus. **The sea was distant.**

7. Tuba tardum exercitum dīriget. **A trumpet will direct the slow army.**

8. Edisne crūstulum sīve mālum? **Are you eating a cookie or an apple?**

9. Spēluncae erunt latebrae bonae. **The caves will be good hiding places.**

10. Metum amō vincere. **I love to conquer fear.**

I. In each sentence, first find the main verb. Then underline subjects, circle direct objects, and draw a box around predicate nouns. Finally, translate each sentence into Latin.

1. The <u>soldier</u> is a | giant. | **Mīles est gigās.**

2. The <u>knights</u> are | friends. | **Equitēs sunt amīcī.**

3. The <u>robber</u> was avoiding the (province.) **Latrō provinciam vītābat.**

4. The <u>sea</u> was the | boundary. | **Pontus erat terminus.**

5. <u>Rome</u> is not often conquered. **Rōma nōn saepe vincit.**

6. The <u>free towns</u> will change the (law.) **Mūnicipiī legem mūtābunt.**

7. The <u>brother</u> is not able to avoid the (neighbors.) **Frāter fīnitimōs nōn potest vītāre.**

8. The <u>boys</u> will be good | apprentices. | **Puerī erunt discipulī bonī.**

9. Did <u>you all</u> see a horrible (griffin?) **Vidētisne foedum grȳphem?**

10. Proclaim the (story!) **Pradīce (*or* pradīcete) fābulam!**

J. On the lines below, label what each animal is called in Latin.

1. **camēlus**   2. **noctua**   3. **lupus**   4. **bālaena**

Week 32 Quiz name:

A. Vocabulary

For each noun, give its genitive singular, gender (M, F, or N), declension (1, 2, 3, or 4), and English meaning.

	NOUN	GENITIVE	GENDER	DECLENSION	ENGLISH
1.	vadum				
2.	patella				
3.	fulmen				
4.	carcer				
5.	pardus				
6.	genū				
7.	manus				
8.	rādix				

For each verb, write its infinitive and which conjugation (1, 2, or 3) it's in.

9. dīrigō _____

10. vincō _____

11. tondeō _____

12. equitō _____

13. praedīcō_____

14. pōnō _____

In each sentence, find the main verb. Then underline subjects, circle direct objects, and draw a box around predicate nouns and predicate adjectives. Finally, translate each sentence into English.

15. Exercitus spērat vincere Brittaniam. _____

16. Īnsulae extrēmae sunt longinquae. _____

17. Frātrēs audent astāre rēgem. _____

18. Potesne emere pēgasum sīve grȳphem? _____

19. Argūmentum captīvum nōn līberābit. _____

20. Māter flōrēs nōn videt statim. _____

B. Derivatives

Use your knowledge of Latin to match the English derivatives on the left with their definitions on the right! Write the letter of the correct definition in the blank.

_____ 1. saccharine

_____ 2. deposit

_____ 3. tonsure

_____ 4. carrion

_____ 5. genuflect

a) a monk's haircut

b) money placed in the bank

c) rotten meat, usually a dead animal

d) to momentarily kneel on one knee

e) sweet, in a fake or unnatural way

C. Chants

Complete the noun ending chants.

3RD DECLENSION

	SINGULAR	PLURAL
NOM.		
GEN.		
DAT.		
ACC.		
ABL.		

4TH DECLENSION

SINGULAR	PLURAL

4TH DECLENSION NEUTER

SINGULAR	PLURAL

Week 32 Quiz: Answer Key

A. Vocabulary

For each noun, give its genitive singular, gender (M, F, or N), declension (1, 2, 3, or 4), and English meaning.

	NOUN	GENITIVE	GENDER	DECLENSION	ENGLISH
1.	vadum	**vadī**	**N**	**2**	**ford, shallows**
2.	patella	**patellae**	**F**	**1**	**plate, dish**
3.	fulmen	**fulmenis**	**N**	**3**	**lightning, thunderbolt**
4.	carcer	**carceris**	**M**	**3**	**prison**
5.	pardus	**pardī**	**M**	**2**	**panther, leopard**
6.	genū	**genūs**	**N**	**4**	**knee**
7.	manus	**manūs**	**F**	**4**	**hand**
8.	rādix	**rādīcis**	**F**	**3**	**root**

For each verb, write its infinitive and which conjugation (1, 2, or 3) it's in.

9. dīrigō   **dīrigere (3)**　　12. equitō   **equitāre (1)**

10. vincō   **vincere (3)**　　13. praedīcō   **pradīcere (3)**

11. tondeō   **tondēre (2)**　　14. pōnō   **pōnere (3)**

In each sentence, find the main verb. Then underline subjects, circle direct objects, and draw a box around predicate nouns and predicate adjectives. Finally, translate each sentence into English.

15. Exercitus spērat vincere Brittaniam. **The army hopes to conquer Britain.**

16. Īnsulae extrēmae sunt longinquae. **The outermost islands are far away.**

17. Frātrēs audent astāre rēgem. **The brothers dare to stand near the king.**

18. Potesne emere pēgasum sīve grȳphem? **Are you able to buy a pegasus or a griffin?**

19. Argūmentum captīvum nōn līberābit. **The evidence will not set the captive free.**

20. Māter flōrēs nōn videt statim. **The mother does not see the flowers immediately.**

B. Derivatives

Use your knowledge of Latin to match the English derivatives on the left with their definitions on the right! Write the letter of the correct definition in the blank.

E 1. saccharine

B 2. deposit

A 3. tonsure

C 4. carrion

D 5. genuflect

a) a monk's haircut

b) money placed in the bank

c) rotten meat, usually a dead animal

d) to momentarily kneel on one knee

e) sweet, in a fake or unnatural way

C. Chants

Complete the noun ending chants.

3RD DECLENSION

	SINGULAR	PLURAL
NOM.	x	-ēs
GEN.	-is	-um
DAT.	-ī	-ibus
ACC.	-em	-ēs
ABL.	-e	-ibus

4TH DECLENSION

	SINGULAR	PLURAL
NOM.	-us	-ūs
GEN.	-ūs	-uum
DAT.	-uī	-ibus
ACC.	-um	-ūs
ABL.	-ū	-ibus

4TH DECLENSION NEUTER

	SINGULAR	PLURAL
NOM.	-ū	-ua
GEN.	-ūs	-uum
DAT.	-ū	-ibus
ACC.	-ū	-ua
ABL.	-ū	-ibus

Unit 4 Test

name:

Chants

A. Conjugate the following words in the present, future, and imperfect tenses.

Present Active

FIRST CONJUGATION			SECOND CONJUGATION			THIRD CONJUGATION		
	SINGULAR	PLURAL		SINGULAR	PLURAL		SINGULAR	PLURAL
1ST	domō		1ST	caveō		1ST	pōnō	
2ND			2ND			2ND		
3RD			3RD			3RD		

Future Active

FIRST CONJUGATION			SECOND CONJUGATION			THIRD CONJUGATION		
	SINGULAR	PLURAL		SINGULAR	PLURAL		SINGULAR	PLURAL
1ST			1ST			1ST		
2ND			2ND			2ND		
3RD			3RD			3RD		

Imperfect Active

FIRST CONJUGATION			SECOND CONJUGATION			THIRD CONJUGATION		
	SINGULAR	PLURAL		SINGULAR	PLURAL		SINGULAR	PLURAL
1ST			1ST			1ST		
2ND			2ND			2ND		
3RD			3RD			3RD		

B. For each noun, give its declension and gender, then decline it.

DECLENSION _____ GENDER _____

	SINGULAR	PLURAL
NOM.		
GEN.	satyrī	
DAT.		
ACC.		
ABL.		

DECLENSION _____ GENDER _____

	SINGULAR	PLURAL
NOM.		
GEN.	bovis	
DAT.		
ACC.		
ABL.		

DECLENSION _____ GENDER _____

	SINGULAR	PLURAL
NOM.		
GEN.		
DAT.		
ACC.		būtūra
ABL.		

DECLENSION _____ GENDER _____

	SINGULAR	PLURAL
NOM.	īnsula	
GEN.		
DAT.		
ACC.		
ABL.		

DECLENSION _____ GENDER _____

	SINGULAR	PLURAL
NOM.		
GEN.		
DAT.		
ACC.		frūctūs
ABL.		

DECLENSION _____ GENDER _____

	SINGULAR	PLURAL
NOM.		
GEN.	capitis	
DAT.		
ACC.		
ABL.		

C. Below, decline the adjective/noun phrase. To the right, give the declension and gender of the noun, and the gender of the adjective.

	SINGULAR	PLURAL
NOM.	magnum pecū	
GEN.		
DAT.		
ACC.		
ABL.		

NOUN

Declension: _____

Gender: _____

ADJECTIVE

Gender: _____

1. What does this phrase mean? _____

D. Conjugate *sum* in the present, future, and imperfect tenses.

Present Active

	SINGULAR	PLURAL
1ST		
2ND		
3RD		

Future Active

	SINGULAR	PLURAL

Imperfect Active

	SINGULAR	PLURAL

Vocabulary

E. Fill in the blanks.

1. The _____ case is used for subjects and predicate nouns.

2. A predicate noun _____ or _____ the subject.

3. Predicate nouns and predicate adjectives both follow a _____ verb.

4. The _____ case is used for direct objects.

5. A direct object _____ the action of the verb.

6. A verb expresses _____ or a state of _____ .

7. The second principal part of a Latin verb is also called the _____ .

8. Does every Latin verb have an infinitive? _____

9. To form a question in Latin, _____ is added to the first word in the sentence.

10. When you tell a dog, "Roll over!", you're giving it a _____ .

11. What is another word for "command"? _____

12. To give a singular command, you use the _____ of the verb.

13. To give a plural command using a first or second conjugation verb, what do you add to the

stem? _____

14. How do you give a plural command using a third conjugation verb? _____

_____

F. Give the English translation for each word. The nouns are all in the singular nominative form.

1. villa _____

2. pirum _____

3. nix _____

4. nucleus _____

5. morbus _____

6. valeō _____

7. mannus _____

8. intrō _____

9. aliēnus _____

10. crūs _____

11. iūs _____

11. flōs _____

12. āridus _____

13. satis _____

14. lingua _____

15. somnus _____

16. coma _____

17. verbum _____

18. terra _____

19. laxō _____

20. pulvis _____

22. querēla _____

23. ēgregius _____   25. consecō _____

24. aestās _____   26. numquam _____

G. On the lines below, label what each thing is called in Latin.

1. _____   2. _____   3. _____   4. _____

H. Label the parts of each sentence: V for main verbs, S for subjects, DO for direct object, PA for predicate adjectives, and PN for predicate nouns. Then translate the sentence into English.

1. Pontus est terminus extrēmus. _____

2. Cȳgnus quiētus tubam cantābit. _____

3. Porcus parvus et aranea sunt amīcī. _____

4. Eques salsus patriam servābit. _____

5. Potestne amāre mīnōtaurus labyrinthum? _____

6. Ōvum est album et flavum. _____

7. Māter patrem expectat mox. _____

8. Verū carnem odōrātam coquēbat. _____

9. Gigantēs erant fessī et tardī. _____

10. Sīmiae improbae ālās et vestīmenta rubra habent. _____

_____

I. In each sentence, underline the main verb and circle the direct object. Then translate the sentence into Latin.

1. The greedy robber owes money. _____

2. Do not eat the cookies! (plural) _____

3. Ought Rome to conquer Carthage? _____

Derivatives

J. Use your knowledge of Latin to complete the definitions of these derivatives.

1. A *unicorn* is a horselike creature whose name means "one _____."

2. Something that is *tangible* is something that you can _____ .

3. A *vigilant* soldier is _____ .

4. When a criminal is *incarcerated,* it means he is living in _____ .

5. If someone has a *simian* face, it means her face reminds you of a _____ !

Quotations

K. Translate the Latin quotations and answer the questions about them.

1. *Frūctū cognoscitur arbor:* _____

2. What is the case and number of *arbor?* _____

3. *Ecce homō!:* _____

4. What is the case and number of *homō?* _____

5. *Mihine crūstula coquēs?:* _____

6. What is the case and number of *crūstula?* _____

Unit 4 Test: Answer Key

Chants

A. Conjugate the following words in the present, future, and imperfect tenses.

Present Active

FIRST CONJUGATION

	SINGULAR	PLURAL
1ST	domō	domāmus
2ND	domās	domātis
3RD	domat	domant

SECOND CONJUGATION

	SINGULAR	PLURAL
1ST	caveō	cavēmus
2ND	cavēs	cavētis
3RD	cavet	cavent

THIRD CONJUGATION

	SINGULAR	PLURAL
1ST	pōnō	pōnimus
2ND	pōnis	pōnitis
3RD	pōnit	pōnunt

Future Active

FIRST CONJUGATION

	SINGULAR	PLURAL
1ST	domābō	domābimus
2ND	domābis	domābitis
3RD	domābit	domābunt

SECOND CONJUGATION

	SINGULAR	PLURAL
1ST	cavēbō	cavēbimus
2ND	cavēbis	cavēbitis
3RD	cavēbit	cavēbunt

THIRD CONJUGATION

	SINGULAR	PLURAL
1ST	pōnam	pōnēmus
2ND	pōnēs	pōnētis
3RD	pōnet	pōnent

Imperfect Active

FIRST CONJUGATION

	SINGULAR	PLURAL
1ST	domābam	domābāmus
2ND	domābās	domābātis
3RD	domābat	domābant

SECOND CONJUGATION

	SINGULAR	PLURAL
1ST	cavēbam	cavēbāmus
2ND	cavēbās	cavēbātis
3RD	cavēbat	cavēbant

THIRD CONJUGATION

	SINGULAR	PLURAL
1ST	pōnēbam	pōnēbāmus
2ND	pōnēbās	pōnēbātis
3RD	pōnēbat	pōnēbant

B. For each noun, give its declension and gender, then decline it.

DECLENSION ___2___ GENDER ___M___

	SINGULAR	PLURAL
NOM.	satyrus	satyrī
GEN.	satyrī	satyrōrum
DAT.	satyrō	satyrīs
ACC.	satyrum	satyrōs
ABL.	satyrō	satyrīs

DECLENSION ___3___ GENDER ___M/F___

	SINGULAR	PLURAL
NOM.	bōs	bovēs
GEN.	bovis	bovum
DAT.	bovī	bovibus
ACC.	bovem	bovēs
ABL.	bove	bovibus

DECLENSION ___2___ GENDER ___N___

	SINGULAR	PLURAL
NOM.	būtūrum	būtūra
GEN.	būtūrī	būtūrōrum
DAT.	būtūrō	būtūrīs
ACC.	būtūrum	būtūra
ABL.	būtūrō	būtūrīs

DECLENSION ___1___ GENDER ___F___

	SINGULAR	PLURAL
NOM.	īnsula	īnsulae
GEN.	īnsulae	īnsulārum
DAT.	īnsulae	īnsulīs
ACC.	īnsulam	īnsulās
ABL.	īnsulā	īnsulīs

DECLENSION ___4___ GENDER ___M___

	SINGULAR	PLURAL
NOM.	frūctus	frūctūs
GEN.	frūctūs	frūctuum
DAT.	frūctuī	frūctibus
ACC.	frūctum	frūctūs
ABL.	frūctū	frūctibus

DECLENSION ___3___ GENDER ___N___

	SINGULAR	PLURAL
NOM.	caput	capita
GEN.	capitis	capitum
DAT.	capitī	capitibus
ACC.	caput	capita
ABL.	capite	capitibus

C. Below, decline the adjective/noun phrase. To the right, give the declension and gender of the noun, and the gender of the adjective.

	SINGULAR	PLURAL
NOM.	magnum pecū	**magna pecua**
GEN.	**magnī pecūs**	**magnōrum pecuum**
DAT.	**magnō pecū**	**magnīs pecibus**
ACC.	**magnum pecū**	**magna pecua**
ABL.	**magnō pecū**	**magnīs pecibus**

NOUN

Declension: __**4**__

Gender: __**N**__

ADJECTIVE

Gender: __**N**__

1. What does this phrase mean? **large cattle**

D. Conjugate *sum* in the present, future, and imperfect tenses.

Present Active

	SINGULAR	PLURAL
1ST	**sum**	**sumus**
2ND	**es**	**estis**
3RD	**est**	**sunt**

Future Active

SINGULAR	PLURAL
erō	**erimus**
eris	**eritis**
erit	**erunt**

Imperfect Active

SINGULAR	PLURAL
eram	**erāmus**
erās	**erātis**
erat	**erant**

Vocabulary

E. Fill in the blanks.

1. The **nominative** case is used for subjects and predicate nouns.

2. A predicate noun **renames** or **identifies** the subject.

3. Predicate nouns and predicate adjectives both follow a **linking** verb.

4. The **accusative** case is used for direct objects.

5. A direct object **receives** the action of the verb.

6. A verb expresses **action** or a state of **being**.

7. The second principal part of a Latin verb is also called the **infinitive**.

8. Does every Latin verb have an infinitive? **yes**

9. To form a question in Latin, **-ne** is added to the first word in the sentence.

10. When you tell a dog, "Roll over!", you're giving it a **command**.

11. What is another word for "command"? **imperative**

12. To give a singular command, you use the **stem** of the verb.

13. To give a plural command using a first or second conjugation verb, what do you add to the stem? **-te**

14. How do you give a plural command using a third conjugation verb? **First, find the stem, then change the stem's "e" to an "i," and add -te.**

F. Give the English translation for each word. The nouns are all in the singular nominative form.

1. villa	**farmhouse**	11. flōs	**flower**	
2. pirum	**pear**	12. āridus	**dry**	
3. nix	**snow**	13. satis	**enough**	
4. nucleus	**nut, kernel**	14. lingua	**language, tongue**	
5. morbus	**sickness, disease**	15. somnus	**sleep**	
6. valeō	**I am well**	16. coma	**hair, leaves, wool, mane**	
7. mannus	**pony**	17. verbum	**word**	
8. intrō	**I enter**	18. terra	**land**	
9. aliēnus	**foreign**	19. laxō	**I loosen**	
10. crūs	**leg**	20. pulvis	**dirt, dust**	
11. iūs	**justice, right, law**	22. querēla	**complaint, whining**	

23. ēgregius **outstanding** 25. consecō **I chop, cut up**

24. aestās **summer** 26. numquam **never**

G. On the lines below, label what each thing is called in Latin.

1. **serpēns**   2. **delphīnus**   3. **flōs**   4. **caper**

H. Label the parts of each sentence: V for main verbs, S for subjects, DO for direct object, PA for predicate adjectives, and PN for predicate nouns. Then translate the sentence into English.

   S   V   PN

1. Pontus est terminus extrēmus. **The sea is the last boundary.**

   S   DO   V

2. Cȳgnus quiētus tubam cantābit. **The quiet swan will play the trumpet.**

   S   S   V   PN

3. Porcus parvus et aranea sunt amīcī. **The little pig and the spider are friends.**

   S   DO   V

4. Eques salsus patriam servābit. **The witty horseman will save the native land.**

   V   S   DO

5. Potestne amāre mīnōtaurus labyrinthum? **Is the minotaur able to love the labyrinth?**

   S   V   PA   PA

6. Ōvum est album et flavum. **An egg is white and yellow.**

   S   DO   V

7. Māter patrem expectat mox. **The mother is expecting the father soon.**

   S   DO   V

8. Verū carnem odōrātam coquēbat. **A spit was cooking the fragrant meat.**

   S   V   PA   PA

9. Gigantēs erant fessī et tardī. **The giants were tired and slow.**

   S   DO   DO   V

10. Sīmiae improbae ālās et vestīmenta rubra habent. **The wicked monkeys have wings and red clothing.**

I. In each sentence, underline the main verb and circle the direct object. Then translate the sentence into Latin.

1. The greedy robber <u>owes</u> (money). **Latrō avārus pecūniam dēbet.**

2. <u>Do</u> not <u>eat</u> the (cookies)! (plural) **Crūstula nōn edite!**

3. <u>Ought</u> Rome to conquer (Carthage)? **Dēbētne vincere Rōma Carthāginem?**

Derivatives

J. Use your knowledge of Latin to complete the definitions of these derivatives.

1. A *unicorn* is a horselike creature whose name means "one **horn**."

2. Something that is *tangible* is something that you can **touch**.

3. A *vigilant* soldier is **watchful**.

4. When a criminal is *incarcerated,* it means he is living in **prison**.

5. If someone has a *simian* face, it means her face reminds you of a **monkey**!

Quotations

K. Translate the Latin quotations and answer the questions about them.

1. *Frūctū cognoscitur arbor:* **The tree is known by its fruit**

2. What is the case and number of *arbor?* **nominative singular**

3. *Ecce homō!:* **Behold the man!**

4. What is the case and number of *homō?* **nominative singular**

5. *Mihine crūstula coquēs?:* **Will you bake cookies for me?**

6. What is the case and number of *crūstula?* **accusative plural**

APPENDICES

- Chant Charts
- Glossary
- Sources and Helps

CHANT CHARTS

Chants, in Order of Introduction

The chants in this section are listed in the order they are introduced in this book.

First Declension Noun Endings *(Week 1, p. 6)*

	SINGULAR	PLURAL		SINGULAR	PLURAL
NOM.	-a	-ae		a, the *noun*	the *nouns*
GEN.	-ae	-ārum		of the *noun*, the *noun's*	of the *nouns*, the *nouns'*
DAT.	-ae	-īs		to, for the *noun*	to, for the *nouns*
ACC.	-am	-ās		the *noun*	the *nouns*
ABL.	-ā	-īs		by, with, from the *noun*	by, with, from the *nouns*

Second Declension Noun Endings *(Week 2, p. 17)*

	SINGULAR	PLURAL		SINGULAR	PLURAL
NOM.	-us	-ī		a, the *noun*	the *nouns*
GEN.	-ī	-ōrum		of the *noun*, the *noun's*	of the *nouns*, the *nouns'*
DAT.	-ō	-īs		to, for the *noun*	to, for the *nouns*
ACC.	-um	-ōs		the *noun*	the *nouns*
ABL.	-ō	-īs		by, with, from the *noun*	by, with, from the *nouns*

Second Declension Neuter Noun Endings *(Week 3, p. 27)*

	SINGULAR	PLURAL		SINGULAR	PLURAL
NOM.	-um	-a		a, the *noun*	the *nouns*
GEN.	-ī	-ōrum		of the *noun*, the *noun's*	of the *nouns*, the *nouns'*
DAT.	-ō	-īs		to, for the *noun*	to, for the *nouns*
ACC.	-um	-a		the *noun*	the *nouns*
ABL.	-ō	-īs		by, with, from the *noun*	by, with, from the *nouns*

Present Active Verb Endings

(Week 4, p. 39)

	SINGULAR	PLURAL		SINGULAR	PLURAL
1ST	-ō	-mus		I am *verbing*, I *verb*	we are *verbing*
2ND	-s	-tis		you are *verbing*	you all are *verbing*
3RD	-t	-nt		he/she/it is *verbing*	they are *verbing*

Future Active Verb Endings

(Week 5, p. 50)

	SINGULAR	PLURAL		SINGULAR	PLURAL
1ST	-bō	-bimus		I will *verb*	we will *verb*
2ND	-bis	-bitis		you will *verb*	you all will *verb*
3RD	-bit	-bunt		he/she/it will *verb*	they will *verb*

Imperfect Active Verb Endings

(Week 6, p. 60)

	SINGULAR	PLURAL		SINGULAR	PLURAL
1ST	-bam	-bāmus		I was *verbing*	we were *verbing*
2ND	-bās	-bātis		you were *verbing*	you all were *verbing*
3RD	-bat	-bant		he/she/it was *verbing*	they were *verbing*

Dūcō, *I lead*—Present Active
Third Conjugation or "e" Family Verb

(Week 9, p. 101)

	SINGULAR	PLURAL		SINGULAR	PLURAL
1ST	dūcō	dūcimus		I lead	we lead
2ND	dūcis	dūcitis		you lead	you all lead
3RD	dūcit	dūcunt		he/she/it leads	they lead

Sum, *I am*—Present Active
Irregular Verb

(Week 10, p. 112)

	SINGULAR	PLURAL		SINGULAR	PLURAL
1ST	sum	sumus		I am	we are
2ND	es	estis		you are	you all are
3RD	est	sunt		he/she/it is	they are

Dūcam, *I will lead*—Future Active

Third Conjugation or "e" Family Verb *(Week 11, p. 123)*

	SINGULAR	PLURAL		SINGULAR	PLURAL
1ST	dūcam	dūcēmus		I will lead	we will lead
2ND	dūcēs	dūcētis		you will lead	you all will lead
3RD	dūcet	dūcent		he/she/it will lead	they will lead

Dūcēbam, *I was leading*—Imperfect Active

Third Conjugation or "e" Family Verb Endings *(Week 12, p. 134)*

	SINGULAR	PLURAL		SINGULAR	PLURAL
1ST	dūcēbam	dūcēbāmus		I was leading	we were leading
2ND	dūcēbās	dūcēbātis		you were leading	you all were leading
3RD	dūcēbat	dūcēbant		he/she/it was leading	they were leading

Third Declension Noun Endings *(Week 13, p. 145)*

	SINGULAR	PLURAL		SINGULAR	PLURAL
NOM.	x	-ēs		a, the *noun*	the *nouns*
GEN.	-is	-um		of the *noun*, the *noun's*	of the *nouns*, the *nouns'*
DAT.	-ī	-ibus		to, for the *noun*	to, for the *nouns*
ACC.	-em	-ēs		the *noun*	the *nouns*
ABL.	-e	-ibus		by, with, from the *noun*	by, with, from the *nouns*

Third Declension Neuter Noun Endings *(Week 15, p. 166)*

	SINGULAR	PLURAL		SINGULAR	PLURAL
NOM.	x	-a		a, the *noun*	the *nouns*
GEN.	-is	-um		of the *noun*, the *noun's*	of the *nouns*, the *nouns'*
DAT.	-ī	-ibus		to, for the *noun*	to, for the *nouns*
ACC.	x	-a		the *noun*	the *nouns*
ABL.	-e	-ibus		by, with, from the *noun*	by, with, from the *nouns*

Erō, *I will be*—Future Active of *Sum*
Irregular Verb

(Week 16, p. 177)

	SINGULAR	PLURAL		SINGULAR	PLURAL
1ST	erō	erimus		I will be	we will be
2ND	eris	eritis		you will be	you all will be
3RD	erit	erunt		he/she/it will be	they will be

Fourth Declension Noun Endings

(Week 23, p. 264)

	SINGULAR	PLURAL		SINGULAR	PLURAL
NOM.	-us	-ūs		a, the *noun*	the *nouns*
GEN.	-ūs	-uum		of the *noun*, the *noun's*	of the *nouns*, the *nouns'*
DAT.	-uī	-ibus		to, for the *noun*	to, for the *nouns*
ACC.	-um	-ūs		the *noun*	the *nouns*
ABL.	-ū	-ibus		by, with, from the *noun*	by, with, from the *nouns*

Fourth Declension Neuter Noun Endings

(Week 25, p. 295)

	SINGULAR	PLURAL		SINGULAR	PLURAL
NOM.	-ū	-ua		a, the *noun*	the *nouns*
GEN.	-ūs	-uum		of the *noun*, the *noun's*	of the *nouns*, the *nouns'*
DAT.	-ū	-ibus		to, for the *noun*	to, for the *nouns*
ACC.	-ū	-ua		the *noun*	the *nouns*
ABL.	-ū	-ibus		by, with, from the *noun*	by, with, from the *nouns*

Possum, *I am able*—Present Active
Irregular Verb

(Week 27, p. 317)

	SINGULAR	PLURAL		SINGULAR	PLURAL
1ST	possum	possumus		I am able	we are able
2ND	potes	potestis		you are able	you all are able
3RD	potest	possunt		he/she/it is able	they are able

Eram, *I was*—Imperfect Active of *Sum*
Irregular Verb

(Week 30, p. 347)

	SINGULAR	PLURAL		SINGULAR	PLURAL
1ST	eram	erāmus		I was	we were
2ND	erās	erātis		you were	you all were
3RD	erat	erant		he/she/it was	they were

Verb Chants, applied to Amō, Videō, and Dūcō

The chants in this section follow the conjugations of amō *(1st)*, videō *(2nd)*, and dūcō *(3rd)*. The notation *[PV]* stands for "passive voice." Conjugations without this notation are in the active voice.

LATIN	SINGULAR			PLURAL		
	1ST	2ND	3RD	1ST	2ND	3RD
PRESENT	am**ō**	am**ās**	ama**t**	am**ā**mus	am**ā**tis	ama**nt**
FUTURE	amā**bō**	amā**bis**	amā**bit**	amā**bimus**	amā**bitis**	amā**bunt**
IMPERFECT	amā**bam**	amā**bās**	amā**bat**	amā**bāmus**	amā**bātis**	amā**bant**
PERFECT	amā**vī**	amā**vistī**	amā**vit**	amā**vimus**	amā**vistis**	amā**vērunt**
FUTURE PERFECT	amā**verō**	amā**veris**	amā**verit**	amā**verimus**	amā**veritis**	amā**verint**
PLUPERFECT	amā**veram**	amā**verās**	amā**verat**	amā**verāmus**	amā**verātis**	amā**verant**
PRESENT [PV]	amo**r**	amā**ris**	amā**tur**	amā**mur**	amā**minī**	ama**ntur**
FUTURE [PV]	amā**bor**	amā**beris**	amā**bitur**	amā**bimur**	amā**biminī**	amā**buntur**
IMPERFECT [PV]	amā**bar**	amā**bāris**	amā**bātur**	amā**bāmur**	amā**bāminī**	amā**bantur**

ENGLISH	SINGULAR			PLURAL		
	1ST	2ND	3RD	1ST	2ND	3RD
PRESENT	I love	you love	he/she/it loves	we love	you all love	they love
FUTURE	I will love	you will love	he/she/it will love	we will love	you all will love	they will love
IMPERFECT	I was loving	you were loving	he/she/it was loving	we were loving	you all were loving	they were loving
PERFECT	I have loved	you have loved	he/she/it has loved	we have loved	you all have loved	they have loved
FUTURE PERFECT	I will have loved	you will have loved	he/she/it will have loved	we will have loved	you all will have loved	they will have loved
PLUPERFECT	I had loved	you had loved	he/she/it had loved	we had loved	you all had loved	they had loved
PRESENT [PV]	I am loved	you are loved	he/she/it is loved	we are loved	you all are loved	they are loved
FUTURE [PV]	I will be loved	you will be loved	he/she/it will be loved	we will be loved	you all will be loved	they will be loved
IMPERFECT [PV]	I was being loved	you were being loved	he/she/it was being loved	we were being loved	you all were being loved	they were being loved

LATIN	SINGULAR			PLURAL		
	1ST	2ND	3RD	1ST	2ND	3RD
PRESENT	vide**ō**	vid**ēs**	vide**t**	vidē**mus**	vidē**tis**	vide**nt**
FUTURE	vidē**bō**	vidē**bis**	vidē**bit**	vidē**bimus**	vidē**bitis**	vidē**bunt**
IMPERFECT	vidē**bam**	vidē**bās**	vidē**bat**	vidē**bāmus**	vidē**bātis**	vidē**bant**
PERFECT	vid**ī**	vid**istī**	vid**it**	vid**imus**	vid**istis**	vid**ērunt**
FUTURE PERFECT	vid**erō**	vid**eris**	vid**erit**	vid**erimus**	vid**eritis**	vid**erint**
PLUPERFECT	vid**eram**	vid**erās**	vid**erat**	vid**erāmus**	vid**erātis**	vid**erant**
PRESENT [PV]	vidē**or**	vid**ēris**	vid**ētur**	vidē**mur**	vidē**minī**	vidē**ntur**
FUTURE [PV]	vidē**bor**	vidē**beris**	vidē**bitur**	vidē**bimur**	vidē**biminī**	vidē**buntur**
IMPERFECT [PV]	vidē**bar**	vidē**bāris**	vidē**bātur**	vidē**bāmur**	vidē**bāminī**	vidē**bantur**

ENGLISH	SINGULAR			PLURAL		
	1ST	2ND	3RD	1ST	2ND	3RD
PRESENT	I see	you see	he/she/it sees	we see	you all see	they see
FUTURE	I will see	you will see	he/she/it will see	we will see	you all will see	they will see
IMPERFECT	I was seeing	you were seeing	he/she/it was seeing	we were seeing	you all were seeing	they were seeing
PERFECT	I have seen	you have seen	he/she/it has seen	we have seen	you all have seen	they have seen
FUTURE PERFECT	I will have seen	you will have seen	he/she/it will have seen	we will have seen	you all will have seen	they will have seen
PLUPERFECT	I had seen	you had seen	he/she/it had seen	we had seen	you all had seen	they had seen
PRESENT [PV]	I am seen	you are seen	he/she/it is seen	we are seen	you all are seen	they are seen
FUTURE [PV]	I will be seen	you will be seen	he/she/it will be seen	we will be seen	you all will be seen	they will be seen
IMPERFECT [PV]	I was being seen	you were being seen	he/she/it was being seen	we were being seen	you all were being seen	they were being seen

LATIN	SINGULAR			PLURAL		
	1ST	2ND	3RD	1ST	2ND	3RD
PRESENT	dūcō	dūcis	dūcit	dūcimus	dūcitis	dūcunt
FUTURE	dūcam	dūcēs	dūcēt	dūcēmus	dūcētis	dūcent
IMPERFECT	dūcēbam	dūcēbās	dūcēbat	dūcēbāmus	dūcēbātis	dūcēbant
PERFECT	dūxī	dūxistī	dūxit	dūximus	dūxistis	dūxērunt
FUTURE PERFECT	dūxerō	dūxeris	dūxerit	dūxerimus	dūxeritis	dūxerint
PLUPERFECT	dūxeram	dūxerās	dūxerat	dūxerāmus	dūxerātis	viderant
PRESENT [PV]	dūcor	dūcēris	dūcitur	dūcimur	dūciminī	dūcuntur
FUTURE [PV]	dūcar	dūcēris	dūcētur	dūcēmur	dūcēminī	dūcentur
IMPERFECT [PV]	dūcēbar	dūcēbāris	dūcēbātur	dūcēbāmur	dūcēbāminī	dūcēbantur

ENGLISH	SINGULAR			PLURAL		
	1ST	2ND	3RD	1ST	2ND	3RD
PRESENT	I lead	you lead	he/she/it leads	we lead	you all lead	they lead
FUTURE	I will lead	you will lead	he/she/it will lead	we will lead	you all will lead	they will lead
IMPERFECT	I was leading	you were leading	he/she/it was leading	we were leading	you all were leading	they were leading
PERFECT	I have led	you have led	he/she/it has led	we have led	you all have led	they have led
FUTURE PERFECT	I will have led	you will have led	he/she/it will have led	we will have led	you all will have led	they will have led
PLUPERFECT	I had led	you had led	he/she/it had led	we had led	you all had led	they had led
PRESENT [PV]	I am led	you are led	he/she/it is led	we are led	you all are led	they are led
FUTURE [PV]	I will be led	you will be led	he/she/it will be led	we will be led	you all will be led	they will be led
IMPERFECT [PV]	I was being led	you were being led	he/she/it was being led	we were being led	you all were being led	they were being led

GLOSSARY

A

accūsō, accūsāre *I accuse, blame* [1st conj., Wk. 14]

administrō, administrāre *I help, manage* [1st conj.,Wk. 14]

adulēscēns, adulēscentis (m) *young man* [3rd decl., Wk. 18]

aedificium, -ī (n) *building* [2nd decl., Wk. 3]

aequus, -a, -um *level, even, calm* [Wk. 6]

aestās, aestātis (f) *summer* [3rd decl., Wk. 29]

aeternus, -a, -um *eternal* [Wk. 11]

agō, agere, *I do, act* [3rd conj., Wk. 12]

agricola, -ae (m) *farmer* [1st decl., Wk. 5]

āla, -ae (f) *wing* [1st decl., Wk. 9]

albus, -a, -um *white* [Wk. 6]

alga, -ae (f) *seaweed* [1st decl., Wk. 6]

aliēnus, -a, -um *foreign* [Wk. 9]

ambulō, ambulāre *I walk* [1st conj., Wk. 3]

amīcus, -ī (m) *friend* [2nd decl., Wk. 1]

amō, amāre, *I love* [1st conj., Wk. 3]

ancora, -ae (f) *anchor* [1st decl., Wk. 9]

antīquus, -a, -um *ancient* [Wk. 10]

appāreō, appārēre *I appear* [2nd conj., Wk. 5]

appellō, appellāre *I name, call, call by, name* [1st conj., Wk. 24]

apricus, -a, -um *sunny* [Wk. 2]

aptus, -a, -um *suitable, fit, ready* [Wk. 9]

aqua, -ae (f) *water* [1st decl., Wk. 1]

aquila, -ae (m/f) *eagle* [1st decl., Wk. 5]

aranea, -ae (f) *spider* [1st decl., Wk. 15]

arbor, arboris (f) *tree* [3rd decl., Wk. 26]

architectus, -ī (m) *architect, inventor* [2nd decl., Wk. 22]

arcus, -ūs (m) *bow, arch, rainbow* [4th decl., Wk. 23]

argūmentum, -ī (n) *proof, evidence* [2nd decl., Wk. 16]

āridus, -a, -um *dry* [Wk. 6]

ariēna, -ae (f) *banana* [1st decl., Wk. 2]

ariēs, arietis (m) *ram* [3rd decl., Wk. 13]

armentum, -ī (n) *herd* [2nd decl., Wk. 5]

arō, arāre *I plow* [1st conj., Wk. 14]

asinus, -ī (m) *donkey* [2nd decl., Wk. 21]

astō, astāre *I stand near, stand by* [1st conj., Wk. 1]

astrum, -ī (n) *star, constellation* [2nd decl., Wk. 9]

audeō, audēre *I dare* [2nd conj., Wk. 8]

augeō, augēre *I increase* [2nd conj., Wk. 7]

aurōra, -ae (f) *dawn* [1st decl., Wk. 9]

avārus, -a, -um *greedy* [Wk. 27]

avia, -ae (f) *grandmother* [1st decl., Wk. 12]

avus, -ī (m) *grandfather* [2nd decl., Wk. 12]

B

bālaena, -ae (f) *whale* [1st decl., Wk. 6]

balatrō, balatrōnis (m) *jester, clown* [3rd decl., Wk. 13]

beātus, -a, -um, *happy, blessed* [Wk. 10]

bestiola, -ae (f) *insect* [1st decl., Wk. 15]

bibō, bibere, *I drink* [3rd conj., Wk. 30]

bonus, -a, -um, *good* [Wk. 11]

bōs, bovis (m/f) *ox, bull, cow* [3rd decl., Wk. 18]

Brittania, -ae (f) *Britain* [1st decl., Wk. 31]

brūnus, -a, -um, *brown* [Wk. 4]

būtūrum, -ī (n) *butter* [2nd decl., Wk. 30]

C

cadō, cadere *I fall, sink, drop* [3rd conj., Wk. 26]

caecus, -a, -um *blind* [Wk. 11]

caelum, -ī (n) *sky, heaven* [2nd decl., Wk. 1]

caeruleus, -a, -um *blue* [Wk. 15]

caldus, -a, -um *warm, hot, fiery* [Wk. 23]

camēlus, -ī (m) *camel* [2nd decl., Wk. 28]

candēla, -ae (f) *candle* [1st decl., Wk. 20]

cantō, cantāre *I sing, play (music)* [1st conj., Wk. 20] cantus, -ūs (m) *song, singing* [4th decl., Wk. 24]

caper, caprī (m) *billy goat* [2nd decl., Wk. 13]

captīvus, -ī (m) *captive* [2nd decl., Wk. 17]

captō, captāre *I hunt* [1st conj., Wk. 22]

caput, capitis (n) *head* [3rd decl., Wk. 15]

carcer, carceris (m) *prison* [3rd decl., Wk. 27]

carmen, carminis (n) *song, poem* [3rd decl., Wk. 20]

carō, carnis (f) *meat, flesh* [3rd decl., Wk. 28]

Carthāgō, Carthāginis (f) *Carthage* [3rd decl., Wk. 29]

cauda, -ae (f) *tail* [1st decl., Wk. 13]

cavea, -ae (f) *cage, animal den* [1st decl., Wk. 13]

caveō, cavēre *I guard against, beware* [2nd conj., Wk. 27]

celsus, -a, -um *tall, high, lofty* [Wk. 29]

cēna, -ae (f) *dinner, meal* [1st decl., Wk. 3]

censeō, censēre *I estimate* [2nd conj., Wk. 7]

centaurus, -ī (m) *centaur* [2nd decl., Wk. 22]

certātim, *eagerly* [Wk. 12]

cervus, -ī (m) *stag, deer* [2nd decl., Wk. 5]

cibō, cibāre *I feed* [1st conj., Wk. 7]

cibus, -ī (m) *food* [2nd decl., Wk. 1]

circus, -ī (m) *circle, racecourse* [2nd decl., Wk. 13]

clam, *secretly* [Wk. 23]

clāmō, clāmāre *I shout* [1st conj., Wk. 5]

cōgitō, cōgitāre *I think* [1st conj., Wk. 11]

colōnus, -ī (m) *settler* [2nd decl., Wk. 1]

coma, -ae (f) *hair, leaves, wool, mane* [1st decl., Wk. 5]

commemorō, commemorāre *I remember, mention, call to mind* [1st conj., Wk. 17]

commendō, commendāre *I commit, entrust* [1st conj., Wk. 24]

commūnicō, commūnicāre *I share, inform* [1st conj., Wk. 22]

consecō, consecāre *I chop, cut up* [1st conj., Wk. 30]

contentus, -a, -um *satisfied, content* [Wk. 16]

coquō, coquere *I cook, bake* [3rd conj., Wk. 30]

coquus, -ī (m) *cook, chef* [2nd decl., Wk. 4]

cor, cordis (n) *heart* [3rd decl., Wk. 20]

cornix, cornicis (f) *crow* [3rd decl., Wk. 15]

cornū, -ūs (n) *horn* [4th decl., Wk. 25]

corpus, corporis (n) *body* [3rd decl., Wk. 15]

crās, *tomorrow* [Wk. 12]

crēdō, crēdere *I believe* [2nd conj., Wk. 24]

crescō, crescere *I grow, arise* [3rd conj., Wk. 10]

crūs, crūris (n) *leg* [3rd decl., Wk. 15]

crūstulum, -ī (n) *cookie, small cake* [2nd decl., Wk. 30]

crux, crucis (f) *cross* [3rd decl., Wk. 21]

culter, -trī (m) *knife* [2nd decl., Wk. 25]

cumulō, cumulāre *I pile up, fill up* [1st conj., Wk. 4]

cunīculus, -ī (m) *rabbit* [2nd decl., Wk. 2]

cūrō, cūrāre *I care for* [1st conj., Wk. 25]

currō, currere *I run* [3rd conj., Wk. 13]

cyclops, cyclōpis (m) *cyclops* [3rd decl., Wk. 22]

cȳgnus, -ī (m) *swan* [2nd decl., Wk. 28]

D

dēbeō, dēbēre *I owe, ought* [2nd conj., Wk. 27]

dēclārō, dēclārāre *I declare, explain* [1st conj., Wk. 11]

dēliciōsus, -a, -um *delicious* [Wk. 2]

delphīnus, -ī (m) *dolphin* [2nd decl., Wk. 6]

dēmonstrō, dēmonstrāre *I show* [1st conj., Wk. 19]

Deus, -ī (m) *God* [2nd decl., Wk. 11]

dīrigō, dīrigere *I direct* [3rd conj., Wk. 32]

disciplīna, -ae (f) *instruction, training* [1st decl., Wk. 17]

discipulus, -ī (m) *apprentice, student* [2nd decl., Wk. 16]

dō, dāre *I give* [1st conj., Wk. 18]

dominus, -ī (m) *lord, master* [2nd decl., Wk. 3]

domō, domāre *I tame, subdue* [1st conj., Wk. 28]

domus, -ūs (f) *home, house* [4th decl., Wk. 24]

dracō, dracōnis (m) *dragon* [3rd decl., Wk. 22]

dubitō, dubitāre *I doubt, hesitate* [1st conj., Wk. 14]

dūcō, dūcere *I lead* [3rd conj., Wk. 9]

dux, ducis (m) *leader* [3rd decl., Wk. 21]

E

edō, edere *I eat* [3rd conj., Wk. 18]

ēgregius, -a, -um *outstanding* [Wk. 27]

elephantus, -ī (m) *elephant* [2nd decl., Wk. 13]

emō, emere *I buy, purchase* [3rd conj., Wk. 30]

epistula, -ae (f) *letter* [1st decl., Wk. 3]

eques, equitis (m) *horseman, knight* [3rd decl., Wk. 31]

equitō, equitāre *I ride (horseback)* [1st conj., Wk. 31]

equus, -ī (m) *horse* [2nd decl., Wk. 1]

eram, *I was* [Wk. 30]

erō, *I will be* [Wk. 16]

errō, errāre *I wander* [1st conj., Wk. 5]

et, *and* [Wk. 6]

Eurōpa, -ae (f) *Europe* [1st decl., Wk. 29]

exanimō, exanimāre *I kill* [1st conj., Wk. 7]

exerceō, exercēre *I train, exercise* [2nd conj., Wk. 19]

exercitus, -ūs (m) *army* [4th decl., Wk. 31]

explōrō, explōrāre *I find out, explore* [1st conj., Wk. 14]

exspectō, exspectāre *I wait, wait for, expect* [1st conj., Wk. 23]

exsultō, exsultāre *I leap up, dance, rejoice* [1st conj., Wk. 3]

extrēmus, -a, -um *last, farthest, outermost* [Wk. 31]

F

fābula, -ae (f) *story, legend* [1st decl., Wk. 3]

famēlicus, -a, -um *hungry* [Wk. 10]

familia, -ae (f) *family, household* [1st decl., Wk. 11]

farīna, -ae (f) *flour* [1st decl., Wk. 30]

fēmina, -ae (f) *woman* [1st decl., Wk. 3]

ferus, -ī (m) *wild animal* [2nd decl., Wk. 17]

fessus, -a, -um *tired, weary* [Wk. 18]

fīdus, -a, -um *faithful, trustworthy* [Wk. 24]

fīgō, fīgere *I fasten, attach, make firm* [3rd conj., Wk. 15]

fīlia, -ae (f) *daughter* [1st decl., Wk. 3]

fīlius, -ī (m) *son* [2nd decl., Wk. 3]

fīlum, -ī (n) *thread, string* [2nd decl., Wk. 22]

fīnitimus, -ī (m) *neighbor* [2nd decl., Wk. 29]

firmus, -a, -um *strong, firm, steadfast* [Wk. 16]

flagellum, -ī (n) *whip* [2nd decl., Wk. 13]

flagrō, flagrāre *I blaze, flame, burn* [1st conj., Wk. 26]

flavus, -a, -um *yellow, blond* [Wk. 15]

fleō, flēre *I weep* [2nd conj., Wk. 16]

flō, flāre *I blow, breathe* [1st conj., Wk. 11]

flōreō, flōrēre *I flourish* [2nd conj., Wk. 21]

flōs, flōris (m) *flower* [3rd decl., Wk. 20]

flūmen, flūminis (n) *river* [3rd decl., Wk. 17]

fluvius, -ī (m) *river, stream* [2nd decl., Wk. 9]

foedus, -a, -um *horrible, ugly* [Wk. 10]

folium, -ī (n) *leaf* [2nd decl., Wk. 2]

forum, -ī (n) *public square, marketplace* [2nd decl., Wk. 3]

foveō, fovēre *I cherish, love, esteem* [2nd conj., Wk. 23]

frāgum, -ī (n) *strawberry* [2nd decl., Wk. 2]

frangō, frangere *I break* [3rd conj., Wk. 30]

frāter, frātris (m) *brother* [3rd decl., Wk. 24]

frūctus, -ūs (m) *fruit, profit* [4th decl., Wk. 23]

fulmen, fulmenis (n) *lightning, thunderbolt* [3rd decl., Wk. 26]

fungus, -ī (m) *mushroom, fungus* [2nd decl., Wk. 4]

fuscina, -ae (f) *harpoon, trident* [1st decl., Wk. 6]

G

Gallia, -ae (f) *Gaul* [1st decl., Wk. 29]

gaudeō, gaudēre *I rejoice* [2nd conj., Wk. 11]

gelidus, -a, -um *cold, icy* [Wk. 9]

gelū, -ūs (n) *chill, frost* [4th decl., Wk. 25]

genū, -ūs (n) *knee* [4th decl., Wk. 25]

germāna, -ae (f) *sister* [1st decl., Wk. 11]

Germānia, -ae (f) *Germany* [1st decl., Wk. 31]

germānus, -ī (m) *brother* [2nd decl., Wk. 11]

gigās, gigantis (m) *giant* [3rd decl., Wk. 22]

grex, gregis (m) *flock, herd* [3rd decl., Wk. 25]

grȳps, grȳphis (m) *griffin* [3rd decl., Wk. 22]

gustō, gustāre *I taste* [1st conj., Wk. 2]

H

habēna, -ae (f) *strap, rein* [1st decl., Wk. 17]

habeō, habēre *I have, hold* [2nd conj., Wk. 20]

habitō, habitāre *I live in, dwell, inhabit* [1st conj., Wk. 31]

harēna, -ae (f) *sand* [1st decl., Wk. 6]

hasta, -ae (f) *spear, lance* [1st decl., Wk. 19]

herba, -ae (f) *herb, grass* [1st decl., Wk. 28]

herī, *yesterday* [Wk. 12]

hiemō, hiemāre *I spend the winter* [1st conj., Wk. 9]

hiems, hiemis (f) *winter, bad weather* [3rd decl., Wk. 29]

hippopotāmus, -ī (m) *hippopotamus* [2nd decl., Wk. 28]

Hispānia, -ae (f) *Spain* [1st decl., Wk. 31]

hodiē, *today* [Wk. 12]

homō, hominis (m) *man, human being* [3rd decl., Wk. 29]

honestus, -a, -um *honorable* [Wk. 14]

hortus, -ī (m) *garden* [2nd decl., Wk. 2]

hyaena, -ae (f) *hyena* [1st decl., Wk. 28]

hydrus, -ī (m) *sea serpent* [2nd decl., Wk. 6]

I

iaceō, iacēre *I lie down* [2nd conj., Wk. 27]

Iesus, -ūs (m) *Jesus* [4th decl., Wk. 24]

imber, imbris (m) *rain* [3rd decl., Wk. 26]

imperō, imperāre *I order* [1st conj., Wk. 21]

improbus, -a, -um *wicked* [Wk. 14]

incendō, incendere *I kindle, set on fire* [3rd conj., Wk. 26]

inimīcus, -ī (m) *personal enemy* [2nd decl., Wk. 7]

insidiae, -ārum (f) *ambush, trap, plot* [1st decl., Wk. 14]

instō, instāre *I pursue eagerly, follow closely* [1st conj., Wk. 6]

īnsula, -ae (f) *island* [1st decl., Wk. 17]

intrō, intrāre, *I enter* [1st conj., Wk. 14]

Ītalia, -ae (f) *Italy* [1st decl., Wk. 29]

iter, itineris (n) *journey* [3rd decl., Wk. 21]

iūdicō, iūdicāre *I judge* [1st conj., Wk. 11]

iungō, iungere *I join, unite, yoke* [3rd conj., Wk. 18]

iūs, iūris (n) *justice, right, law* [3rd decl., Wk. 16]

iūstus, -a, -um *just, righteous* [Wk. 11]

L

labor, labōris (m) *work, labor* [3rd decl., Wk. 18]

labōrō, labōrāre *I work, toil* [1st conj., Wk. 5]

labyrinthus, -ī (m) *labyrinth, maze* [2nd decl., Wk. 22]

lāc, lactis (n) *milk* [3rd decl., Wk. 30]

lacrima, -ae (f) *tear* [1st decl., Wk. 16]

lacus, -ūs (m) *lake, tub, hollow* [4th decl., Wk. 23]

laetus, -a, -um *happy, joyful* [Wk. 11]

latebra, -ae (f) *hiding place* [1st decl., Wk. 1]

latrō, latrōnis (m) *robber* [3rd decl., Wk. 27]

lātus, -a, -um *wide, broad* [Wk. 9]

latus, lateris (n) *flank, side* [3rd decl., Wk. 18]

laudō, laudāre *I praise* [1st conj., Wk. 3]

laxō, laxāre *I loosen* [1st conj., Wk. 17]

lēgātus, -ī (m) *lieutenant* [2nd decl., Wk. 17]

leō, leōnis (m) *lion* [3rd decl., Wk. 25]

lēx, lēgis (f) *law* [3rd decl., Wk. 27]

liber, librī (m) *book* [2nd decl., Wk. 11]

līberō, līberāre *I set free* [1st conj., Wk. 14]

lībō, lībāre *I sip, taste* [1st conj., Wk. 5]

lignum, -ī (n) *wood, timber* [2nd decl., Wk. 26]

lingua, -ae (f) *tongue, language* [1st decl., Wk. 3]

littera, -ae (f) *letter of the alphabet, PLURAL: letter, epistle* [1st decl., Wk. 12]

longinquus, -a, -um *far away, distant* [Wk. 31]

lūceō, lūcēre *I shine, am bright* [2nd conj., Wk. 5]

lūdō, lūdere *I play, tease, trick* [3rd conj., Wk. 20]

lūgeō, lūgēre *I grieve, mourn* [2nd conj., Wk. 11]

lūna, -ae (f) *moon* [1st decl., Wk. 5]

lupus, -ī (m) *wolf* [2nd decl., Wk. 5]

lutum, -ī (n) *mud* [2nd decl., Wk. 26]

lux, lūcis (f) *light* [3rd decl., Wk. 20]

luxuria, -ae (f) *luxury, extravagance* [1st decl., Wk. 19]

lyra, -ae (f) *lyre* [1st decl., Wk. 20]

M

maculōsus, -a, -um *spotted, stained* [Wk. 10]

magister, magistrī (m) *teacher (male)* [2nd decl., Wk. 16]

magistra, -ae (f) *teacher (female)* [1st decl., Wk. 16]

magnus, -a, -um *large, big* [Wk. 2]

mālum, -ī (n) *apple* [2nd decl., Wk. 2]

malus, -a, -um *bad, evil* [Wk. 2]

maneō, manēre *I remain, stay* [2nd conj., Wk. 8]

mannus, -ī (m) *pony* [2nd decl., Wk. 13]

manus, -ūs (f) *hand* [4th decl., Wk. 24]

māter, mātris (f) *mother* [3rd decl., Wk. 24]

matrimonium, -ī (n) *marriage* [2nd decl., Wk. 12]

memoria, -ae (f) *memory* [1st decl., Wk. 17]

mensa, -ae (f) *table* [1st decl., Wk. 3]

mereō, merēre *I deserve, earn, am worthy of* [2nd conj., Wk. 27]

metus, -ūs (m) *fear, dread* [4th decl., Wk. 24]

mīles, mīlitis (m) *soldier* [3rd decl., Wk. 27]

mīnōtaurus, -ī (m) *minotaur* [2nd decl., Wk. 22]

minūtātim, *gradually, bit by bit* [Wk. 12]

mīrus, -a, -um *strange, wonderful* [Wk. 9]

mittō, mittere *I send, let go* [3rd conj., Wk. 15]

moenia, -ium (n, pl) *fortifications, city walls* [2nd decl., Wk. 21]

moneō, monēre *I warn* [2nd conj., Wk. 16]

morbus, -ī (m) *sickness, disease* [2nd decl., Wk. 7]

mordeō, mordēre *I bite, sting* [2nd conj., Wk. 28]

moveō, movēre *I move* [2nd conj., Wk. 21]

mox, *soon* [Wk. 26]

mūnicipium, -ī (n) *free town* [2nd decl., Wk. 19]

mūnus, mūneris (n) *duty, office* [3rd decl., Wk. 27]

mūrus, -ī (m) *wall* [2nd decl., Wk. 1]

musca, -ae (f) *fly* [1st decl., Wk. 15]

mūtō, mūtāre *I change* [1st conj., Wk. 11]

N

narrō, narrāre *I tell, relate, recount* [1st conj., Wk. 14]

nasus, -ī (m) *nose* [2nd decl., Wk. 4]

nausea, -ae (f) *nausea, seasickness* [1st decl., Wk. 6]

nauta, -ae (m) *sailor* [1st decl., Wk. 1]

nāvigō, nāvigāre *I sail* [1st conj., Wk. 9]

nimbus, -ī (m) *thundercloud, storm* [2nd decl., Wk. 1]

nix, nivis (f) *snow* [3rd decl., Wk. 23]

nō, nāre, *I swim* [1st conj., Wk. 22]

noctua, -ae (f) *owl* [1st decl., Wk. 8]

nōmen, nōminis (n) *name* [3rd decl., Wk. 21]

nōn, *not* [Wk. 12]

novus, -a, -um *new* [Wk. 23]

nūbēs, nūbis (f) *cloud, gloom* [3rd decl., Wk. 26]

nucleus, -ī (m) *nut, kernel* [2nd decl., Wk. 4]

numquam, *never* [Wk. 28]

nuntiō, nuntiāre *I announce, declare* [1st conj., Wk. 14]

nuntius, -ī (m) *message, messenger* [2nd decl., Wk. 5]

O

obsecrō, obsecrāre *I beg, implore* [1st conj., Wk. 14]

obsideō, obsidēre *I remain near, besiege* [2nd conj., Wk. 19]

occultō, occultāre *I hide, conceal* [1st conj., Wk. 3]

occupō, occupāre *I seize* [1st conj., Wk. 8]

ōceanus, -ī (m) *ocean* [2nd decl., Wk. 6]

odōrātus, -a, -um *sweet-smelling, fragrant* [Wk. 4]

olefactō, olefactāre *I smell, sniff* [1st conj., Wk. 4]

opācus, -a, -um *dark, shaded* [Wk. 23]

opera, -ae (f) *effort, services* [1st decl., Wk. 7]

oppidum, -ī (n) *town* [2nd decl., Wk. 19]

oppugnō, oppugnāre *I attack* [1st conj., Wk. 7]

ornō, ornāre *I equip, decorate* [1st conj., Wk. 17]

ōs, ōris (n) *mouth* [3rd decl., Wk. 18]

ōvum, -ī (n) *egg* [2nd decl., Wk. 30]

P

pābulum, -ī (n) *fodder, food for animals* [2nd decl., Wk. 13]

pacō, pacāre *I pacify, subdue* [1st conj., Wk. 19]

palma, -ae (f) *palm of the hand, palm tree* [1st decl., Wk. 21]

pardus, -ī (m) *panther, leopard* [2nd decl., Wk. 28]

pāreō, pārēre *I obey* [2nd conj., Wk. 13]

parō, parāre *I prepare* [1st conj., Wk. 7]

parvus, -a, -um *little, small* [Wk. 2]

pastor, pastōris (m) *shepherd* [3rd decl., Wk. 25]

patella, -ae (f) *plate, dish* [1st decl., Wk. 30]

pater, patris (m) *father* [3rd decl., Wk. 24]

patria, -ae (f) *native land* [1st decl., Wk. 17]

pax, pācis (f) *peace* [3rd decl., Wk. 16]

peccō, peccāre *I sin* [1st conj., Wk. 1]

pecū, -ūs (n) *cattle, flock* [4th decl., Wk. 25]

pecūnia, -ae (f) *money* [1st decl., Wk. 27]

pēgasus, -ī (m) *pegasus* [2nd decl., Wk. 22]

perfectus, -a, um *perfect* [Wk. 4]

pēs, pedis (m) *foot* [3rd decl., Wk. 18]

pharetra, -ae (f) *quiver* [1st decl., Wk. 7]

pinna, -ae *(f) feather, wing* [1st decl., Wk. 15]

pirum, -ī (n) *pear* [2nd decl., Wk. 2]

pōculum, -ī (n) *cup* [2nd decl., Wk. 30]

poēta, -ae (m) *poet* [1st decl., Wk. 1]

pōnō, pōnere *I put, place* [3rd conj., Wk. 32]

pontus, -ī (m) *sea, seawater* [2nd decl., Wk. 1]

porcus, -ī (m) *pig* [2nd decl., Wk. 4]

porta, -ae (f) *door, gate* [1st decl., Wk. 3]

portō, portāre *I carry* [1st conj., Wk. 20]

portus, -ūs (m) *port, harbor* [4th decl., Wk. 23]

possum, posse *I am able* [Wk. 27]

praedīcō, pradīcere *I proclaim* [3rd conj., Wk. 32]

princeps, principis (n) *chief* [3rd decl., Wk. 21]

probō, probāre *I approve* [1st conj., Wk. 3]

properō, properāre *I hurry, rush* [1st conj., Wk. 5]

prōra, -ae (f) *prow (of a ship)* [1st decl., Wk. 9]

prōvincia, -ae (f) *province* [1st decl., Wk. 19]

psittācus, -ī (m) *parrot* [2nd decl., Wk. 28]

puella, -ae (f) *girl* [1st decl., Wk. 1]

puer, puerī (m) *boy* [2nd decl., Wk. 1]

pugnō, pugnāre *I fight* [1st conj., Wk. 7]

pulcher, -chra, -chrum *beautiful* [Wk. 10]

pulvereus, -a, -um *dusty, full of dust* [Wk. 18]

pulvīnus, -ī (m) *pillow, cushion* [2nd decl., Wk. 10]

pulvis, pulveris (m) *dirt, dust, powder* [3rd decl., Wk. 18]

pūrpureus, -a, -um *purple* [Wk. 10]

pūrus, -a, -um *pure, clean* [Wk. 10]

Q

quaerō, quaerere *I search for, seek* [3rd conj., Wk. 27]

querēla, -ae (f) *complaint, whining* [1st decl., Wk. 19]

quiescō, quiescere *I rest, sleep* [3rd conj., Wk. 18]

quiētus, -a, -um *quiet, sleeping* [Wk. 10]

quondam, *once, formerly* [Wk. 31]

R

radius, -ī (m) *staff, rod* [2nd decl., Wk. 4]

rādix, rādīcis (f) *root* [3rd decl., Wk. 26]

rāmus, -ī (m) *branch, twig* [2nd decl., Wk. 26]

recuperō, recuperāre *I recover* [1st conj., Wk. 14]

rēgīna, -ae (f) *queen* [1st decl., Wk. 14]

regnō, regnāre *I rule, govern, reign* [1st conj., Wk. 14]

regnum, -ī (n) *kingdom* [2nd decl., Wk. 31]

removeō, removēre *I remove, take away* [2nd conj., Wk. 19]

rēmus, -ī (m) *oar* [2nd decl., Wk. 9]

repente, *suddenly* [Wk. 24]

reptō, reptāre *I crawl, creep* [1st conj., Wk. 15]

repudiō, repudiāre *I reject, scorn* [1st conj., Wk. 16]

respondeō, respondēre *I respond, answer* [2nd conj., Wk. 16]

retineō, retinēre *I hold back, retain* [2nd conj., Wk. 17]

rēx, rēgis (m) *king* [3rd decl., Wk. 14]

rhīnocerōs, rhīnocerōtis (m) *rhinoceros* [3rd decl., Wk. 28]

rīdeō, rīdēre *I laugh* [2nd conj., Wk. 6]

rīdiculus, -a, -um *funny, amusing* [Wk. 10]

rīpa, -ae (f) *riverbank* [1st decl., Wk. 5]

rogō, rogāre, *I ask* [1st conj., Wk. 14]

Rōma, -ae (f) *Rome* [1st decl., Wk. 29]

ruber, -bra, -brum *red* [Wk. 22]

rudō, rudere *I roar, bellow, bray* [3rd conj., Wk. 13]

S

sacchārum, -ī (n) *sugar* [2nd decl., Wk. 30]

sagitta, -ae (f) *arrow* [1st decl., Wk. 7]

salsus, -a, -um *salty, witty* [Wk. 6]

satis, *enough* [Wk. 12]

satyrus, -ī (m) *satyr, faun* [2nd decl., Wk. 22]

saxum, -ī (n) *rock* [2nd decl., Wk. 5]

scalpō, scalpere *I carve, scratch* [3rd conj., Wk. 15]

sciūrus, -ī (m) *squirrel* [2nd decl., Wk. 8]

scrībō, scribere *I write* [3rd conj., Wk. 12]

sedeō, sedēre *I sit* [2nd conj., Wk. 16]

sella, -ae (f) *seat, chair* [1st decl., Wk. 3]

sēmen, sēminis (n) *seed* [3rd decl., Wk. 18]

semper, *always* [Wk. 12]

sepulcrum, -ī (n) *tomb, grave* [2nd decl., Wk. 27]

serēnus, -a, -um *calm, bright, clear* [Wk. 9]

serō, serere *I sow, plant* [3rd conj., Wk. 12]

serpēns, serpentis (m/f) *serpent, snake* [3rd decl., Wk. 28]

servō, servāre *I save* [1st conj., Wk. 17]

servus, -ī (m) *slave, servant* [2nd decl., Wk. 14]

significō, significāre *I indicate, point out* [1st conj., Wk. 7]

silva, -ae (f) *forest* [1st decl., Wk. 4]

sīmia, -ae (f) *ape, monkey* [1st decl., Wk. 28]

simul, *at the same time* [Wk. 12]

sīve, *or* [Wk. 30]

sōl, sōlis (m) *sun* [3rd decl., Wk. 23]

somniō, somniāre *I dream* [1st conj., Wk. 10]

somnus, -ī (m) *sleep* [2nd decl., Wk. 10]

soror, sorōris (f) *sister* [3rd decl., Wk. 24]

spectō, spectāre *I look at, watch* [1st conj., Wk. 9]

spērō, spērāre *I hope* [1st conj., Wk. 11]

spīritus, -ūs (m) *spirit, breath* [4th decl., Wk. 24]

spīrō, spīrāre *I breathe* [1st conj., Wk. 5]

stabulum, -ī (n) *stall, stable* [2nd decl., Wk. 19]

statim, *immediately* [Wk. 6]

stella, -ae (f) *star* [1st decl., Wk. 1]

stimulus, -ī (m) *goad, spur* [2nd decl., Wk. 17]

sub, *below, under* [Wk. 4]

sum, *I am* [Wk. 10]

superō, superāre *I defeat, conquer* [1st conj., Wk. 7]

suprā, *above* [Wk. 4]

T

tangō, tangere *I touch, strike* [3rd conj., Wk. 26]

tardus, -a, -um *slow* [Wk. 10]

taurus, -ī (m) *bull* [2nd decl., Wk. 1]

tectum, -ī (n) *roof, ceiling, dwelling* [2nd decl., Wk. 19]

tellūs, tellūris (f) *earth, ground, land* [3rd decl., Wk. 23]

tempestās, tempestātis (f) *weather, storm* [3rd decl., Wk. 25]

tempus, temporis (n) *time* [3rd decl., Wk. 20]

terminus, -ī (m) *end, boundary, limit* [2nd decl., Wk. 29]

terra, -ae (f) *earth, land* [1st decl., Wk. 1]

terreō, terrēre *I frighten, terrify* [2nd conj., Wk. 25]

tībia, -ae (f) *flute, pipe* [1st decl., Wk. 21]

tigris, tigridis (m/f) *tiger* [3rd decl., Wk. 13]

timeō, timēre *I fear* [2nd conj., Wk. 16]

tondeō, tondēre *I clip, give a haircut, shear* [2nd conj., Wk. 25]

tonitrus, -ūs (m) *thunder* [4th decl., Wk. 26]

trochus, -ī (m) *hoop for games* [2nd decl., Wk. 13]

tuba, -ae (f) *trumpet* [1st decl., Wk. 31]

turba, -ae (f) *crowd, mob* [1st decl., Wk. 3]

tūtus, -a, -um *safe, secure* [Wk. 25]

U

ulmus, -ī (m) *elm tree* [2nd decl., Wk. 4]

ululō, ululāre *I howl, scream* [1st conj., Wk. 5]

umbra, -ae (f) *shadow, shade* [1st decl., Wk. 23]

ūmidus, -a, -um *wet* [Wk. 6]

ūnā, *together, in one* [Wk. 18]

unda, -ae (f) *wave* [1st decl., Wk. 9]

undique, *on/from all sides, from every direction* [Wk. 29]

ursa, -ae (f) *or* **ursus,** -ī (m) *bear*
[1st decl. *or* 2nd decl., Wk. 28]

ūva, -ae (f) *grape* [1st decl., Wk. 2]

V

vadum, -ī (n) *ford, shallows* [2nd decl., Wk. 31]

valeō, valēre *I am well* [2nd conj., Wk. 8]

vastō, vastāre *I devastate, lay waste* [1st conj., Wk. 26]

vehō, vehere *I carry, ride, convey* [3rd conj., Wk. 21]

vēlum, -ī (n) *sail, curtain* [2nd decl., Wk. 9]

venēnum, -ī (n) *poison* [2nd decl., Wk. 7]

ventus, -ī (m) *wind* [2nd decl., Wk. 7]

verbum, -ī (n) *word* [2nd decl., Wk. 11]

verū, -ūs (n) *javelin, spit (for roasting meat)*
[4th decl., Wk. 25]

vesper, vesperis (m) *evening, evening star*
[3rd decl., Wk. 20]

vestīmentum, -ī (n) *clothing, garment*
[2nd decl., Wk. 21]

vexō, vexāre *I annoy, harass* [1st conj., Wk. 29]

vibrō, vibrāre *I wave, shake* [1st conj., Wk. 21]

victōria, -ae (f) *victory* [1st decl., Wk. 19]

vīcus, -ī (m) *village* [2nd decl., Wk. 23]

videō, vidēre *I see* [2nd conj., Wk. 16]

vigilō, vigilāre *I guard, watch over* [1st conj., Wk. 25]

villa, -ae (f) *farmhouse, country house* [1st decl., Wk. 17]

vincō, vincere *I conquer* [3rd conj., Wk. 32]

vir, virī (m) *man* [2nd decl., Wk. 11]

virga, -ae (f) *branch, twig* [1st decl., Wk. 1]

virgō, virginis (f) *maiden* [3rd decl., Wk. 20]

vītō, vītāre *I avoid* [1st conj., Wk. 29]

vīvō, vīvere *I live* [3rd conj., Wk. 12]

vocō, vocāre *I call, summon, invite* [1st conj., Wk. 14]

volō, volāre *I fly* [1st conj., Wk. 5]

vox, vōcis (f) *voice* [3rd decl., Wk. 20]

vulnerō, vulnerāre *I wound* [1st conj., Wk. 19]

vulnus, vulneris (n) *wound* [3rd decl., Wk. 15]

SOURCES AND HELPS

Brunel Jr., Donald J. *Basic Latin Vocabulary.* Oxford: American Classical League, 1989. In the later stages of developing the curriculum, this was my basic source for choosing and defining vocabulary.

Buehner, William J. and John W. Ambrose. *Introduction to Preparatory Latin,* Book I, 2nd ed. Wellesley Hills: Independent School Press, 1977.

Ehrlich, Eugene. *Amo, Amas, Amat, and More.* New York: Harper and Row, 1985.

Greenough, J. B., J. H. Allen, et al., *Allen & Greenough's New Latin Grammar.* Boston: Ginn and Co., 1903.

Mirza, Sumair and Jason Tsang. "Latin Wordstock—Latin Vocabulary and Derivatives." http://www. classicsunveiled.com/romevd/html/index.html. This is a helpful list of derivative possibilities, best paired with an English dictionary for confirmation.

Morris, William, ed. *American Heritage Dictionary of the English Language,* New College Edition. Boston: Houghton Mifflin, 1976. This was my basic reference English dictionary and one I would recommend for the teaching of Latin. My main use for it was to confirm and define derivatives.

Moutoux, Eugene R. "Latin Derivatives: English Words from Latin." http://german-latin-english.com/ latinderivatives.htm. This is another list of derivative possibilities, best paired with an English dictionary for confirmation.

Schaeffer, Rudolph F. *Latin English Derivative Dictionary,* edited by W. C. Carr. Oxford: American Classical League, 1960.

Simpson, D. P. *Cassell's Latin and English Dictionary.* New York: Macmillan Publishing, 1987. This is my most commonly used Latin dictionary, as well as the one the students used in their work.

Weber, Robertus, ed. *Biblia Sacra Vulgata.* Stuttgart: Wurttembergische Bibelanstalt, 1975. I used this and perhaps other versions for Scripture quotations.

Wheelock, Frederic M. *Latin: An Introductory Course Based on Ancient Authors,* 6th ed. revised. New York: Harper and Row, 2005. I depended upon this for Latin grammar, and I would recommend it for Latin teachers who need more of a Latin background.